GOOD KIND THINGS
FOR OTHERS

GOOD KIND THINGS FOR OTHERS

A True Story of Corruption in the Texas Panhandle

Glenn Baxter

Library of Congress Control Number:		2006905103
ISBN:	Hardcover	1-4257-1905-8
	Softcover	1-4257-1906-6

This book was printed in the United States of America.

To order additional copies of this book, contact:
Xlibris Corporation
1-888-795-4274
www.Xlibris.com
Orders@Xlibris.com
33762

Dedication

This book is dedicated to:
Memory of Frank Smith
&
Others who Seek Truth in Hutchinson County.

Some names have been changed but everything else is true
The people in this book are real.
The events actually occurred.

GB.

PREFACE

It was one of the last boxes to fill. A stack of books and pictures lay on the floor in mother's bedroom. She never threw a lot of things away. There was an accumulation of over sixty years of personal belongings in the home. It was sad sorting through aged sentimental family memories. There were childhood pictures of my brother, sister and myself. I missed by brother since his passing on six years ago.

I held pictures of my Father in his sailor uniform and others of my Mama and Daddy when they were first married. "Mama and Daddy" is what children call their parents in small Texas towns.

Absorbed in past reflections, I looked at the next item and reached for it. It was a 1978 membership directory of the First Baptist Church. Turning the pages there was a group picture of the Deacons. Standing on each side of the pastor was the Pharmacist and the Attorney for Golden Plains Community Hospital. I couldn't believe my eyes. Was this a prophecy of the past two years of my life?

I turned more pages of group photos of husbands, wives and family members. Then I saw a solitary photo of my mother. She became a church member without my father. I was proud of her for acting on her own convictions. My father's disdain for the "church going" crowd most likely developed through childhood physiological bruises placed there by his father, a Pentecostal Holiness preacher.

Seeing my father from the eyes of a child, I was blind to his imperfections. He was my hero. Now as an adult with my eyes open, he became the most hurtful experience in my life.

Soon, the trailer would be packed and we would be moving to North Central Texas. Mother was 78 years old, after 60 years of marriage, her divorce had been finalized.

*We have kept on praying and asking God to help you understand what He wants you to do, **you will always be doing good kind things for others**, all the time learning to know God better and better. We are praying too, that you will be filled with His mighty, glorious strength so that you can keep going no matter what happens—always be full of the joy of the Lord."*

—The Living Bible, Collossians 1:9-11*

*   From Pastor's Message in 1978 First Baptist Membership Directory, Borger, Texas

CHAPTER ONE

PUBLIC CORRUPTION IN THE NAME OF JESUS.

In January, 2005, no one was more shocked than Rick Roach, District Attorney, when a team of plainclothes FBI agents walked into the courtroom in Pampa, Texas. Roach was conducting a forfeiture hearing when the agents arrived to serve him an arrest warrant. The FBI had uncovered Roach's use of methamphetamines with intent to distribute and possession of more than 30 firearms.

John Mann, the former District Attorney, who was voted out of office in 2000, was not surprised about the arrest of Rick Roach. During a 1996 campaign for District Attorney of the Thirty-first district, it was brought to the public's attention that Roach had undergone treatment for alcohol and drug abuse. Roach admitted in the Canadian Record that he "allowed peer pressure to get him involved with marijuana and some amphetamines" and he had undergone treatment. Although, Roach admitted "it was wrong and I made a mistake," he lost that election.

Apparently, Rich Roach wasn't discouraged and he never moved his sights from becoming a District Attorney. After all, he was living in a small Texas Panhandle town where people like to think the best of others, forgive and often look the other way. It's no secret that the largest church in small towns usually has a large enough congregation to support a shoe-in for any member ambitious enough to run for political office.

By 2000, Roach was performing regularly in a Christian Gospel Band. He was looking good, clean cut, well dressed and well forgiven. He was convincing to the church going crowd and played the "Church Card" in narrowly winning the election. Drunk on power, the new District Attorney accelerated out of control down a road of arrogance, greed, deception, illegal drugs and public corruption.

Once in office, he built a hypocritical front of being tough on drugs. He used the press to build an image as the strongest, most unforgiving prosecutor in the Texas Panhandle. When it was released to the Amarillo Globe-News that a habitual DWI offender was sentenced to serve life, the editorial read, "We gain hope from this story because of the hard work of prosecutors like Rick Roach." Even the press was snowed.

Until his arrest, Rick Roach was the District Attorney for the Thirty-first District of Texas. This District includes Gray, Hemphill, Lipscomb, Roberts, and Wheeler Counties. The adjacent 84th District includes Hansford and Hutchinson Counties. Here's where my story takes place.

HUTCHINSON COUNTY

Hutchinson County stands in the North Central area of the Texas Panhandle. Borger, Fritch and Stinnett are the three main towns. The County Courthouse is located in Stinnett.

There are no major interstate highways running through the county. Barb wire lines both sides of paved and dirt roads. The local accent is a nasal twang different to the ear from other areas in Texas. The majority of folks are blue collar and wear western or work boots, gimmee caps, Stetsons and wrangler jeans. Beef cattle and other livestock are raised in addition to wheat, corn, alfalfa, and grain sorghums. The land is rolling plains, and the views extend to expansive horizons with cobalt blue skies. White grain elevators and pump jacks rise up against the stark vistas. Yucca, prickly pear cactus, coyotes, pronghorn antelope, prairie dogs, horned toads and rattlesnakes populate a landscape that was once referred to as part of the "Great American Desert." The average annual rainfall is a scarce 19.9 inches. Dust storms and tornadoes intimidate inhabitants.

The Canadian River cuts through the county exposing canyons of red earth and boulders. In the 1800's this isolated source of water attracted tribes of Comanches, Kiowas, Apaches and Cheyenne's. Buffalo roamed the grasslands and Buffalo hunters arrived in the vicinity around 1840 to take hides. A trading post, known as Fort Adobe, opened in 1843. Friction between the Indians and Buffalo hunters ensued and two battles were fought. On November 25, 1864, Colonel Kit Carson and a detachment of United States Calvary troops were nearly massacred by 3000 angry Comanches and Kiowas. On June 27, 1874 a second battle of Adobe Walls occurred.

By 1876, the spirit of the Plains tribes was broken and white settlement moved into the county.

BOOMTOWN

Oil was discovered in 1926 and independent oil producers and companies rushed in to strike it rich. Town sites spring up overnight. The toughest and wildest of these oil towns was Borger, named after Ace Borger. Ace was a town promoter who placed sensational advertising featuring the lure of "Black Gold." Boomtown fever brought in 45,000 men and women within ninety days. Buildings were hastily put up. Oil money flowed down Borger's main street. Roughnecks, opportunist, bootleggers, card sharks, dope peddlers, and a criminal element sought fast dollars and fast entertainment after dark. Prostitution, gambling, drinking and bar fights were an every night occurrence. After rain or the thaw of snowfall, the streets turned into thick, deep mud. The town wasn't a pretty site, but it was a place where a man who was tough and brave enough to gamble on a wildcat well could become rich overnight.

Nicked named "Booger Town," Borger became a refuge for fugitives running from the law. The town government quickly fell into the grasp of organized crime led by Mayor Miller and enforced by "Two-Gun Dick" Herwig a convicted murderer from Oklahoma.

Herwig and his boys, including W.J. (Shine) Popejoy, the King of Texas Bootleggers, controlled the brothels, speakeasies, dance halls, gambling and illegal moonshine stills. Robberies and murders were an everyday occurrence.

In 1927, The Governor of Texas sent in the Texas Rangers led by Captain Hamer to declare martial law and clean up the town. Many undesirables left town but crime continued up to 1930. The District Attorney, John A. Holmes, was murdered by an unknown assassin on September 18, 1929. State Troopers were sent in and martial law was declared for one month. On August 31, 1934, Arthur Huey shot to death his longtime enemy Ace Borger when the two men ran into each other in the middle of the day on the steps of the post office. There are those who have written and believe that this marked the end of the lawless organized crime element in Borger and Hutchinson County. One can only wonder.

Borger has the unique distinction as being the only town in the State of Texas where martial law has been declared twice in its history.

CHAPTER TWO

MY HOMETOWN

In May 1945, I was born in Pampa, Texas. When War World II ended, my father returned from the Navy and we moved 28 miles North into a small two bedroom wood frame in Borger.

My father was hired at the Carbon Black Plant and later at the Sante Fe Railroad Depot as a bookkeeper. There were no passenger trains running through town, only freight trains transporting mostly petroleum products and equipment. As years passed, Dad opened his own oil field mud company and later became an independent oil man.

He grew up during the depression in a poor family of five brothers and one sister. His father was a preacher who believed in the old proverb that if you spare the rod you spoil the child. In the name of Jesus' love, and with leather strap he would beat the living daylights out of his children. According to my father, "When I was sixteen years old my Dad whupped me six times in the same day. That's when I left home."

As a result, my father grew up to be independent, tough minded, two fisted and determined. He controlled everything in his life with an iron will that led him to financial success. Everything was "his way or the highway".

Mother's family were immigrants from Germany. My Great Grandfather was an early settler and farmer of the wheat Plains surrounding Groom, Texas.

The Ritters were a very closely knit family. Mother grew up on the farm with three sisters and one "baby" brother. She carried on the farm tradition into being a small town homemaker. Three home cooked meals a day were placed on the table. Family plans or problems were discussed at the dinner table. She was all heart and spent every waking hour taking care of my father, brother, sister and myself. Our family life reminded me of "Leave it to Beaver." There was a simplicity of love and closeness. Mother became a den mother for cub scouts and brownies. My father taught my brother and myself how to box, fish, play baseball, and football.

I remember Mother doing laundry by hand and hanging out everything to dry by clipping clothes pins on clothes' lines. She would wipe the line with a wet cloth and would often get upset when specks of carbon drifted on the clean clothes from the Carbon Black Plant. Large, black, ugly smoke stacks ascended over the town. Smoke billowed out of them daily. Back then, the newspaper proudly displayed on the front page masthead, "THE CARBON BLACK CAPITAL OF THE WORLD". It was a time when it was politically correct to be proud about pollution.

My brother, sister, and I would play outside each day and our legs became black from the sock line up. Undressing for a bath at the end of each day we would look down to see white feet. There was always a black ring surrounding the tub when the used bath water drained out.

Borger can be seen from far distances, especially at night. The town lights from the Phillips Petroleum Plant appear to stretch for miles and can fool visitors into thinking they are driving toward a larger city. The smell of sulfur and oil distinctly identifies the town. It's always been described as "the smell of money" in defense of the putrid odors.

By 1960, Borger was one of the largest suppliers for petrochemical products, oil, and carbon black production in Texas. Approximately 20,000 folks inhabited the town. These people were very content living an ordinary life. Simply parking down town on Main Street on Saturdays to watch people, friends and neighbors walk past was entertainment. Almost everyone knew each other. It seemed like there were no strangers, only family.

Located in the Bible Belt, there has always been an abundance of churches in town. Our family attended the First Baptist Church. It was formed in 1926 and has always had the largest congregation in the city.

At sixteen years old I was driving my brother and sister to the First Baptist every Sunday. My mother insisted we go even at times when she didn't attend. I was never comfortable with the Sunday school teacher who preached at us as "being sinners". He would proclaim fire and brimstone. "We are all sinners. Ask God for forgiveness or go to Hell!" After church, I would anxiously drive home with a guilt trip over my sins (whatever they were). I usually repented over looking through the women's garment's section in the Sears Roebuck catalog.

I always noticed the difference in some of the adults in the church. There were those who took great pride in showing off their best dresses and suits every Sunday. Some members were humble while others thought in their arrogant minds that "looking good" made them better and more righteous. The First Baptist Church became a place to worship for some and a status symbol for others.

Everyone liked the pastor of the church. He was a tall, handsome man with a natural confidence that disarmed members of the congregation. In later years, the rumor was that he had an affair with his secretary resulting in a divorce. I don't know what happened to this man or where he is today. I'm sure God forgave him even if some of his congregation secretly did not.

One Sunday, my friend Teddy rode with me to church. Following the services, we walked to the parking lot and got into my car. The first thing I did was to reach for the tuner on the radio. What a shock when my hand went into an empty space! A thief had stolen my radio while we were in church. All kind of cuss words came to mind and spewed forth. Teddy saw and heard how angry I was and did his best not to laugh when he said, "Man, I'm sorry that happened."

I tried to use the theft of my radio as a guilt trip on my mother. In an attempt to get out of going to church, I told her it was a bad omen. She just looked at me, rolled her eyes upward and said, "Go to Church!"

Going North down Main Street at one end of town was the Morley and Rex Theaters. The grownups called them "picture shows", and at the opposite end of town was the Hitching Post Drive Inn. Most of the students in High School drove 50 era model Fords and Chevrolets with loud glass pack mufflers, pipes and dumps. Main Street was a straight strip of asphalt with traffic lights on every block. Dragging Main and driving endless circles around the Hitching Post while honking and stuffing greasy fries in our mouths was the usual Friday and Saturday night small town recreation.

Gasoline was affordable at only 14 cents per gallon and drag racing from light to light on Main was a frequent occurrence. One night while stopped at a light in my 1954 Ford, the car next to me begin to rev up its engine. I accepted the challenge by reving up and getting ready to race. Turning to see who was driving the other car, I looked into the eyes of my Uncle. He was pointing his finger at me and had a smile on his face. I was so busted! It's easy to get caught in a small town.

Sex education originated behind fogged over car windows at the Buenavista and Plains Drive Inn theaters a few miles outside of town. This was the preferred place to smooch a girl, or hang out with buddies on weekends to watch a movie and check out who was there.

In the Winter of 1962, on a Saturday night, three buddies and I drove to the Buenavista Drive Inn. We all wanted to sneak in except for Gerald. So he got behind the wheel of my car. His brother Rick hid in a blanket in the back floorboard, and Johnny and I climbed into the trunk. The back end of the car sunk suspiciously low and almost touched the ground. When Gerald drove up to the ticket window, a fellow student was taking tickets that night. He asked, "Why are you driving Baxter's car?" The reply was, "My car is in the shop and he loaned me his."

Gerald paid for a single ticket and drove through. When Gerald pulled up next to the speaker stand, he got out and opened the trunk. We crawled out and got into the car. The four of us sat smugly watching the movie when we heard a knock on the window. Mr. Fagen, the owner stood outside saying, "Boys, get out of the car." We all stepped out and he asked for our ticket stubs. Gerald immediately handed over his stub while the three of us held our hands in our pockets.

Johnny spoke up, "We threw our stubs away!" Fagen was a big intimidating man. He looked Johnny in the eye and replied, "You threw your ticket stubs away on cash gift drawing night?" Without blinking, Johnny replied, "My Momma told me not to gamble." Fagen's face turned red and he demanded that we cough up money for three tickets. He took our money and told us to leave. We drove off with our tails between our legs while laughing over what Johnny had said.

That night was the last time I ever saw Johnny Baker. Years later, he may have gambled and lost to become one of the biggest mysteries in Borger, Texas.

Upon graduation in 1963, my father asked if I would like to attend The University of Oklahoma. Dad finished High School with a GED. Many of his business associates in the oil patch were engineering graduates from O.U. I looked at my Dad and said, "I'll go anywhere to get away from here." I'd never been to a big city and was ready to see more of the world. This would be the last time I would live in Borger for the next 40 years.

I will always be grateful to Dad for encouraging and supporting me in getting a college education. Upon graduation, I moved to Dallas, Texas where I spent over 30 years as an entrepreneur and owner of an advertising agency. I was fortunate to work with clients who are among the wealthiest companies in the world. My company was responsible for creating and sustaining professional corporate images starting with logos, advertising and public relations campaigns. In a large part we were accountable for how these companies looked to the outside world.

Over the years, I returned home to visit my family during the Holidays. It was jarring to see the city deteriorate. The population decreased and more abandoned buildings cropped up. It was an affront to my boyhood memories of what I recalled as a normal small Texas town. A hometown I had grown up to love.

CHAPTER THREE

COMING HOME

Near the middle of August 2003, I received a call from my sister saying that my mother was admitted to BSA Hospital in Amarillo, Texas. Mother was 86 years old and unable to walk due to severe back pain. She was also diagnosed with pneumonia. An MRI was performed to see if surgery would be necessary. In addition to osteoporosis, mother had suffered for years with high blood pressure and obesity.

I was in North Central Texas at the family lake house with my father when the call came. He wasn't happy about having to drive back home. The next day, we packed and headed out on the road. He drove his new Cadillac Escalade and I followed in my pickup. It was an eight hour drive to the hospital. When we got to mother's room, she was unconscious from heavy medications. The nurse explained that she was in extreme pain. I became worried that she wouldn't recover and walk again. Looking down at her, she opened her eyes. With tears in my eyes, I hugged her and said, "I'm sorry you're in here. I love you and I'm here to help."

It was decided that I would spend the night in the room and that my father would drive 50 miles to Borger to spend the night at home. Over the next week, I stayed with my mother and spent nights in the hospital with her. My sister and brother-in-law had to work, so they would come to visit in the evenings and on weekends.

It became embarrassing whenever my father was at the hospital because he would yell and scream at my mother over various meaningless things. At one point, a nurse said to my sister, "I'm thinking about telling your father to leave the room and the hospital." I felt horrible for my mother and sad over my father.

Years earlier, my father was diagnosed with cancer and had his prostate removed. He also had diabetes and was taking numerous medications. He's a big man of 6 foot 2 inches and weighs over 250 pounds. Walking had become a problem, but his vanity prevented him from using a cane for support.

He reminded me of my grandfather when he shuffled around and suffered from dementia. It saddened me to see my father abilities fade in old age. I had always been proud of my father's steadfastness, determination and ability to reason. He had a been a good provider for the family. Elder age was robbing him of everything physical and mental. He wasn't taking it gracefully. His golden years were being tarnished by stubborn pride and outrageous anger.

Surviving several falls, Dad always needed someone to help him stand upright. One day in the hospital room, he approached mother's bed and fell in the floor. Several nurses came running into the room to see if he was okay. My mind was going crazy imagining both my mother and father in hospital beds at the same time. Thank God he was not badly hurt!

My mind flashed back when I was four years old and Dad would put boxing gloves on me. He'd say, "Son, I don't want you to ever start a fight. But if someone starts a fight with you, I want you to know how to finish it." Then he would go on to say, "I don't want to ever hear you cussing or telling lies." He was passing on the teachings of his father, on how to become a man. Like many other men in his era, my father's image of manhood was showing up tough on the outside and never showing weakness on the inside. He believed, "a man stands on his own and never cries".

Just the thought of his going out swinging in his elder years would be overwhelming for our family. In his state of mind, rage was the only thing he had to fight the frustration and fear of losing control over his image of manhood.

The first week in September my mother transferred to Plum Creek to start rehabilitation. We would push her in a wheel chair down the halls each day to the physical therapy room. I'll always remember her courage in learning to use her hands, arms and legs in physical therapy. I stayed for over a week until I had to return to my business.

An eight hour drive gave me time to think things over. My mother had given her life to our family. She was a giver who put everyone else first and always worried about her children and grandchildren. For sixty years, father had always depended on her to cook and take care of his every need. She did everything for him. Now, he didn't show appreciation toward her in their retirement years. He was bitter, angry, totally selfish and behaving like a child.

Previously, he paid over fifty thousand dollars for his new Cadillac and refused to buy a new mattress for my mother. He would rather rant at her because she couldn't hear him rather than buy her new hearing aids.

Sadly, my sister is not in good health and suffers from obesity and diabetes. Every day, Monday through Friday, she teaches school. Her husband works for my father and has arthritis. They have been there to help my parents throughout the years. Now the stress on them was building because of my mother's condition.

Being unmarried, there was no one holding me back from moving home to help my family. I would need to close my landscaping business, but at some point it would be easy to reopen in Amarillo. The time had come to repay my mother for all the things she sacrificed in her life for the family and me. The thought of moving back to my hometown was appealing. I would be able to help my family and grow closer to my parents in their last years. It was a chance to reacquaint myself with some childhood friends.

By November, I was able to make the move. My parent's home has a downstairs with bedrooms and a bath that's been vacant for years. This would enable me to be there to help 24/7 with cooking, housework, landscaping and taking my mother out to run errands.

In the weeks ahead I drove my mother to Wallmart and the Grocery Stores. She would ride in a wheelchair while I pushed her down the isles. Eventually, she advanced to driving the motorized shopping carts. It was funny seeing her accidentally run into an isle of can goods. We both laughed about her driving. Care giving to a parent was new to me and I took pride in helping her walk again.

BORGER BETTERMENT COMMITTEE

Articles in the newspaper were covering a movement for a recall election of the city council. The city manager was in the middle of the controversy. This new group called "Borger Betterment Committee" was formed by Garrett Spradling. Garret was 24 years old and just graduating from college with a degree in political science. His grandmother owned the family business, Spradling Oil. I kept up with the articles about how they wanted the City Manager to resign.

The following is an excerpt from an opinion article I submitted to the newspaper:

"It's interesting to read about the unrest among citizens and the formation of the Borger Betterment Committee. As a newcomer, I don't know who is more right or more wrong. In my mind it really doesn't matter because change is often good. Change brings in new ideas that can make a difference. In my opinion, city councils and committees sometimes get bogged down in meetings where little is accomplished.

Which brings me to what inspired me to write this opinion letter. Last week, I drove around Borger taking photos of the city to promote my new business venture. I couldn't find a good sign or first impression leading into Borger. Finally, I took a photo of the red and white water tower with the wording Borger Bulldogs on its side. The tower was a proud sign at the entrance of Borger back in 1963.

Today, the paint has deteriorated so badly that it's hard to read. It looks like one of the abandoned buildings on Main Street. I've read and heard about the BEDC spending tax dollars to encourage new businesses to move here. Shouldn't this water tower, one of the most visible signs of Borger, Texas, look new to create a favorable first impression to potential business newcomers?"

It was surprising these comments created controversy. I considered it feedback for making improvements. Some others took it as criticism.

Later in the week, I had lunch with Jim Harder, the City Utilities Manager. We have known each other all our lives. I have fond memories when his father was our Scout Leader.

The water tower came up in our conversation. I responded, "I didn't mean to put anyone on the spot. My comments were meant to get people to look at ways to improve the looks of our town."

Continuing to talk about the city, he said the same person had been mayor for 17 years. The mayor is appointed by the council members and not elected. I said, "Most other cities or towns elect the mayor. It's only democratic. It brings in new life, new ideas and new leadership."

He went on to explain, "people never seem to mind how things are done. The majority of folks serving on the council are retired from Phillips Petroleum. The mayor used to work there too. I worked as a Phillips engineer and expected to retire from there. Like many others, I was laid off before my retirement benefits kicked in. Thank God, I was hired by the City."

PHILLIPS PETROLEUM COMPANY

In 1927, Phillips was the largest refinery in the world. Throughout the years, Borger has been a company town under the control of Phillips as the biggest employer. The better salaries in town are paid to engineers and managers at the refinery. This gives these individuals financial means and status. Phillips has always had several employees and retired employees pulling strings on the city council and local boards. Many of these people retire in Borger. Others stay a few years before transferring out. I've heard it said that some transferred Phillips executives refer to Borger as the "armpit of the Phillips World"

I remember in the 1960's when Phillips was an independent town with its own school district. Later, this changed, all the homes were moved away from the refinery and the school was closed. Negotiations started to consolidate the school districts. The Borger negotiators got into a heated deadlock with Phillips negotiators. Phillips abandoned the negotiations and went on to consolidate with Stinnett. To this day, Stinnett schools have benefited from Phillips taxes while Borger has suffered as a poor school district.

Through a contract agreement, The City of Phillips paid the City of Borger $320,000 to stay outside of the city limits. Phillips has paid the same amount for about 20 years without an increase until 2004. The contract had terms that it would increase by the cost of the CPI each year. It was never enforced. Last year (2004) was the year it was increased. If it had been increased by the CPI every year, Borger would be receiving about $700,000 a year from Phillips. If the refinery was annexed into Borger city limits, Borger would be receiving six to ten million dollars per year. This would double today's city budget and go a long way in improving the appearance of Borger.

Naturally, Phillips has a fear of annexation while inhabitants fear that if Phillips closed its refinery, the town would die over night. This fear combined with Phillips employees influencing the city council and has resulted in tax rebates that other companies in Borger do not receive.

Fear of closing is probably baseless. I've been told that if the refinery closed to a minimum operating standard with skeleton crews, it would require approximately $50 million dollars to clean up the facility per EPA requirements. Fifty million dollars is a lot of money to cough up especially when the refinery makes profits every year.

Today, Phillips has merged into two different companies. Conoco Phillips and Chevron Phillips. Rumor has it that the control has lessened from what it was in the past.

Until 2004, the appointed mayor for the preceding 17 years was a Phillips employee. Although the mayor is a good person, new ideas and changes come from new leadership. Everyone knows that's just one of the reasons the President of the United States and other elected government leaders have term limits. Electoral limits and majority rules established by our Constitution protects citizens from being ruled by Kings or Dictators.

A unique fact is that there has never been an election for mayor in the City of Borger.

CHAPTER FOUR

BORGER TODAY

Anyone coming through Borger probably wouldn't remember much about the town. If asked to list the benefits of living in Borger, one would probably list "friendly people" at the top of the list. They might say it's a good place to raise kids. They may be right, but most of the kids leave when they graduate because they can't find a decent job.

The Main Street today has been changed with planters and trees. Following this redesign, Borger was designated as the All American City. There are no longer flashing stop lights on each block. Many of the buildings are abandoned and have unsightly plywood over the windows. It looks like there has never been a sign ordinance. The majority of the store front signs look hand painted by the store merchant or an amateur sign painter.

At the South end of town is the abandoned four story Phillips Building with broken windows and at the North end of town is the abandoned 4 story Hotel Black in the same condition. Both buildings contain asbestos and would be very expensive for the city to tear down.

There is no zoning in many of the neighborhoods. A wood frame shack may be next door to a brick home. There are even some trailer homes on lots between residences. Many of the lower end neighborhoods have old tires and an assortment of junk in their front yards. The prestigious neighborhood is adjacent the Country Club where class distinctions are apparent. Here is where one's class status is populated by many member's of the First Baptist Church. It never hurts to be a Republican and a first family member to have status in Borger, Texas.

There are those who like to think of everyone as equal, but deep in their minds lurk bigotry. Many inhabitants remember the era of segregation and the everyday use of the "N" word. At one time Booker T. Washington was the only school for blacks to attend.

We lived in a neighborhood near Booker T. Washington. Every day when school let out, I would walk home past the baseball field. I recall days when I was the solitary white boy "honkey" on the outfield. The Tillman and Coffer boys were great ball players. When I came in to bat, arguments and scuffles ensued over who was going to use my glove.

When integration came, local citizens were horrified when blacks started swimming with whites at the community pool. Then, I was too young to understand that superstition and bigotry feeds hate and mistrust that corrodes communities.

A segment of the wealth in the city is derived by the independent oil producers. These individuals don't have to answer to the powers that be. This is the same mind set of risk takers that originally built the town. It's been said that some Phillips employees and retailers are jealous of these people because they don't have to answer to anyone. Unlike the retail business owners, the independents can't be boycotted or threatened when they speak their minds about local politics. I've heard it said, "The oil trash pay cash and the snobs charge on credit cards."

The "little guys" blue collar workers and office workers who consist of the majority of the population live in resignation. These are down to earth, honest people who sweat out a living every day. Many are cynical and feel they do not have a voice. Comments are heard on the street like, "Nothing is ever going to change here."

Anyone who enters any barber shop or beauty shop in town can listen and find out what's on these local's minds. Sitting in barber chairs and waiting on the sidelines, opinions are voiced whether they be truth or rumor. These are honest felt opinions expressed without arrogance. They know who got in a bar room brawl, who's sleeping with whom, and so forth. Some of these stories grow through exaggeration into rural myths. Often, they bring out anger, smiles and laughter among the participants.

REMOVAL OF CITY MANAGER AND RECALL ELECTION

In mid February, Chris Coffman, City Manager pled his case to the City Council through a published letter in the newspaper. He presented his case to council members that they resist political pressure to terminate him. The last sentence in the paper said it all. "Locks were changed at City Hall on Tuesday morning." The Borger Betterment Committee successfully moved against Hoffman and pressured him out of office.

Earlier in January 2004, the BBC had moved swiftly to organize and file recall petitions against Mayor Judy Flanders, Mayor Pro-tem Meryl Barnett and Councilman Jeff Brain. This came about because of their unyielding support of Coffman. Chris Coffman had made derogatory and unprofessional statements toward Terry Don Webster during an interview for a position on the police department. The council refused to reprimand Coffman for his statements. Garrett Spradling said, "How can the city council do that? No one is perfect. No one is 100%."

Another BBC member, Chuck Litterell said, "Whatever Chris wants he gets." He went on to say, "I have talked to several people in the previous months, and they feel they don't have a voice anymore. They feel like the council won't listen. Many people want a change, and we need to effect a change for the betterment of Borger. We want to replace the city council with people who care."

It wasn't published in the paper that Coffman stepped on "bigger toes in cowboy boots" and that led to his being kicked out of Borger. This was a major victory for the BBC even when a very close recall election in May failed to remove the three council members. The waters had been stirred in Borger, Texas.

COMMITTEE VOLUNTEER

When mother got better, I started taking her to Keeler Baptist Church. Dr. Paul Anderson is the minister. I immediately liked Brother Paul. His genuine smile and kind manner are very appealing. He is a human being who compassionately listens to people. Mother really likes him as well as the members in the church.

One evening, there was an opinion article in the newspaper where someone was driving their "BMW". I'm not referring to driving an automobile. We're talking about Bitching, Moaning, and Whining about a community problem. I thought this person needs to organize a committee or volunteer with others to solve the problem.

The matter inspired me to submit my opinion to the newspaper.

"We all get paid in "good feelings" for volunteering our time and giving to causes that help others. We receive prestige and recognition for doing a good job. If you're one of those who have been pointing a finger, maybe you should ask yourself what have you done to contribute. If you haven't, then you should volunteer and give your time to earn the right to criticize."

A week later, there was an unrelated article in the newspaper announcing the formation of an arts committee. The name of the person to contact was Mary Zan Warren. I called her number and she told me the first meeting would be at the Hutchinson County Museum. I said, "Put me on the list."

There were probably 12 people at the first meeting. The meeting was about organizing the first Art Festival in Borger. One woman on the committee worked at the museum and was on the Chamber of Commerce Board. She felt the best date for the Art Fest would be on Mother's Day weekend. Others agreed and it was settled. I thought differently, but didn't want to be outspoken since I was a newcomer. My advertising company had planned many similar events in the past. We would allow 6 months lead time for planning. There was only 3 months planning for this event. In the end, only three of us remained and the Festival was canceled.

The next committee was to create an art coop in an empty historic building on Main Street. Several artists in conjunction to the Museum Director and a City Councilman worked on this project. The Borger Economic Development Corp. owned the building and sold it to the Huffines who owned the building next door before we could complete our plans.

Before one of the meetings, a City Council Member told me a story of Borger's first fire truck. He said,

"There was a salesman from up North who came to meet with the city fathers about buying a fire truck. They decided to purchase the fire truck from the salesman. When he presented them the price they asked, "What's in it for us?" This shocked the salesman and he said he needed to talk with the president. The president of the company agreed. The city submitted the payment and some individuals got their kickback.

The fire truck arrived with no hoses. It wouldn't work. The city contacted the salesman who informed them they would have to pay more for the hoses. By the time all was said and done, the city paid a lot more for their first fire truck than expected."

The salesman got the last laugh!

In June, I joined the Borger Chamber of Commerce and became more involved by serving on a tourism committee. A local printer invited me to join the Rotary Club and I became a member. Years previously, I was a Rotary Club member in Fort Worth, Texas.

Dr. Paul Anderson was the president of the Borger Rotary Club. It felt good in getting to know others in business and become involved in the community.

The Rotary Club meets every Tuesday at noon. Each week I saw community leaders Conny Moore, Norm Lambert, Commissioner R.D. Corneilson and County Judge Jack Worsham attending the meetings. They appeared to be close friends and business associates.

CHAPTER FIVE

INVEST IN YOURSELF COMMITTEE

In July, 2004, Paul Anderson approached me about becoming a committee member of Invest in Yourself. He explained that Invest in Yourself was a group of citizens who were working together toward building a new hospital. He said they meet every Thursday morning at 7:00 a.m. I was eager to participate and told him I would attend the next meeting.

On Thursday morning I walked into the Borger Chamber of Commerce conference room for my first meeting. In attendance were Beverly Benton-Chamber Director, Conny Moore-President of the Chamber, Leon Mitchell—hospital attorney, Norm Lambert-hospital CEO, Susan Rawlins-hospital Marketing Director, Elaine Feese-hospital Human Resources Director, Jock Lee-Veterinarian, Debra Wells-Publisher of Eagle Press, Judy Flanders-Past Mayor of Borger, Cliff Stevens-Superintendent of Schools, and David Brandon-President of the Hospital Board, Scott Mills-Investment Counselor and Steve Williams-Contractor.

A handful of materials were handed to me. I briefly looked through them while Conny Moore started the meeting by addressing the advertising campaign. All the advertising materials were thorough and well organized. There was a slide presentation with a schedule of speaking meetings at civic clubs, city councils, and churches in the county. Mr. Moore said there was ten years in planning to build a new hospital.

The following Saturday morning I attended an orientation meeting. Garrett Spradling was seated next to me. My mind replayed all the newspaper articles covering Spradling's Borger Betterment Committee, the demise of the City Manager, and the recall election.

It was the intent of the IIY committee to gain Garrett's support by enlisting him as a committee member. The hope was to curtail any BBC opposition toward the bond election. He was asking very specific questions about surveys conducted, tax increases, etc. This was the second time I had met Spradling. I was impressed with the questions he asked. Although, he was only 24 years old, he wasn't someone who could be controlled.

The next Thursday morning meeting, I agreed to produce a web site for Invest in Yourself. I was very enthusiastic about donating this web site because I had already developed a business directory web site and was selling advertising to local businesses. As a newcomer, it was important to become acquainted with others in business. Surely, being on this committee carried prestige in supporting growth and goodwill for everyone in the community.

Previously, I had written an opinion article in the News-Herald in support of the hospital.

"It's interesting to read in recent GPCH advertisements published in the News-Herald that approximately 34% of health care dollars go to Amarillo that could be spent in Borger. The ad reads, If 55% to 65% of the Hutchinson County patients used their community hospital, this would provide an additional 5 million dollars to Golden Plains Community Hospital annually.

When one reads the qualifications of the doctors pictured in the ad, it doesn't make sense to drive 48 miles for the same quality medical care. It makes less sense to throw 5 million dollars out of our local economy to help Amarillo grow bigger and richer.

I would like to commend the hospital for presenting their professional staff of doctors in the newspaper ads and on the billboard."

I was naive of the past hospital history and I didn't know any of the doctors or their qualifications. I accepted the advertising at face value. After all, I thought, what could be wrong with a community hospital.

During the meeting there was a discussion about Nancy Young, editor of the Borger News-Herald. The consensus among the members was to recruit the newspaper editor to join the committee as a tactic to gain favorable press. There was fearful concern over the newspaper coverage of the demise of the City Manager and the recall election. One of the members volunteered to invite Nancy Young to the next meeting.

The next Thursday, Nancy Young attended the meeting and became a member of Invest in Yourself? This neatly wrapped up both newspapers in the county when editors of the Borger News-Herald and the Eagle Press were both officially committee members. Mission to control the press accomplished!

On Wednesday evening, July 7th, I picked up the newspaper and read the following headline.

25 Million Hospital Bond Election Called. Hospital District Board calls election for new hospital on September 11, 2004
by Nancy Young

Voters in Hutchinson County Hospital District will go to the polls September 11. To decide whether they want to build a new hospital to replace the present structure. Also planned, with medical facility is a medical office complex to house 10 physicians.

Two proposals will be on the ballot to be voted on by registered voters in the Hutchinson County Hospital District. Proposition one will be for the issuance of a 25 million hospital bond and leading a tax and payment and while proposition two were being for the levying of taxes at .25 cents per $100 valuation.

All but one of the Hutchinson County District Board of Directors were present at their monthly meeting. They were board members Kenneth Benton, Ed Davis, Jock

Lee, DVM; Glen Buckles, Julia Barker, and Jason Vance. Absent was board president David Brandon.

Leon Mitchell, hospital attorney and a member of the Invest In Yourself committee, said citizens in the hospital district have been circulating a petition for an increase in taxes. The petition was presented to Annette Ehrlich, board secretary for certification. The maximum number of signatures required to validate the petition was 100, and local citizens received 418 signatures prior to the meeting. The petition was certified by Ehrlich, and Mitchell said it was an opportunity for the board to approve and that the petition, which was a notice for a Hutchinson hospital bond and tax election, which is set to take place on September 11, 2004.

Attorney Leon Mitchell said the community and Fritch had been overwhelmed in working with Invest In Yourself on setting out meetings and had seen positive response from the community, thanks to the work of Jock Lee, DVM, and other Fritch citizens. Lee read the following resolution drafted by the City of Fritch concerning their support of Invest In Yourself and the bond election.

"Whereas, Golden Plains Community Hospital, currently 37 to 67 years old, and whereas, Golden Plains Community Hospital is in need of major renovations, and whereas, Golden Plains Community Hospital in his current state may not be able to serve this community indefinitely due to aging infrastructure, and whereas, the great city of Fritch needs a local Medical Center to care for its citizens now and in the future, therefore been resolved that the city of Fritch be a full supporter and backer of Invest in Yourself and a new Medical Center. Be it further resolved that the city of Fritch encourage all citizens of Hutchinson County Hospital District to vote yes for the bond election on September 11, 2004 to have a new Medical Center built."

The board opened up discussion from the floor for public comment and heard from local residents Mr. and Mrs. Lloyd Gooch. Mr. Gooch said he had crunched some numbers concerning the increase in taxes. He said he knew the citizens had received over 400 signatures on the petition, but he wanted to know if they were property owners, since they were the ones who would see their taxes rise. He said that even if enough people on the petition were registered voters, not all them with see a raise in taxes. He said that his Social Security had increased $17.05 a month and his Medicare supplements had also gone up. After estimating his property value, he said if taxes went up 150%, he and his wife would be paying possibly three dollars a month in increased taxes, which adds up to $36 a year. He said he would have a net loss of $1.75 dollars per month.

He went on to say he felt like he and his wife were the only ones who were speaking out against the new facility. He said that Hutchinson County can get by with a much less elaborate campus than was being proposed. He said it needed to be more than a first aid station, but not nearly as fancy as was being planned. The board, mentioned that 25 beds was being proposed for the new facility. Gooch asked them if that many beds could be filled and the board said it had a census of 32. He mentioned the motto of Invest in Yourself, which is "Your Health, Your Education, and Your Future". He wanted to know if the board had anything to do with possibly building new schools. They said they were not behind that. *(Note: Not an entirely true statement.)*

Gooch expressed his concern that in order to bring new schools into the community, a new bond election would have to be called, which in turn would bring in a new increase in taxes. He wanted to know if the plan was to bring up the new hospital and then look into refurbishing the schools.

Lee said that the first proposal was to look into what could be done to improve the health care system over the next 10 years and that it was something that they had been looking into for sometime already. He reiterated the fact that Invest in Yourself was merely a citizen's committee. He said their goal was to promote the county through making possible improvements in the hospital district and school system. He said it would be up to the voters to make those decisions when the time came.

Gooch said that he had talked with people in the community to see what their feelings were about a new facility, just to get some answers on his own.

"I can tell you this. I've asked the question, 'Are you for this new hospital?' of several people. I found one person is for it, but guess what? They're not a taxpayer," Gooch said.

"No matter if you get a gold plated hospital here, you will not get the two of us, because of the experiences we have had with doctors, and X-ray technicians," Gooch said.

He said that his wife had a mammogram back in 1994 at Golden Plains Community Hospital. They said that technician said she had nothing more than a mass and it was not cancerous. They got that word, and then when to Baptist Saint Anthony's in Amarillo, where Mrs. Gooch had another mammogram done. Immediately, the technician got them in with a doctor, who scheduled her for surgery the following day. She ended up having a lumpectomy because the mass was cancerous.

In the same News-Herald edition, Lambert said that the choice of people in the community had was that there needed to be a new bond issue and tax rate, along with a new medical center, because renovating the aging facility simply didn't make sense. He said that 20 million to renovate the old facility was not there, and that a bond issue and increase in taxes, would have had to be set in place to bring this to fruition.

"I think people have missed that point. I think there are some people that are thinking we just want 25 million to build a new hospital, and if we can just choose not to do that, everything will be wonderful," Lambert said. But we don't have 20 million to renovate, just like we don't have the 25 million."

He said that eventually, the present facilities will close, and if nothing is done, the building will continue to deteriorate, the money will not be there to fix it, and accreditation for me building could be lost. Once that happens, the Texas Department of Health, could come and revoke the county's license if the facility does not meet proper standards. He said, if the building continued to deteriorate, it would be more difficult to attract physicians to the community and keeping physicians that are already here. In Lambert's words," it's a never ending spiral downward."

He said there had been examples a good, solid primary and secondary care that had been given at the Golden Plains facilities, and that people constantly traveling to Amarillo, could result in loss lives, because of the time it takes to get from here to there.

He said that a 15 cents raise in taxes would mean about $66 for the average household in Hutchinson County. He said the cost of traveling one time to Amarillo, about the same as this number.

Lambert went on to say that if the hospital were to close today, the tax burden would not go away, and that money will go to indigent and charity care somewhere else. The board also talked about how the loss of the hospital could result in the decrease in property value, which they did not want to see happen either.

Lambert said that the community needed to know this election was not just about making the choice for a new hospital. "It's the choice of a new hospital or no hospital," he said.

I recognized Mr. Gooch as a member and deacon at the Keeler Baptist Church. How unusual that he would speak out against a hospital bond issue where his pastor, Dr. Paul Anderson was a leading member of Invest in Yourself?

Mr. Gooch made some good points about how the tax increase would affect him and other retired people on fixed incomes. Earlier, I had looked at local demographics and seemed to recall a population of over 3,500 over age 65 in Hutchinson County.

ANTENNAS RISING

During the following Thursday morning meetings, it bothered me the way some things were presented. When Mr. Moore went over the presentation in training sessions, it was reminiscent of sales people presenting canned land deals with a close for every objection. I mentally cringed whenever he would say, "The Amarillo developer had made a generous offer of 11 free acres if we build the hospital on it."

Throughout my career, I had written multimedia sales presentations for developers, recreational property sales organization, and all other types of corporations. I seldom worked for "generous" developers. They get into deals to make money. Many are not above awarding kick backs to those who help them put a deal together. I don't know if this was the case and probably never will know. But, what I do know is that my antennas were raised. Since the beginning of time, "FREE" is the biggest confidence word in the history of marketing. Nothing is ever free.

Another thing that made me uneasy was the plan to spend or what I considered waste three million dollars to tear down the old building. The old building is made of brick. Two of my past clients were brick companies. Brick doesn't deteriorate and will last hundreds of years. I couldn't believe my ears when one of the IIY members stood up and proclaimed in the style of an evangelist, "The building is in such bad condition, IT'S TURNING TO DUST EVERYDAY!

The canned response for tearing down the building was, "WE DON'T WANT ANOTHER EMPTY BUILDING IN BORGER ACROSS FROM THE HIGH SCHOOL THAT COULD BECOME A CRACK HOUSE!"

Was this an exaggeration and "injection of fear" sales technique to justify tearing down a building? What about other adjacent medical buildings that would eventually become vacated when the hospital was moved elsewhere? Wouldn't these also need to be torn down to avoid crack houses across from the High School?

HAVING SECOND THOUGHTS

I was placed on the schedule to speak in behalf of Invest in Yourself with Paul Anderson on air at the local radio station KQTY on July 20, 2004.

A few days beforehand, I had breakfast with Brother Paul and expressed my hesitation in continuing to serve on the Invest in Yourself committee. I brought up my concerns over people on the committee who appeared to have conflicts of interest. When I mentioned Conny Moore, he assured me that Mr. Moore was doing everything in the best interest of the community, it wasn't about money, and he was sort of retired. I told Brother Paul that I would continue and meet him at the radio station. I didn't want to let him down, but in the back of my mind remained serious reservations.

At the Borger Town Hall Meeting held at the High School Auditorium on July 22, there was one woman who asked a question that stood out. She identified herself as a retired nurse. She asked, "Has the hospital board looked into other ways to build the hospital that wouldn't increase taxes? Like a private hospital group?"

The IIY committee person answering the question stumbled and hesitated before responding, "We use Quorum as a consulting firm. They have told us no one would be interested and that we are under the radar."

I didn't feel good about how the question was answered and wondered if others present felt the same way. There was way too much indecision in the answer.

At the next Thursday morning meeting, I recall Conny Moore pointing out his concern over the exact question asked at the High School meeting. He proceeded to coach those present how to be very positive and affirmative in responding to that question whenever it was asked again.

Had there been a true effort to find other sources to build a new hospital, or was this just a canned response to close the deal with a 25 million dollar burden on taxpayers? Was there nothing to tell and everything to sell?

THEY CALL THIS DEMOCRACY

The next Thursday, I arrived at the Chamber Offices shortly before seven a.m. When I entered the conference room, Beverly Benton, Chamber Director and Conny Moore were there. We exchanged greetings as I walked toward the coffee pot to pour a cup and pick up a granola bar before taking a seat at the back of the room. I placed my brief case on the table in front of me. Soon the room began to fill as others arrived. Cliff Stevens, Superintendent of Schools sat to my left and Jock Lee the Veterinarian from Fritch sat on my right a few chairs away from me. Dr. Paul Anderson entered the room and took a place across from me. It was good to see Brother Paul because his friendly demeanor always made me feel better.

The Chairman, Conny Moore called the meeting to order. Seated around the table were Norm Lambert, hospital CEO, Susan Rawlins, marketing director, Elaine Feese, human resources director, Leon Mitchell, attorney and David Brandon, president of the board for the hospital.

The opening discussion was about a group from Mississippi coming to town. An irritated hospital CEO said, "Garrett Spradling and the BBC contacted this group from Mississippi who will be here to tour the hospital." He continued to say, "I believe this has to do with Dr. Holland and others."

This was the first time Dr. Holland or any others were mentioned. I had only seen these Doctors pictured across a billboard on the way out of town. Lambert's comment puzzled me because I knew nothing about of the past history of Golden Plains Community Hospital.

Then one of the committee members who was also a hospital board member spoke. He said, "Why do we even have to recognize these people from Mississippi? Can't we just keep them out of the building?"

This statement went all over me. Why would anyone even think or say they could keep someone from touring a public facility. The idea made me boil and went against every democratic principle in my body. My mind was telling me to stay cool but I had to speak up.

"I don't think it's right trying to control anyone from touring a public hospital supported by tax dollars. What's wrong in this town is everyone on the street I talk to feels the situation is hopeless in Borger, Texas. All I've heard on the street is cynicism. Too many people believe and say, "Nothing is ever going to change here".

"What's the problem is with the BBC? A city needs different opinions and ideas if it is ever going to grow." I continued speaking until a saw a redness in the face of the hospital board president, sitting across from me. He begin to address my comments. I really don't recall his exact words. I was at a point of trying to regain my composure.

After all, I joined this committee to become a part of the community. These were the leaders of the community. I had started a new business and needed support from these people for my business to grow.

I was relieved when the meeting was over and glad to leave that morning. It was awkward telling Paul Anderson goodbye and saying, "I'll talk with you later." It felt like I let down a man I respected.

EYES WIDE OPEN

That evening, I called a "Borger Native". We talked about what happened in the meeting. She said, "You should resign from the committee. Things are not right there with the management. Go look at the pre-fabricated doctors building on McGee Street next to the hospital." "Why?" I asked.

"It cost $600,000. There's no way . . . something's wrong. You'll understand when you see it."

I said, "Okay, I'll take a look at it. Is there anything else?"

"The eleven acres that's being donated to the hospital from the developer in Amarillo. It's in a flood plain. It wasn't that long ago when the developer approached the city to foot the bill for dirt work in order to build a Townhouse project there. I recall the developer making presentations to several real estate firms in town."

"What did the city do," I asked. "Turned the developer down. Refused to spend taxpayer dollars to float the deal," he said. "Anything else," I responded.

"Oh Yeah! I went to the hospital emergency room when I cut my hand. When I got the bill, they charged me several hundred dollars a stitch on my insurance."

"You got to be kidding me. I'll go look at the Doctor's building in the morning. Talk to you later," I said.

The next morning I drove to the Doctor's building. My first thought from seeing the building was, "No way did this building cost $600,000 to build." It was a prefabricated structure that reminded me of a "cracker box." I suspected something was wrong. So, I called some other people in town and they concurred somewhere between $550,000 to $600,000.

Later that day, I drove to look at the eleven acres. The first thing I noticed was a major drainage ditch cutting through the property. The land is located where all the other adjacent developed property drains across the acreage.

Thinking back over the Invest in Yourself meetings, I couldn't recall anyone mentioning the cost of excavation to prepare the site for the proposed building.

Considering these circumstances and my gut feelings from listening to how the Invest in Yourself members were presenting the deal, I began to regret being on the committee.

CONTROVERSY BEGINS

On the weekend of August 14 and 15th 2004, the front page of the News-Herald, read:

Hospital District Voting Begins Soon. One of the most controversial elections ever faced by voters in Hutchinson County is less than a month away. Early voting begins August 20 and ends September 7. Voters wishing to cast ballots by personal appearance must go to Golden Plains in the hospital, 200 South McGee, in Borger between the hours of eight A. M. and five P.M. been beginning August 25.

Hutchinson County clerk Beverly Turner contacted the News-Herald Friday and said she has received numerous inquiries about the upcoming election, with many people asking why the balloting is being conducted at the hospital. Turner explained that the Hutchinson County hospital district is the taxing entity in charge of the election, not the county. She added that each taxing entity is always in charge of their own elections.

Many citizens did not like or trust going to the hospital for early voting.

WHO IS JERRY STRECKER?

There was a letter to the editor with unusual insight. It was uncanny how many things pointed out in the letter were the very ones bothering me.

Wants new medical facility; opposes election.

Dear editor:

To begin, let me say that I am strongly in favor of the wonderful hospital in Borger and strongly opposed to this bond election on September 11. I am very much in favor of a long range plan for excellent health care in Hutchinson County, if these plans include the right kind of hospital for our community.

Everyone seems to admit that our present hospital is adequate for the near future, even for five years or more, so why the sudden rush to action? Our whole community deserves to have some time to think about our future, to talk to each other, to share ideas and come up with the best plan we can envision to take care of our own and our neighbors' health care.

This kind of grass-roots process is exactly what the Texas Hospital Association recommends before any plans are finalized for building a new hospital. I know because I called and asked them.

My understanding is that the three town meetings where loaded with pro-hospital people and designed to be a sales job and not an open discussion. True public discussion takes place before decisions are made, not after the bond election is already set. I, for one, want to thank the Borger-News Herald for providing a true open forum of shared ideas. I think I have read every single letter that has appeared in the paper, both in favor and against this bond election. It seems obvious that a whole lot of people are interested in this issue, and I know I have learned so much from what each of you has written.

I wish the hospital board had not rushed into forcing us, the public, to make a decision of either a $25 million facility or supposedly no hospital in all. I wish the board would have given us that respect and the time to look at all the options, like: (1) What do we really need (top priority); (2) What can we afford it? (Big issue, when this raises taxes 150%), and (3) How do we best negotiate together what we need and what we can afford in such a way, that it builds a positive consensus within our community, instead of causing such divisiveness.

I wish people felt united and excited over what we are deciding about our long-range future. Instead, it seems that fear has become the prime motivation in many people's minds. Many letters express deep fear that unless we vote "for" this bond election, we will end up with no hospital at all, including emergency care when it is so critical. And if I were a hospital employee, I would also be terribly scared of losing my livelihood in Borger. Others have expressed an equally deep fear that unless we do vote" against" this bond election, we will be left with a $25 million debt, a facility, we do not really need, and a 150% increased tax burden on those barely able to make their expenses now. Records prove that barely one third of our people choose to use GPCH because they consider its standard of care to be less than what they want or need for their families. People are afraid of pouring more tax money into a hospital that already loses up to $700,000 a year, and what if this brand new hospital eventually closed its doors in bankruptcy. We taxpayers are still stuck with the bill.

In my opinion, both sides have legitimate fears. On September the 11, one group is going to win and the other group is going to lose. We will have been forced into bitterly combating among ourselves over something that is so good and so important to our whole community. It saddens me that our hospital board has chosen to set this bond election under such a short time frame, and forcing people to make either/or decisions, as if the only option is either close the hospital" or" to build a $25 million medical complex that includes a hospital, several doctors' offices, and even possibly a retirement center and nursing home. For me, I do not like either choice. I will not vote for 150% tax increase on those who can barely afford food and medicine. Likewise, I don't ever want to vote not to have medical care, especially emergency care, for the people of our county.

The tragedy of this election is we could have all of what we really need. We can have a new hospital that truly fits our needs, and our budget. We can have jobs for those who take care of our sick and elderly. We can have a hospital that truly listens to any complaints about care that is less than satisfactory and then do something about it. We could have 80% of our people using our hospital instead of 30%. We could talk to each other and turn our fears into mutual understanding. We can get all the ideas possible from as many people as possible; we could sort through all these ideas and possibilities to come up with the best options; and we could believe that the Lord will guide us in this endeavor if we first gathered in prayer to ask for his help. We need and deserve all of this in Hutchinson County if we are doing a good job of caring for the sick and the dying.

But our hospital board has chosen to use a slick campaign instead of real communication. They call it" Invest In Yourself!" I am surprised that our government in Washington didn't come up that slogan. a long time ago. Think of all the good reasons that they could come up with for asking to invest in ourselves by raising our taxes. A few people hit the pork barrel and the rest of us pay for it at the rate of a 150% tax increase.

When I was a little boy on a farm, my Dad used to say about politicians and taxes: "if it looks cow manure; and it smells like cow manure; and it feels like cow manure; it probably is cow manure!" I know this much. There is something about this whole bond election that does not add up and it certainly does not smell right.

I wish the hospital board would have gone about this whole issue in a very different way. But now it seems that since the board is unwilling to rescind this September 11th election, so we the public have to do it for ourselves. Our vote against this bond election is a vote to" start over", not a vote against good medical care for our people. We need to insist on our right to speak and be heard before decisions are made. There are many opinions and options, and we deserve better than a yes or no to one possibility. When people have honest comments about the past or real questions about the future, they deserve better than to have fear, guilt, and shame dumped on them for their viewpoints.

So, I am asking all of you to care enough to vote; to vote proudly; and vote against the bond election. We need to get this $25 million millstone off our necks. Then we can start over, and give this issue of future health care the due diligence it deserves.

Jerry Strecker . . . Borger

CHAPTER SIX

RESIGNING FROM INVEST IN YOURSELF

On Monday morning, August 16, I went to Keeler Baptist Church to meet with Dr. Paul Anderson and submit my letter of resignation from Invest in Yourself. I told Brother Paul that I could not in good conscious continue as a committee member. I handed him Jerry Strecker's opinion letter and asked if he had read the letter because it touched on many things troubling me.

I said, "The past management decisions made by the hospital administrator shocks me."

Brother Paul said, "The management can be changed after the bond issue is passed. This community needs a new hospital and assisted living facility"

I responded, "I agree the need is there, but my business experience tells me not to invest $25 million dollars into poor management. Change the management, then invest the money."

After further discussion, we respectively shook hands and I left his office to return home where I e-mailed the resignation letter to the editor of the Borger News-Herald.

MY TIMING FOR GOING TO THE NEWS-HERALD WAS FORTUITOUS.

On Tuesday morning I stopped by the newspaper to make sure the editor received my e-mail. When I walked through the front door, there was Conny Moore, Chairman of Invest in Yourself, sitting next to editor Nancy Young's desk. I was taken aback when the two looked up at me. I said, "Nancy, I e-mailed you and this is a hard copy." She took the copy in hand and I quickly turned to leave with my "ears a burning". Moore never said a word. I wondered if they were as surprised to see me. Had the editor contacted Moore about my resignation? Was he sitting there giving his rebuttal to my letter?

RESIGNATION HITS THE NEWS-HERALD

The headline on the front page of Tuesday, August 17, paper read **"Hospital Issue Arouses Increasing Agitation**." Baxter resigns from Invest in Yourself committee; Moore, Williams respond," By Nancy Young, editor.

The article began, "Stating he has not seen evidence that a new hospital is the best option for the Hutchinson County Hospital District, a member of the Invest in Yourself Committee resigned from the committee Monday afternoon.

IIY is supporting the passage of a bond issue to construct a new medical facility. Glenn Baxter, a local businessman, notified the News-Herald he has submitted his resignation to Dr. Paul Anderson, who is also a member of the committee. He also gave a copy of the resignation letter to the News-Herald. The letter cites numerous reasons for his decisions.

The entire text of his letter is printed in today's edition. Also, comments from Conny Moore, chairman of the group, will follow. The News-Herald also contacted Steve Williams, a local businessman, for comments as Baxter referred to him in the resignation letter.

The Baxter letter reads as follows:

Dear Invest in Yourself Committee Members:

I have decided to resign from the Invest in Yourself Committee. My decision is based on the following reasons:

1. I believe that it is inappropriate for insiders or people who have personal and private interest in the hospital activities to personally profit from the hospital. It has bothered me that Conny Moore, who is known to be the pharmacist for the hospital, is the leader of Invest in Yourself Committee. Being the sole pharmacist in a new facility away from the other pharmacies in town would certainly provide a strategic benefit to Mr. Moore.

2. I am not certain about Steve Williams, but I am told that his construction company does asbestos removal. A 3 million dollar contract for demolishing the old facility could provide profit to his company and would result in a personal gain.

3. In my opinion, The Borger Chamber of Commerce is an organization for all business members. I know for a fact that not all chamber members are in favor of a new $25 million hospital. Since Mr. Moore is also President of the Chamber, this creates another problem for those members of the chamber like myself who feel uncomfortable in disagreeing with the goals of Invest in Yourself. I feel that the Borger Chamber has placed itself into taking a political position that is not in the best interest of all members.

4. I don't really see the members of Invest in Yourself as a true mix of people in our community. There are no senior citizens on a fixed income or blue-collar workers serving on the committee. In my opinion, the committee does not represent the whole community.

5. I have not seen nor have I been told of any focus groups conducted or research conducted by the committee to find out what the people in Hutchinson County as a majority would really prefer in a Health Care System. As a committee, you have predetermined what is best for the majority of citizens in Hutchinson County and launched an aggressive marketing sales pitch and strategies to overcome all objections. Leading this sales pitch is the Chamber President and the pharmacist for the hospital who in my opinion is attempting to control the attitudes of the committee and how individuals respond to questions.

6. As stated "community-leaders", Invest in Yourself Committee has assumed that it already knows what is best for the community. You're obviously operating in a very unscientific manner by not taking time to ask people by conducting surveys to test out your assumptions. You've already made a plan set in concrete with a strategy to manipulate and overrun any opposition. The committee is taking this plan to town meetings with the guise of answering questions in a democratic spirit. Did anyone ever consider that it might be better to have town meetings and gathering input from citizens before creating the plan?

7. I don't think that opposition surprised anyone on the committee. I would expect everyone to be aware of the numerous complaints about the services and the management of the hospital. I became concerned when I started asking people about their experiences at the hospital. It's alarming to know that no one told me about a really positive story. In fact, a high-ranking county official told me a horror story about what happened to a close relative. I was not totally aware of the past problems until I conducted my own research this last week. At this point, I am shocked by some of the past management decisions that have occurred at the hospital over the last 6 years. Never in my career in marketing have I seen an attempt of an orchestrated few to sell a majority of citizens on trusting them to place negative luggage into a new facility with expectations that everything will change into a bright and shining future.

8. In the past two meetings, I have heard members refer to opposition as "radicals." Another member suggested that the committee not recognize opposition and refuse them permission to tour the facility. The audacity of this comment lit my fuse. Wake up people and "get this" . . . we live in a democracy. Committees should not try to control and rule as kings. The name of the hospital is Hutchinson County Community Hospital. A community of citizens supports it. The hospital board is in place to serve the welfare of the community of citizens. It is not there to support bad management decisions and poor quality service. The board should not be a "good old boy society" and behave in a righteous manner in response to an outcry of citizens about poor quality whether it is real or perceived.

9. I am not convinced nor have I seen evidence to convince me that remodeling the existing hospital facility would not be the best choice for the community. (Even the committee's presentation states a savings of $7 million by remodeling.) The existing hospital is located in the central business district and supports several other businesses that occupy surrounding buildings. At present, there are 4 buildings vacant or abandoned. Moving the hospital to the new location would surely create other vacant buildings. And demolition of the hospital would surely leave a vacant lot eye sore for residents and visitors. A recognized negative distraction in small towns is abandoned buildings. These buildings are the signs of a dying town as seen from the eyes of visitors and those who looks at small towns as a place to move into with new business. They create a "rural ghetto".

10. The hospital building is brick and brick will last for centuries. Brick buildings in small and large cities preserve the unique heritage for future generations. Many cities have opted to renovate their hospitals rather than tear them down . . . even with asbestos problems. In the past most major cities let the buildings in their central business district deteriorate. Today, they have restored their older buildings and central business districts are thriving. The real opportunity in Borger and Hutchinson County is to create a plan to stop abandoning and tearing down buildings and begin restoring to build a healthy and unified community. Why live the past mistakes that other cities have learned from experience?

I resign from what I feel is best in my heart. My personal goal is excellence for my hometown and every citizen in it.

Sincerely, Glenn Baxter

The article goes on to say that Conny Moore issued the following statement Tuesday morning:

"I would like to first respond to the statement that being the pharmacist for the hospital would provide a strategic benefit to myself. It would be much better if people would get the true facts before they make public statements. The hospital pharmacy only dispenses medications to patients in the hospital and there is no benefit as it being in a new or old pharmacy.

"As for the Borger Chamber of Commerce being involved in the hospital campaign, the meeting room that is used for the meeting is also available to other organizations in the community. The fact that I am presently serving as the chairman is only indicative of the lifestyle I have embraced ever since I moved to Borger. I have always served on committees and organizations to benefit others and our area, and I find that others who give of themselves unselfishly are a lot less quick to complain and condemn.

"The process of looking at the needs of our community and county began with a meeting of about 100 elected leaders in our county with an open invitation to anyone who would like to attend.

"All meetings of the Invest in Yourself campaign have been open to anyone who would like to attend. To the best of my knowledge all the meetings have been open to the public and all questions that anyone asked have been answered.

"There are many advantages and opportunities for our community at this time. One of the greatest is the opportunity to have someone build a retirement center in our community.

"If we will just look at other communities and counties and not make the same mistakes here, then we can benefit greatly. Clarendon, Texas is a good example.

"About 30 yeas ago the state closed their hospital. The community divided instead of joining together. As a result, the doctors chose not to continue their practice and part of the hospital board resigned. The disgruntled citizens then built a new hospital at the taxpayers expense, but to their surprise then could not open it without doctors and during those 30 years the hospital has been open less than six months.

"All efforts of the Invest in Yourself are open to county residents and are backed with 10 years of research. I encourage everyone in the county to get involved by working together to make Hutchinson County the best it can be.

Steve Williams, who is also active in IIY, issued the following comment Monday afternoon regarding Baxter's statement.

"Regarding the comment about whether my construction company does asbestos removal, I can say flat-out, that my construction company does NOT do asbestos removal in public facilities such as the hospital," he said.

When asked if his company would do any work on the construction of the hospital he responded, "Given any opportunity we might bid it, but I rather doubt it. We really aren't qualified by experience to do any of the work that would come up on this building."

YOU CAN BS THE TOURIST!

Mr. Bobby Brantwein, a 20 year resident, responded to the newspaper article with his half page opinion letter the following day. However, his letter did not appear until seven days later on August 24th.

I was very appreciative when reading his (Baxter's)statement . . . "Wow! I've got to say that Baxter's decision to resign from the IYY committee was an act of integrity, and his revealing "insider's look" to the public was an act of bravery. Thank you, sir for your efforts to offer those of us outside the committee other reasons to consider casting our votes."

Mr. Brantwein went on to say, "One of the reasons Baxter mentioned is something that I too, have had concerns about: the fact that the IYY committee is largely made up of members of our communities who have high paying/or high ranking jobs, OR, are closely with or employed by the Hospital District. Can someone say, "conflict of interest?"

Regarding those on the committee who are somehow involved/employed by the Hospital District, or may otherwise profit from the proposed issue, where is the integrity there? (Mr. Steve Williams, IIY Committeeman-your company, SERCO, does perform asbestos abatement as one of its contractual services. How is an old hospital's asbestos any different than the type found in petroleum manufacturing?? Are you saying that if the old building's abatement job goes up for bid, that you will not bid on it?) And does anyone believe Conny Moore, in his position as hospital pharmacist will not benefit in some way.

"Guys, you can B.S. the tourists, but I live here."

I smiled at reading the last sentence. Maybe I had been a gullible tourist who mistakenly joined Invest in Yourself.

CHAPTER SEVEN

PHONE RINGING OFF THE HOOK

That evening and the next two days I received approximately 30 phone calls. These were left on my voice mail.

"Mr. Baxter, thank you so much for your letter. I greatly appreciate it."

"Glenn, this is Roy Haley and I read the paper today and I wanted to call you and complement you on your fine letter and for what you did. I'm glad you saw these people for what they are. I was born and raised here in Borger, and what you wrote, I feel the same as you do. Thank you again.

"This is Gerry Holland calling for Glenn Baxter and I just want to thank you for your article in the paper. Thank you very much."

"If this is the Baxter residence I just wanted to call and thank you for the letter that you wrote against Invest in Yourself committee. I am a senior citizen and my husband is a senior citizen. We have felt this is something that is being forced on Borger. I appreciate you and I appreciate the courage that it took to present this letter to this committee. My name is Sue Tindall.

"Glenn, this is Dr. Jerry Strecker. I just got home and saw your article. I heard about it at the office from several people saying how special your letter is and it's exactly what's needed to be said. I appreciated the powerful truth you expressed and again thank you for your courage."

"Glenn, this is Bill Klien here in Borger. If you're the one that put that article in the paper, I want to thank you from the bottom of my heart. It was something I could see, but not being an insider there wasn't anything I could do about it. Good luck to you and don't take any flack."

"This is Pat Cleveland a former member of the hospital board. I just want to thank you for your letter in last night's paper. It needed to be said and there is a lot more going on down there."

"Mr. Baxter, this is Olin Holliman. I just wanted to thank you for stepping away from that hospital committee. We would appreciate any kind of help you could give us to stop that. I've been retired from Huber for 16 years and I think there's a better way. Thank you."

These supportive calls from "real" people reinforced my decision to step on toes and go against what others called the "Click" in Borger.

When I went in the bank lobby the following day, many of the ladies behind the desks complimented the resignation article. The consensus was that they had often wished they could speak their minds but were afraid of repercussions that might lead to losing their jobs.

It was gratifying hearing people complimenting my actions. How democratic is a small town that suppresses and controls people through fear? How did people get into power who can prevent free speech through boycotting and intimidating retail business owners ?

At one point, I had considered walking away from the committee and into the woodwork. But, the injustice handed out to Doctors and others should be spoken out against. I would rather have my personal integrity than money from business. This is my hometown. I was determined to join with others and do everything in my power to make a difference.

MEETING JERRY STRECKER

I wanted to respond to Dr. Strecker's voice message so I looked up his phone number in the directory and found him listed as a doctor of psychology. When the receptionist answered the phone, I asked, "Can I speak to Doctor Strecker?" She replied, "Who's calling please." I replied, "Glenn Baxter" and she said, "one moment please."

"Hello, this is Doctor Strecker."

"Dr. Strecker, you left a message on my voice mail about my resignation from Invest in Yourself and I was impressed by your letter to the editor. Would you be able to meet with me this evening? I have some questions for you."

Strecker replied, "I would really like meeting you. How about the Pizza Hut on the way to Fritch at 6:00 PM?"

"I'll see you there. Goodbye."

When I walked in the door of Pizza Hut, there was a man about 6 foot tall, gray hair and slight build. I asked, "Are you Doctor Strecker?" He extended his hand replying, "Yes, good to meet you."

We moved to a table and exchanged courtesies. I looked at Dr. Strecker and said, "I really appreciated your letter. It was amazing how what you wrote touched on many things troubling me as a committee member. I grew up here but only returned about 6 months ago."

Dr. Strecker informed me that he was a past hospital board member. Our meeting continued for about an hour in which the Doctor told me the entire background story about Golden Plains Community Hospital. I was shocked over many things he told me, especially about one disturbing incident at the hospital that had haunted him for years.

Strecker was mild mannered and seemed sincere in everything he told me. I had no reason not to believe him. He wasn't telling to sell, he was telling because he cared.

CITIZENS WHO CARE ABOUT HUTCHINSON COUNTY

My mind kept going over Strecker's story as I drove home that evening. There was no time to waste. The hospital election was scheduled on September 11th. I had less than 30 days to produce a marketing attack that would help defeat the $25 million hospital bond. GPCH and the Invest in Yourself committee claimed there were 10 years spent into planning and creating their campaign. That night, I wrote and e-mailed the following press release that appeared in the newspaper on Wednesday, August 18, 2004.

NEW COMMITTEE FORMED ABOUT MEDICAL CENTER
Glenn Baxter announces the formation of "CITIZENS WHO CARE ABOUT HUTCHINSON COUNTY".

The goal of this specific purpose committee is to work together where each citizen may prosper and benefit from an inspired community life based on a shared vision for all citizens and not only a few who decide for others. The "CITIZENS WHO CARE ABOUT HUTCHINSON COUNTY" strongly supports voter turnout for the upcoming bond election on September 11, 2004. The members oppose the $25 Million Bond Election as formulated by Invest in Yourself Committee. "We strongly believe in excellence in health care for all citizens in Hutchinson County.

We believe that there is more than one choice as presented by IIYC for the Hutchinson County voters to consider and we are concerned for the 3,672 Senior Citizens in Hutchinson County over the age of 65. Many of these citizens are on fixed incomes and would needlessly suffer financially, should the present bond proposal be passed. We want time to explore and present several health care service options to the community." said Glenn Baxter, Chairman of the Committee. Any citizen in Hutchinson County

Anyone interested in joining or contributing to the committee may contact Glenn Baxter online at . . . or by mail at "CITIZENS WHO CARE ABOUT HUTCHINSON COUNTY" PO Box, Borger, Texas 79008.

GETTING ARMED WITH FACTS

In marketing and political warfare, the more one knows about an opponent the better. My next step was to find out everything about the past history of Golden Plains Community Hospital.

When the phone rang on Thursday morning, it was like a prayer being answered. On the line was a source who asked to remain anonymous concerning a box of records and documents pertaining to the hospital. I thought it was odd that Frank Smith's name was mentioned in connection to these documents. Frank Smith was a dominate leader in

Borger who had passed away years ago. I agreed to meet the source to take possession of the records and hold in safe keeping.

What I couldn't find in the box of documents, I would research at the Library. Old newspaper stories can tell a lot about individuals who were pulling strings in the past and how they are linked to today's events. It would be like placing links in a chain and looking for a pattern of events that expose the story.

In addition to my financially contributing to the campaign, I would need to contact business people with an interest in defeating the bond proposal and ask for contributions.

1989 to August, 2004

Searching for Past Links

CHAPTER EIGHT

THE HOSPITAL DISTRICT

I enjoyed the smell of old books and newspapers in a back room of the Hutchinson County Library. Newspapers chronicled the Hospital District formation in 1989. Starting that year and searching forward in newspapers provides glimpses of local history and events. According to 1989 newspaper articles, legislation had been passed in Austin to form the Hutchinson County Hospital District. The county commissioner's court of 4 commissioners overseen by County Judge Tom Wicker representing four precincts would appoint 3 members to the Board of Directors and the other 4 would be elected.

It was Monday, November 13, 1989 when the ribbon was cut and the crowd applauded in celebration of opening the new Golden Plains Hospital District. The Borger High School Band was playing the Star Spangled Banner while the United States and Texas flags were raised.

Seven temporary members were appointed to the first Board of Directors. Jerry Waggoner served as president. Other directors included Dr. Ed Quiros, Jack King, Mark Mayberry, Dr. Dane Welch, Deborah Summers and Tambre Lumpkin

Throughout 1989, present day 94th District Attorney, Clay Ballman was prominently mentioned throughout editions of the News Herald as being involved in forming of the hospital district. Ballman was representing Precinct 1 as a County Commissioner. This is the same precinct that R.D. Cornelision was elected to fill when Clay Ballman vacated the spot by winning the election for District Attorney.

I found the link to the present day District Attorney to be very interesting. At the time, I didn't realize how this link could possibly influence future decisions concerning Golden Plains Community Hospital.

PANHANDLE DRUG TRAFFICKING

While looking through the newspapers, I ran across an interesting article with the Headline: PANHANDLE FAVORED BY SMUGGLERS. "The seizure of nearly a ton of cocaine from a plane forced to land in the Texas Panhandle is evidence of the steadily increasing air smuggling traffic between northern Mexico and one of the state's remotest areas, federal authorities said.

The 1,940 pounds of cocaine onboard a Queenaire Beechcraft was the largest cocaine seizure ever in Northern Texas. The Panhandle's remote level farm roads have long been favorite clandestine landing sites for Mexico based smuggling rings. Restrictions on flights through Cuban air space in recent months have prompted the Colombian Medellin cartel smugglers to turn to West Texas routes.

Interstate 40 cutting through the Panhandle has been a mainline for small time drug dealers and big time drug mules driving vehicles loaded with coke and marijuana. Cocaine trafficking was prevalent throughout the 80's and 90's in the Panhandle. Easy money was indiscriminate and tempting. The need and greed for power became the order of the day. During this time period in Borger's history, another boom of white oil and white powder corrupted and busted some of the perceived morally upstanding citizens.

Bankers played fast and loose with depositor's funds. High stakes poker games and gambling ruined some political careers including the removal from office of a Hutchinson County District Attorney who was arrested in an illegal gambling raid by the Sheriff's department. Distinctions between good and evil faded to gray while many good "Christian Citizens" looked the other way.

When District Attorney Rick Roach was arrested in 2005, it was revealed that one of the suspicions leading to the FBI investigation was when Roach started offering DPS officers Rolex watches as an incentive for making more money seizures when they stopped drug traffickers along I-40. The DA knew that any confiscated money went into bank accounts controlled by his office. Up to 30% of the money went to the prosecuting attorney's office. More than three million dollars seized and controlled by Roach's office would tempt any criminal mind to embezzle some of the money.

Today, cocaine busts are seldom mentioned in the local press. Since my return to Borger two years ago, the majority of drug articles in the Borger News Herald cover an epidemic of methamphetamine labs cropping up in oil fields and other locales in Hutchinson County.

PHARMACISTS AND ILLEGAL DRUGS

I had not spoken to my High School classmate Johnny Baker since 1963. He left Borger to become a Pharmacist and returned to open the John Baker Pharmacy in Megert shopping center.

I ran across newspaper articles where his mother reported him missing on June 21, 1994 at 10:00 a.m. When Police Officers searched his residence they found no evidence of anything missing. According to Chief of Police, Mike Smith, "Baker's billfold, credit cards, personal items and vehicle were still at the residence. At the time we do not know if his absence is voluntary or involuntary."

Rumors were that Johnny was gambling and involved with drugs. Others believe that he entered the witness protection program. To this day the whereabouts of John Baker is unknown.

In the same newspaper reporting the missing pharmacist another article covered the warrants being issued for 50 people in the Texas Panhandle charged with delivery of crack cocaine, cocaine, and marijuana purchased over the past year by undercover agents.

I was told by a very reliable source about another Borger pharmacist who was reported to have committed suicide. They said this pharmacist toted three hand guns because he was paranoid and heavily involved in illegal drugs and gambling.

Could the involvement of these two white collar pharmacists with others making money illegally on drugs be remnants of the past criminal elements of Boomtown Borger?

CHAPTER NINE

NEW DECADE AT GOLDEN PLAINS

Norm T. Lambert was hired as CEO of Golden Plains Community Hospital in 1995. Lambert was originally from Houston, Texas in Harris County. He received his BS in Biology/Medical Technology at the University of Houston in 1975. He received a Masters from the University of Houston Baylor College of Medicine in 1976. His marriage to Pamela Lambert ended in divorce in March of 1997 for undisclosed reasons, and in December of 1997, he married Sherrill Janke.

According to Pat Cleveland, "I came on to the board in 1970 and again in 1994, when Mr. Brown was CEO. The next year in 1995, Ken Crain, President of Amarillo National Bank of Borger came onto board. At that time, we needed a new administrator, CEO. Crain handled the search and found one in Arkansas. He went and talked to the Cub Scouts where Norm Lambert was involved and so forth. Ken Crain said he was really good. So, he was hired.

A year afterwards, Norm Lambert was doing anything and everything he seemed to want and if a doctor or anyone else didn't agree with him, he would want to get rid of them. Norm Lambert has always gotten people on the board, who say yes to him and if they don't, he'll find ways to get them off the board."

During this time period, the hospital board members were Jock Lee, a veterinarian, served as president, Kenneth Benton, retired, served as Vice President, Pat Cleveland, retired nurse, served as Secretary, Tom Zeni was a Phillips executive, Connie Ferricks was a business woman, and Ken Crain was Bank President and Dr. Gerry Holland was a general practitioner.

"Upon Lambert's arrival in Borger, he immediately instructed the Emergency Room Group to exclude from the Emergency Room Schedule, Dr. Juan Viola, a Filipino doctor who worked as an Emergency Room Physician. Allegedly, his reason for firing Viola was that Dr. Viola was not of their kind and he did not fit into the community."

Lambert's firing of Dr. Viola raised concerns of other Filipino doctors including Dr. Ed Quiros who was respectively appointed to the board of trustees when the Hospital District was formed in 1989. Further actions by Lambert and others would be taken against the Filipino doctors developing into a lawsuit filed in June 2002.

FINANCIAL CRISIS OF 1997

Near the end of two years under the management of Norm Lambert, Golden Plains Community Hospital faced a deficit approaching two million dollars.

This "period of austerity" commenced on June 26, 1997, when Lambert instituted his Financial Action Plan and lasted until May of 1998. Lambert dealt with this financial crisis by freezing and later cutting salaries and hours to 32 hours per week for hospital employees. During this period of time, Lambert managed to convince the board that he deserved a bonus and raises of over $24,000. A majority of the board agreed and Lambert was awarded for his unbelievable request.

How often are CEO's rewarded by a board of directors in bad times when the employees they lead are suffering financially? Where was the empathy for employees? What happened to the business school principle where; "a leader leads by example"

By 2000, conditions were not much better. At that time, hospital board president Pat Cleveland reported, "A firm out of Springfield, Missouri, Baird, Kurtz & Dobson, were contracted to audit the books. This little guy, he was a very nice little guy, would come each year to perform our audit. At that time, I knew we were in the red up to our eye balls.

The guy from the audit firm presented the financials to the board. I'm sure he took out a lot of garbage to sugarcoat his report. When he finished his presentation, I asked him, 'I just want to ask you one question. Tell me if we are 2 million dollars in the red? He started to say, "ARR" and I said, 'Don't look at Norm, you answer me. You should know because you've just audited the books. Are we two million or more in the red? It's a YES or NO answer.' Finally, he said 'YES'. I responded, 'THANK YOU', now do any of you board members want to talk about our being over two million in the red?" No one said anything. I do not know if they did not understand what was going on."

A THORN IN LAMBERT'S SIDE

In 1997, the Borger News-Herald publisher was Tom Quinn and the editor was Gary Edmondson. These guys weren't afraid to write it how they saw it and became thorns in the side of Lambert and GPCH. An excerpt from an October 18, 1997 editorial reads . . .

Hospital Board Must Regain Public Trust . . . He (Lambert) says that the steering committee is exploring an increased partnership with Baptist-Saint Anthony's Hospital in Amarillo and involving local industries as a third partner in building a new facility. A new health care facility might make it easier to recruit new doctors to Borger, which could address another problem that Mr. Lambert faces.

These developments provide hope for the future of health care in the county. *The key to gaining voter acceptance for any plan rests on the managers' ability to regain the trust of the people. Much work needs to be done on this front.*

After the September meeting received its first coverage in a while, the hospital district's finance meeting finance committee met this month without notifying the press. When the News Herald asked for minutes and tapes of this committee meeting—which generally sets the tone for the next board of managers' meeting—Mr. Lambert refused repeatedly to provide these obviously open records. We received them following the managers' meeting when Finance Committee Chairman Ken Crain supplied them after a news story pointed out the district's violation of open record provisions of state law.

Also, the board of managers-appointed steering committee which will ultimately ask county voters to support its recommendation with tax dollars, has been meeting since May, with its work just now being acknowledged.

Secrecy does not build trust. Refusing to provide open records increases doubts as to what is transpiring in private public meetings. Claiming, as Mr. Lambert did, that he did not know the whereabouts of the tapes the News-Herald requested can, at best, be regarded as stonewalling against public scrutiny. At worst, it raises the same question of competency that arose when the district established a tax discount policy that did not comply with state law.

At various times, Messrs. Lambert and Crain have assured us of their good intentions and their willingness to help keep the public informed. Mr. Crain's providing the requested minutes speaks well on this point. Mr Lambert's agreeing to sit down with our reporter and bring everyone up to date on hospital plans is similarly encouraging.

But such efforts at damage control only impact the recent damage that necessitated them. The larger problem of the district being perceived as unresponsive, arrogantly secretive or mismanaged persists. This must be resolved before people will feel comfortable with entrusting the district with more money and greater responsibilities.

If snowfall on a glacier exceeds its rate of melting, the glacier will continue to grow. Those who would restore public confidence in the hospital are in the position of standing in front of such a glacier of bad public perception and working with ice picks as a blizzard rages around them. If the district continues to generate mistrust and doubts, those working to combat that impression will be in constant retreat.

The News-Herald needs public information to present to county readers—and we demand that public agencies adhere to open meeting and open record laws. The public needs this information even more so that its members can weigh all of the facts, understand the issues and make intelligent choices at the polls.

But, more than either the press or the public, the hospital district needs to make sure that all of its happenings—bad as well as good, fiscal problems as well as informative features—are put before county residents. Before the hospital board can convince us that its recommendations for our health care further deserve our support, it must convince us that it is credible and competent and that it cares about us as more than the source of its revenue.

Hospital board managers and steering committee members have a monumental job before them to restore public confidence in the hospital and its future. Battening down the bunker to repel all inquiry will only ensure their failure. And, if they fail this crucial test, everyone in Hutchinson County loses, too.

Over the ensuing months other articles and an editorial on Sunday, April 11, 1999 protesting closed meetings attacked and rankled the CEO and his supportive board members. Nothing changed!

Mr. Edmonson's last paragraph gave good advice to board members about restoring public confidence. Maybe the future would have been different if board members had paid attention, sat aside their egos, became more open with the public and acted in the best interest of the taxpayers.

THE NEW DOCTORS ARE COMING

In May 1998, Norm Lambert acted to revamp the hospital by recruiting new doctors. Six new doctors were hired and granted salaries of between $165,000 and $350,000 per year, in addition to bonuses, paying off their student loans, paid offices and staff. Five of the six recruited doctors left the hospital at the end of one year in spite of the lucrative and generous recruitment packages.

In the year 2000, another six new doctors were recruited. It was noted that except for two physicians, the doctors enticed into Golden Plains throughout 1998 and 2000, were Caucasian males under the age of 40 with guaranteed salaries up to $350,000 per year.

Previously, the Senior Medical Staff doctors had agreement privileges to work as independent contractors, paid directly by patients solely for work performed. These doctors had built private practices on their own merits by caring for their patients rather than caring about getting paid guaranteed incomes from the hospital. They were recruited by the hospital between 1977 and 1994.

What was the rationale behind continuing hiring doctors who couldn't commit more than one year to the community? Why didn't management realize the unrest it was creating between doctors? Did management establish a revolving door where doctors are not a priority but rather an expendable necessary evil to run the hospital? Did management ever consider that their actions were discriminating and violating equal rights?

CHAPTER TEN

MR. LARRY LANGLEY, CHIEF FINANCIAL OFFICER

On May 12, 1997, Larry Langley was hired by Norm Lambert. Mr. Langley was offered a salary of $72,000 per year paid in 26 equal payments. His start date was on June 9, 1997. Item 6 on the employment letter stated: *Should your employment at Golden Plains Community Hospital be severed without your consent, except for cause, the following severance compensation will be provided to you and be based on your current salary.*

Lambert's hiring of Larry Langley evolved into a major debacle that would shake the foundation of Golden Plains Community Hospital and bring in the FBI on two separate occasions.

LANGLEY RECOMMENDS PREFABRICATED DOCTOR'S BUILDING

In the Board Meeting notes from October 5, 1999, Norm Lambert reported there was a need for additional office space to house physicians that the hospital was trying to recruit to Borger. He is quoted in the minutes as saying, "Management would like to set up a group practice of four Family Practice/OB housed in one building. This would assure patients that there is a physician available to see them to take care of their medical needs if their physician is gone.

The office building presently occupied by Dr. Mitchell Preston will need to be torn down and the property located across the street, which houses Hospice of the Panhandle will need to be torn down or moved. Clearing both property sites will make room for the office building and additional parking.

Larry Langley and I visited a modular building that was constructed in Dumas to house physicians. I would like to recommended a time be set aside for the Board to view the very well built building. When a new hospital is built, the building can be moved. *The estimated cost is $552,789. This includes furnishings and equipment.*"

> *Note: Later, the above underlined statement surfaces as false and deceptive.*

The meeting minutes continue:

Tom Zeni spoke, "I make the motion to grant administration approval to receive information from PREFAB Inc.,* that built the Dumas office building. All the Board members should visit the Dumas site ASAP. Then we should receive bids, reasonable cost estimates in lieu of actual bids to tear down/move buildings and putting in a parking lot. I also recommend that Mr. Lambert visit community functions to sell the idea of the office building and do a public forum on expenditures of the communities' money."

Ken Benton said, "I second the motion." The motion was carried!

In the November 2, 1999 board meeting, Lambert presented an architectural drawing of the proposed office space for four physicians. He also presented a general description of the building and a preliminary pricing schedule.

Danny Courtney, Engineering Manager for the hospital reported, "My perspective of viewing the building was very positive on the overall workmanship and materials that went into the building. The modular building is structurally very sound."

The comment "the modular building is structurally very sound" is noteworthy when one reads a copy of this letter mailed to Dr. Strecker while he was serving as a board member. This letter was mailed to Dr. Strecker about one year after construction was completed.

In this letter, Ms. Jackson presents an account claiming herself and another older employee were being degraded because of age. She also makes comments on the "sound structure" of the building.

March 12, 2001

Dear Dr. Strecker;

I am writing in response to our phone conversation of March 8, 2001. I would like to convey to you some of the problems I faced during my employment at the new office plaza. Myself and another older employee were constantly being degraded due to our age. I have been a nurse since 1967 having graduated from the second nursing class from North Plains Hospital. I have worked in ICU and ER at Northwest Texas Hospital, St. Anthonys, and High Plains Baptist Hospital as well as the Methodist Hospital System in Houston, and as a private nurse for Mrs. Francis Withers, under the direction of Dr. Smythe, dean of the University of Texas Medical School at that time. Her sons are Dr. George Withers and Dr. Ed Withers. My fellow older employee was employed by Dr. Joel Fondren for approximately seventeen years until his death. I was also employed by Dr. Rex D. Prewit until his death last April.

I realize that might be considered, "from the old school", but I still believe the patients deserve to be treated in a professional atmosphere. The new office building is anything but, sound proof. Everything that is said is heard by everyone in the office. I experienced everything from running, giggling in the halls, to having a small Raggedy Ann type doll hung over my head by a tourniquet with a large syringe stuck in the back of it's head. The doll was taken from my desk drawer. The next day I found the doll with it's head closed and file cabinet, next to my work station. The third day the doll was laying face down floating in a sink of water, when I went to wash my hands.

Being the old geezer that I am, I didn't enjoy the conversations about the Doctor's sex life or vulgar sex talk about 69 points. Even the Christmas party turned into the drunken vulgar brawl to the extent that the staff at the country club closed the door to keep from disturbing the diners in the other part of the club.

There were pranks such as putting dry ice in the doctors toilet to make it smoke and frequent discussions about the Doctor stopping up the toilet and passing gas. When I was away for a day in January, they took a razor blade and slashed my desk calendar. Or may I say, the hospital's calendar, since it was paid for by the hospital.

As I said, previously, the new building is not sound proof, everyone can hear everything that is said, extra caution should be maintained to give patients as much privacy as possible under the bad circumstances. The floor is uneven, and not very solid when horseplay is going on and everyone in the building knows about it.

I visited with the director of nurses, the last part in November, about the problems that we were having at the new medical building. She appeared to being outraged at what was going on. The way they tried to solve the problem was to move the office manager to the position of receptionist. That only exacerbated the problem because it left no one in charge. General chaos ensued for about three months. Problems were to be resolved with the appointment of another person from the administration office to the position of office manager at the medical Plaza.

Instead of solving the problems, this person proceeded to set up for an office in one of the extra doctor's offices well away from the problems of the front office. The computer was disconnected, and the line taken back in the new office. She couldn't use the computer at the front desk to help. Then they had new office staff come in and run another line to reconnect the computer so that the desk could be used. She bought a new desk and all the frills were set up. Still all of the problems continued.

Whenever, the receptionist would threaten to quit, someone would help her. Frequently the waiting room was full, but no charts are there where the physicians could start because she could only do so much at one time. Their resolution to the problem was to hire more staff. Never was the problem of unprofessional staff addressed. The office manager was aware of the vicious attack on me and she never suggested they stop their unprofessional behavior.

This is just a small amount of the problems I experienced while working there. The administration was very aware of the problems going on there and everything they did made the situation worse.

Mary Eileen Jackson

When the Doctor's Building was completed in May, 2000, it attracted immediate attention from many locals. Barber shop comments were heard like, "What is going on at that hospital? How in the world can 6 trailer homes locked together cost that much?"

MRI MYSTERY-WHERE DID THE MONEY GO?

It was in the month of March in 1999 that Langley approached Lambert with the idea of reducing the MRI expense at GPCH. Langley claimed that $100,000 per year could be saved by purchasing a refurbished MRI. At that time the hospital was paying $25,000 per month for a mobile service and a MRI machine could be purchased for approximately $8000 per month. Technicians and supplies to operate the machine would make the total monthly expenditure about $12,000 per month.

The meeting notes from the November 2, 1999 Board meeting state that management reviewed proposals for a refurbished MRI unit costing $615,000 from Advanced Diagnostic Systems. First National Bank of Borger offered the best financing package at a 5 year cost of $855,405. In October, 1999, Ken Crain moved to approve the purchase and finance of the MRI through First National Bank. Ken Benton seconded and the motion was carried.

Ken Crain was Chairman of the Finance and Planning Committee with Jock Lee and Tom Zeni. This committee reviewed all purchases brought before the board. "Ken Crain, Tom Zeni, and Jock Lee would all get together with Norm Lambert and have their budget meeting. The three of them had reviewed the MRI purchase before making a motion to the board," said Pat Cleveland.

Documents show that the typewritten date on the contract with Advanced Diagnostic Systems was September 27, 1999. The contract was signed by Norman T. Lambert with a hand written date next to his signature of 11/4/99 and James Gandy signed for the company. This was two days following the Board's approval.

Page 3 of the contract is marked as an Addendum. A cash price was quoted of $625,000 and marked out and substituted with $615,000 net per phone conversation on 11/4/99 @ 3:56 p.m. for James Gandy/ Denette Ehrlich.

Page 4 is also marked Addendum as a buy back policy providing that if the unit is not able to realize a profit in 180 days of full-time service that Advanced Diagnostic Solutions will buy the unit back. What's unusual about page 4 is that it is signed solely by James Gandy with a date of 9/27/99 hand written under his signature. Apparently no representative from Golden Plains Community Hospital signed this document.

When the contract was signed by Lambert on 11/4/99, why was this contract signed solely by Gandy with a 9/27/99 date? Why didn't Lambert sign on the lines provided?

The Service Contract dated January 7, 2000 (3 months 10 days later) stated that under the *Warranty Disclaimer* that: "ADS's full contractual obligations are provided in the Agreement. *There are no warranties, written or oral provided otherwise: All service and parts covered under this Agreement are provided as is.* No warranty of merchantability or fitness for a particular purpose applies to anything provided by ADS or its service contractor.

Why wasn't this Service Contract executed the same date at the contract that was signed by Lambert and Gandy? Did the terms no warranties, written or oral provided otherwise: and are provided as is absolve Gandy from any responsibility?

THE BIG QUESTION: Did the hospital's attorney review all the documents before they were signed by the administrator? Where in Lambert's explanation does he state, he initially sent the contracts to the hospital attorney to review? Did the attorney review and approve the Service Contract?

LAMBERT SAYS DON'T BLAME ME!

The hospital CEO presented his account of "what happened" on April 26, 2000. This overwrought report explains his actions and events to the Board of Directors. Is there a sentence where the CEO concedes his culpability?

"Larry was instructed by me to proceed, but with caution to pay attention to details and involve the necessary persons so as not to be making a decision purely based on financial consideration.

During June, 1999, Larry brought to my attention that we were required to give 90 day notice prior to the end of the current mobile imaging company's contract in order to make changes in that contract. A letter was sent to Alliance Imaging notifying them that we were going to cancel that contract in 90 days and seek to re-negotiate a new contract. This opened the door to any avenue for providing MRI services in the future.

Rumors started throughout the hospital that we had already made a decision to change the MRI service and to immediately cancel the service of the mobile service. I instructed Larry to meet with Dr. Maza and his staff to inform them of what we had done with the contract and to assure them that they would be totally involved in the development of any alternative contract or purchase choice of a MRI.

Stories still persisted that Administration was not considering Dr. Maza's nor his staff input into the decision. I, therefore, met myself with Dr. Maza and Dr. Nelson sometime in August. I informed them about the contract change and that it was merely a formality to notify the mobile vendor prior to the 90 day period or else we could not change the contract. I also tried to assure them that we had no intention of making a decision about a MRI purchase without their full involvement because only they and Steve Price had the technical knowledge to assist in the decision.

Larry Langley spent the rest of the summer preparing the justification for the purchase by contacting vendors including Advanced Diagnostics Solutions (the vendor ultimately recommended), Alliance Imaging (the mobile vendor), and General Electric and requesting proposals from each of these vendors.

At one point during the summer, I asked Larry about the public bidding process and he reminded me that the Enabling Legislation for the Hutchinson County Hospital District only required that on construction projects, it was not necessary to make a public bid. The practical matter is that no local vendor exists for such equipment. I did instruct Larry to seek competitive proposals from local lending institutions for funding of the equipment purchase.

Larry completed his investigation and presented his final information to me in mid-September. I suggested some changes in the presentation format on his proposal before it was presented to the Finance and Planning Committee. *(NOTE: The finance committee consisted of Ken Crain, Chairman, Jock Lee, and Ken Benton.)*

At this time, I again inquired as to how much Dr. Maza and his staff had been involved and was again assured by Larry that they were totally involved. Since I had observed them with Larry in his office on more than one occasion, I had no reason to believe otherwise. I was also told by Larry that Dr. Maza and Dr. Nelson had reviewed MRI films from the machine we were to be purchasing and that they were satisfied with the quality of the films. *I did not know until February, 2000, that those films had actually come from a MRI in Amarillo similar to the one we were to purchase. I was led to believe the radiologists viewed actual films from our machine.*

(NOTE: Is Lambert blaming Larry Langley, Dr. Maza, and Dr. Nelson for deceiving him and the board with false films? If so, why weren't these three people reprimanded and terminated from their positions with the hospital? Who ordered the films from the Amarillo MRI? Who paid for them? Who was responsible for this cover up?

BOARD MEMBER PAT CLEVELAND'S ACCOUNT OF WHAT OCCURRED.

"After the machine arrived at the hospital we were told how good the pictures were the machine was taking and how much money we were making. And come to find out it was not working nor taking pictures. In fact of the matter, the machine caught on fire, under the bottom, and it was repaired with bungee cords. In order to try to prove to us we were getting really good pictures, they went over to the BSA in Amarillo and had some pictures taken on the machine there and tried to palm them off on us. They got caught, and finally had to admit they were trying to bamboozle us. Then we found out it wasn't taking a picture at all.

I called Norm Lambert, on January 6th and he said, "It wasn't any of my business. No, it wasn't taking any pictures."

I said, "Why haven't you let us know and why haven't you done anything about it?"

Lambert said," you expect me to take care of things?"

I said," for the amount of money you draw you're expected to take care of things."

The next day, Lambert sent out a Memo saying that Pat Cleveland was kind enough to bring it to his attention that the MRI was not taking pictures. If that was the first time it was ever brought to his attention, there was something wrong."—Pat Cleveland

Lambert's explanation continues:

"The story still persisted that Dr. Maza was not being involved in the decision even after my personal meeting on two occasions in his office with Dr. Maza and Steve Price regarding this matter. At one time I stepped in to again say that we need their input in order for us not to *buy a piece of junk.*"

Note: Isn't it odd for Lambert to use the term "piece of junk?" At that time, how would he have known the MRI was a piece of junk?

"At one time, other members of the medical staff were being told by Dr. Maza that administration was not involving him in the decision. Other physicians voiced their disfavor about not being involved in the decision. On the most part, however, physicians were not usually asked about capital items that do not specifically involve/impact them on a day-to-day basis. Dr. Maza was the obvious utilizer of this equipment just as other surgical equipment has been considered for specific surgeons and not the medical staff in general. I presented information to the Medical Executive Committee and sent out a "Leak-of-the-Week" in early October describing our efforts and Dr. Maza's involvement. By this time the strategy had already been preliminarily presented to the Board.

Just before the final decision was made to recommend the purchase to the Finance & Planning Committee, a meeting was held in Patty Wilhite's office with myself, Larry, Patty, Steve Price, Richard Sandoval, Dr. Nelson and Dr. Maza regarding some questions over certain capabilities of the machine we were proposing to purchase. I instructed Steve Price who was most familiar with MRI's to contact the vendor and his technical representatives directly to insure that all of technical questions were answered. I was later told that the chosen vendor had given all of the necessary information to Steve.

Patty Wilhite had previously had little involvement in the matter in part because she did not become a GPCH employee until June, 1999, after the project had been begun by Larry Langley and in part because Larry again had the MRI experience.

Patty Wilhite, Larry Langley, Steve Price, Richard Sandoval and Dr. Maza held a conference call with James Gandy of Advanced Diagnostic Solutions regarding the specifications of the MRI we were buying to confirm that this machine met all of the similar specifications as provided by the mobile service. Gandy confirmed that it did indeed do all of the similar imaging. At this point all involved believed we were to receive the MRI as per our specifications.

On October 27, 1999 the Finance and Planning reviewed the proposal to purchase the MRI. The proposal, as prepared by Larry Langley's investigation and supported by the Radiology Department's/ personnel's involvement, demonstrated

A. Purchase the MRI from Alliance Imaging for "$615,000
B. Financing through First National Bank of Borger
C. Machine would do all of the necessary scans
D. Save $100,000 per year.

On November 2, 1999, the proposal was taken to the Board and was approved. The machined arrived on November 17, 1999 and was first put into service by James Gandy on December 6, 1999. It was then discovered on December 6 that the machine's imaging quality was not as good as expected and promised. After further investigation, it was found that the machine was found not to have all the components on it to perform all of the required images.

Gandy verified to Patty Wilhite that the equipment was not as promised, blamed the vendor that he bought the machine from, and promised to fix the machine and bring it to our specification. Gandy had procured the MRI from another broker in Los Angeles without verifying the components on the machine.

Note: The machine was sold with 6 components missing with an "as is" service warranty agreement.

At this time I assigned Patty Wilhite to rectifying the problem for I knew she would take a more detailed, proactive approach to resolving the issue.

During Patty's investigation of the matter, she discovered that:

1. Gandy had received full payment for the equipment as of November 9, 1999 via Larry Langley's supervision, prior to verification that the equipment worked properly; *(Note: Lambert signed the contract on November 4, 1999. That was 5 days before payment was submitted via Langley. Shouldn't Lambert had made sure that the USED MRI worked properly before signing a contract?)*
2. The films reviewed in August had not come from our purchased machine as I was led to believe, but from a similar machine in Amarillo; *(Note: This was 9 months after purchasing the MRI. According to a board member this falsified film was presented the board and represented as being film from the MRI. According to Lambert he knew nothing about it?)*
3. That Gandy's original proposal was for a capital lease and that Larry had sought to purchase the machine to save money.
4. That the other vendors were given only one chance by Larry at proposing to GPCH and may have been willing to "deal" more.

In a meeting with myself, Patty and Larry, James Gandy agreed to replace the machine while at the same time pay the monthly note payments to the bank and to pay for the expense of bringing in a mobile service while he was seeking the replacement.

Gandy sent a copy of a check for the bank payment that he stated "was in the mail." Our bank verification on the check showed insufficient funds. We never actually received the check.

On January 26, 2000, the hospital's attorney was contacted to begin legal proceedings to rectify the problem. Gandy executed another contract on February 10, 2000, describing that he would indeed replace the old machine with a GE model MRI. The new contract listed all of the specifications needed.

A small electrical fire occurred in the MRI unit which did not harm the machine, but did damage a transformer and breakers. After this incident and after Leon Mitchell's advice, the MRI was taken by Gandy to Louisiana for safe keeping. The rationale was that if permanent damage occurred to the MRI while under our care, we may be required to accept the machine "as is." *(NOTE: Does this make sense when the Service Contract stated provided as is.)*

Patty Wilhite and Frank Danielson (GE tech) went to Louisiana to verify the safety of the MRI and to determine if the proposed GE machine's computer was in good working order. The Siemens MRI was secure, but the GE computer was not in working order at that time and its capabilities could not be verified.

At Leon Mitchell's advice and after conferring with the Finance & Planning Committee, an addendum to the newest contract was executed on April 7, 2000 whereby Gandy agreed to provide the new machine by May 10, 2000 or otherwise submit a Performance Bond assuring that he could in deed live up to the agreement. With the performance bond Gandy would have until July 10, 2000, to replace the old MRI with the GE model.

Also, on April 7, 2000, Gandy stated that he had a buyer for the old machine for $250,000 less $18,000 for an upgrade with a 15 mili Tesla Chip. We agreed to allow Gandy to sell the MRI, but that all monies were to be directly wired to First National Bank in Borger, i.e., Gandy would not handle the money.

On April 14, 2000, Gandy proposed that he actually replace the 15 mili Tesla chip and MRA chip (the missing components) at his cost of $55,000. This would either bring the MRI up to the original specifications or at least bring the value of the MRI up for a sale.

On April 24, 2000, Gandy wanted GPCH to pay for the upgrade chips ($55,000), to which we said "no" that we had already paid for the chips.

At this date we are prepared to file a law suit against Gandy in Federal Court seeking repayment of the total $615,000.

According to Lambert's statements, Larry Langley, Dr., Maza and Steve Price were responsible for every mistake made in the purchase of the MRI. It was reported that Langley was linked to Gandy from Houston where the two of them previously worked together. Lambert claims that via Larry Langley's supervision, prior to verification that the equipment worked properly; Gandy had received full payment for the equipment as of November 9, 1999.

Was Langley able to sign, approve and wire a payment for $615,000 without Lambert's knowledge and approval? Was Lambert using Langley and others as scapegoats? Doesn't it seem incredible that any CEO would be so out of the loop over an expensive purchase that enabled gross mismanagement of $615,000? Do things add up?

LAMBERT SAYS, "LANGLEY HAS INTEGRITY."

The following paragraph about Larry Langley from Norm Lambert's, CEO Self Evaluation on November 2, 1999 portrays a different picture and support for Langley.

"When I arrived in late 1995, it was obvious to me early on that the then CFO did not know how to manage the financial administration of this hospital. I replaced him with the current CFO. While Larry Langley does have an abrupt leadership style and at times lets his demeanor get away from him, he has aggressively tackled many critical financial issues and has been of great value to me in achieving this financial turnaround. Larry's integrity has been challenged, in most part from rumors preceding his arrival here. *In working with Larry from day-to-day, he has exhibited only the highest degree of integrity contrary to the rumors.* In fact responding to the negativity of these rumors has cost us additional dollars for unnecessary audits. I have counseled Larry on his demeanor and the need for him to pay more attention to details. However, his more direct style of management has produced positive financial results."—Norm Lambert

The "rumors preceding Langley's arrival" referred to in Lambert's paragraph were that Langley had been terminated from the hospital in Dumas, Texas and escorted out of the building. If this was true, why did Lambert hire him? If it wasn't true, why didn't Lambert clear up the rumors by presenting the facts to the board and general public?

According to Pat Cleveland, "Lambert told me it was none of my business why he hired Larry Langley as CFO. Lambert knew that Larry Langley had been escorted out of the Dumas Hospital. As a matter of fact, I got to where I liked Larry Langley better than I did Norm. In some ways I think Langley was more honest. I don't think either one of them are honest. Why did Norm Lambert hire him when he knew about his getting fired at Dumas? Why didn't Lambert bring the decision to hire Langley before the board? As soon as the MRI fiasco started, someone had to take the rap and Norm began to blame everything on Langley."

Lambert hired Langley to replace an Interim CFO who came from Northwest Texas Hospital in Amarillo, Texas. John Curnutt was friends with this CFO. John stated, "In 1974 when I was in Northwest Texas Hospital following my accident, he came to visit me in the hospital. That's when he found a job in student financial aid and later worked his way up to became CFO." Ultimately he became the CEO of Northwest Texas Hospital District. During his time there, the district built a new hospital. According to a letter in the Amarillo Globe News, the district was never in better shape. The hospital had some 80 million dollars in reserve and had given a tax rebate over the last 5 years. When the hospital was sold, his contract was bought out and he was going to retire. I asked him to help as the interim CFO at Golden Plains and he agreed to take the position."

TEN DOLLARS BUYS A $615,000 MRI MACHINE

The events became more complicated on March 4, 2000 in a document titled ADDENDUM TO CONTRACT FOR SALE OF MRI where the original machine was to be replaced by a General Electric machine and that for and in the consideration of the sum of Ten and No/100 ($10,00) Dollars and other good and valuable consideration, the receipt of which is hereby acknowledged, and the parties agree as follows: Hospital shall allow ADS to remove the MRI machine originally provided under the terms of exhibit "A", ADS agrees that it will provide a MRI machine with the following items. The contract goes on with a detail list of parts with the General Electric machine.

At this point, Charles Gandy bought a $615,000 MRI for $10 and a promise of a General Electric machine. A promise he never kept.

THE RESIGNATION OF LARRY LANGLEY

In January 2000, Lambert informed hospital employees that Larry Langley, Chief Financial Officer of Golden Plains Community Hospital had resigned and moved elsewhere.

Records show a hand written resignation letter presented to Norm Lambert. It read:

January 28, 2000

TO: Norm Lambert, CEO
FROM: Larry Langley

Please accept my resignation from employment as Hutchinson County Hospital District Effective February 25, 2000. This resignation is made freely and voluntarily.

Larry Langley

Received and accepted 1-28-2000 signed Norman T. Lambert

"When Larry Langley was finally let go, Norm finally came out and told us that he was gone. I asked, 'Can you tell us what was his reason for leaving?' Lambert responded, 'No, I can't and I'm not going to.' I said, 'You can't do that!' Lambert stated, 'If you need to know, ask Jock.' I said, 'Okay, Jock you tell me.' Jock responded, 'No, I'm not going to tell you either.' I said, 'Okay, I'll get the Texas Hospital Association in on this. One way or the other, I'm finding out.' 'Why do you need to know Pat?' I said, 'For all I know he absconded with some finances we are responsible for. I have ever right to know where this man went."-Pat Cleveland

TWO MONTHS LATER DR. HOLLAND SPEAKS UP

On April 5, 2000, board member, Dr. Gerry Holland expressed her concerns in a Memo to Jock Lee, board president following a board meeting.

Dear Jock:
I am very concerned about last night's board meeting. I believe we need a special part of the meeting for just board members only to discuss any issues needed that are not on the "agenda".

I have serious concerns regarding the handling of the MRI because Norm approved the contract and the board was never given the contract to review, nor was it reviewed by an attorney to my knowledge.

I do not think the board should have had an attorney present in an open meeting to discuss a potential law suit! It could have gone under executive privilege and been discussed out of an open meeting.

We have serious problems with surgery because we only have one surgeon on ER back up call, he is gone often and he is not always available to back up Orthopedics, FP, Internal Medicine, etc. We are bringing 4 new doctors in with one surgeon . . . we need another full time surgeon. Inala is not going to stay here and he is not getting enough referrals to stay.

The other issue you need to be aware of is the cost to radiology department for supplies and the tech's time and Ribeiro is being paid, not the radiology department. He owes the hospital a great deal of money and his charts alone last month had a $168,000 bill hold due to lack of charting and these two issues are not being addressed that I am aware of.

Norm told MED that he has spoken with him about the bill hold and I am unaware of any discussions about the radiology issue. The physicians perceive this as preferential treatment and that he (Dr. Ribeiro) is being carefully treated due to the income he is bringing to the hospital. I think Patty tried to address this issue in the past? It does not seem to be fair. I am also concerned about the cost of suing for the MRI. I think the board needs to know how and why we have $615,000 gone with an incomplete and inferior MRI.

Thanks,
Dr. Holland.

Was Dr. Holland's Memo forwarded to Norm Lambert? If so, how did Lambert perceive this memo? Did he consider it feedback from a concerned board member or criticism? Was this the point where Dr. Holland became targeted as a "non-supportive" Doctor?

CHAPTER ELEVEN

HOSPITAL BOARD ELECTION IN MAY, 2000

By May, 2000, the news of the MRI that didn't work and the loss of over $615,000 had filtered throughout Hutchinson County. The hospital CEO became a target for public pressure by concerned taxpayers in the county. There was a movement to replace two of the board members with new members who would act in seeing to it that Norm Lambert became accountable for his actions as CEO of Golden Plains Community Hospital.

On Friday, May 5, 2000, Lambert's stated paragraph in a Borger News Herald opinion article read, "Have you ever bought some type of appliance that did not work? If you did, did you blame yourself for buying the appliance or did you hold the vendor responsible? The answer is obvious, and we have held this vendor to the original purchase agreement. Additionally, we are prepared to take whatever additional steps are necessary to insure that either the appropriate equipment is delivered or the purchase price is refunded as per the written agreements."

Lambert's explanation of the MRI in this article ran the night before the Saturday election. It was an attempt to defend his management against an outrage of criticism over the MRI purchase that in his own words was a "piece of junk".

John Curnutt, a private citizen was on the ballet running against Chamber of Commerce Executive Director, Joe Frank Wheeler. When Curnutt read Lambert's paragraph he exclaimed, "How can any executive explain away a $615,000 purchase by comparing it to a used appliance that costs only several hundred dollars. The MRI has never worked. Lambert is more responsible than the vendor because he did not inspect the MRI. He did not perform his fiduciary duties in behalf of the taxpayers. This is an outlandish excuse. It's typical Lambert to place the blame elsewhere. I only hope that the vendor comes through for the hospital. It would be a shame to lose all that money."

The next morning, the polls were open from 7 a.m. to 7 p.m. At the end of the day, John Curnutt lost to Joe Frank Wheeler by a mere 6 votes. John was sorely disappointed. He had been outspoken about the administrator and the machine that didn't work. He was on a mission to change the administration at the hospital. Curnutt joked about the outcome of the race by saying, "It's pretty bad when a disabled person in a wheelchair can almost outrun the Chamber of Commerce president."

Dr. Jerry Strecker won over Jock Lee in precinct 2 and commented, "I want to build on what the board has already done. The top order of business is improving the hospital's credibility so the community will believe in it and have it as their hospital of choice."

What Dr. Strecker did not know was the shock awaiting him as a new board member. In an orientation as a board member, he was told by Leon Mitchell, hospital attorney, that, "the legal confidentiality levels required within executive meetings of the Board were of a higher level than Strecker's profession (psychologist) and under no conditions was he allowed to speak of information received in these meetings."

Strecker would be burdened with keeping a secret that would haunt him the rest of his life and lead to his resignation from the hospital board.

The News Herald reported that Dr. Strecker thanked Lee for his years of service on the board. Lee had no comment. According to Dr. Strecker, "Lee never called me to congratulate me for winning."

Throughout his term as a board member, Jock Lee had been an avid supporter of Norm Lambert. Although Lee lost, he would be back on board a lot sooner than many people thought.

The new board consisted of Pat Cleveland, Connie Ferricks, Gerry Holland, Jerry Strecker, Joe Frank Wheeler, Paul Ruhlman, and Ken Crain.

Following the election, Pat Cleveland was made president of the board. This would be her last year to serve. A year of frustration she would never forget.

When I interviewed Mrs. Cleveland, she said, "I guess that Lambert thought he could control me when I was placed as chairman of the board. Norm's a charmer for these women, but it takes a lot more than his silver tongue to charm me. He found that out."

She continued saying, "We had four new members come onto the board, so I wanted to Xerox some information about the MRI, etc. so they would know what was going on and wouldn't have to ask questions about everything. I didn't invite Norm to the meeting and his board members said I couldn't do that. I told them I didn't have to have Lambert there. After that, they started fighting it so hard that one of the board members wrote a letter stating that I would be thrown in jail because they claimed I disregarded the open meetings act. They were frantic about me telling what I knew to these new board members. I finally told them, fine throw me in jail. Just have television channel 10 and 4 there to take a picture of me and give me a book to read. They quickly backed down."

That whole last year was a farce. Lambert would bring in people from the offices and tell them to bring their families to board meetings. It became a circus. They would disrupt the whole meeting. You couldn't really talk or get anything done. I would go faithfully down to Norm's office on Fridays before board meetings and say do you have something for the agenda. He'd say, "NO" and get up and turn his back to me while looking out the window. I would ask, "Is there any old business we need to discuss?" and he would respond "NO".

That last year I would come home from a board meeting sick at my stomach. There were 4 new members on the board and I finally had hope there was a way to govern to save some money and not spend frivolously. But, Lambert already had the new members sucked into his good old boy club. It was frustrating to see Jerry Strecker make a motion and no one would even second it."

FEDERAL LAW SUIT FILED AGAINST ADVANCED DIAGNOSTIC SOLUTIONS

On May 24, 2000, a Federal Lawsuit was filed against James Gandy, Individually and D/B/A Advanced Diagnostic Solutions.

In a letter to the hospital's attorney dated August 4, 2000, Lambert stated, "I do, however want to insure that my neutral position be maintained during this effort. Thus, could you please make a recommendation for any local, state or federal agency that would be appropriate to investigate this manner. We want to be able to determine whether any current or past employee may have had any wrong doing or criminal activity, whether there was less than an "arms length" relationship, or whether sole responsibility belongs to James Gandy, the vendor, including his possible criminal activity."

On October 11, 2000, Pat Cleveland, Leon Mitchell, Patty Wilhite and Norm Lambert met with Agent Vandiver regarding an FBI investigation. Vandiver said that there was definitely evidence of a technical violation of the law and there would be an investigation of James Gandy's intent to defraud GPCH through wire and mail fraud statutes.

At the end of the day, the hospital was out $615,000 for the purchase of the MRI and legal fees in access of $200,000. The total loss was approaching one million dollars wasted in behalf of the taxpayers in Hutchinson County.

PETITION FOR FORENSIC AUDIT

Following the May election, John Curnutt kept track of all the activities of the hospital regarding the MRI. John has lived in Borger all his life. He had served on the Department of Human Services volunteer board for 15 years, American Red Cross Board for 5 years, North Hills Paving Project coordinator, Emergency Transportation coordinator for Golden Plains Community Hospital for 2 years, Volunteer Delivery of Commodities to the Aged and Disabled coordinator for 5 years, Citizen's Advisory Committee in 1995, Developed a Head Injury Survivor Project for state wide use in rehabilitation facilities.

In early October, Curnutt organized a Petition to the hospital board and in less than one month had 1,041 signatures. On November 7, 2000, he presented the petition to the hospital board.

The petition stated:

Whereas, in late 1999, GPCH paid an excess of $600,000 for an MRI machine which was not in working condition and has caused considerable financial loss to the hospital, the hospital district, and the taxpayers.

And whereas additional matters, including but not limited to, lack of meaningful financial reporting to the Board seems apparent.

Therefore, we, the undersigned, do petition the Board, to hire and retain an experienced and qualified person or firm to conduct a forensic audit and properly

review and investigate the above described matters and/or such other matters, as the circumstances warrant, and report to the Board its findings and recommendations.

We request that this audit be conducted distinctly and apart from the current auditing function.

The day following the board meeting, the headline in the newspaper read:

MRI SPARKS HEATED DISCUSSION. "Sparks flew at last night's Golden Plains Community Hospital Board meeting. Arguments among board members and the audience were heard. At one point the president of the board engaged in name calling with *two other members* from the public."

Note: The board president, Pat Cleveland reported, "The two members from the public were Jock Lee and Tom Zeni. Both of these men were ex board members andh supporters of Norm Lambert. Once when I was at the Country Club, Tom Zeni was there. I asked him, 'What are you and Jock doing coming to these meetings?' He said, 'to protect Norm.' And I said, 'to protect Norm from what?' 'From you,' he said. Pat responded, 'you mean you think you need to protect him from a little ol' gray headed woman like me?' 'Well, yes . . . you shouldn't have said anything about the $150,000 that Dr. Ribero got in X-rays," said Zeni.

The newspaper article went on to say,

"The heated discussion resulted from a petition presented by John Curnutt. The petition, asking for an inquiry on a MRI purchase made by the hospital, was signed by 1,041 people."

"The majority of the board members felt that there was nothing fraudulent to hide and it would be wise to wait and see the results of the annual hospital audit that is currently being done before asking for an additional audit of the MRI issue."

A foretelling comment in the article was made by new board member Joe Frank Wheeler who said, "the hospital should have nothing to hide and not wanting an audit would come across bad to the public."

Wheeler was right on target with his comment. Who wouldn't think it was arrogant for a few board members to ignore a forensic audit requested in a petition of over 1000 taxpayers? Wouldn't it have been easier to be open to a forensic audit that would have cleared everything up? It was only rational, human nature when citizens began to wonder, what was there to hide and for who's benefit? Was justice being done?

Joe Frank Wheeler was the past president of the Chamber of Commerce where Norm Lambert was a fellow supporting member serving on the board of directors. I wonder if Wheeler's voting record was for or against the forensic audit?

CHAPTER TWELEVE

BORGER NEWS PUBLISHER GETS INVOLVED

A week after the board meeting, Ron Rucker, Borger News Herald publisher, featured an editorial "Publisher Thoughts". The headline read: **HOSPITAL THOUGHTS.**

"I had heard the rumors. People told me it was bad. I had no idea. A number of folks had told me that the meetings could become a bit of a circus. Just out of curiosity, I attended a Golden Plains Hospital Board meeting last Tuesday night. The show I saw certainly deserved to be under the big top.

I didn't get a chance to sit down, before the arguing and the name calling began.

To start the night off, a petition was presented to the board asking for an investigation into the hospital's purchase of an MRI.

For those who have not heard about the MRI; to make a long story short, the hospital bought a lemon and is out at least $300,000. *(Note: The fact was $615,000. Was this sentence a publisher's typo, a misleading statement or a exaggeration to lead the public astray?)*

As reported in this paper, by admittance of the hospital, some poor decisions were made on the purchase. According to Norm Lambert, CEO of the hospital, people and procedures were put in place to make sure it didn't happen again. End of an unfortunate story, right?

Wrong.

After watching the board meeting, it is fairly obvious that the issue is not dead for at least one board member.

It was easy to tell that one of the instigators of the petition was the president of the board. In other words, a member of the board assisted in petitioning the board itself. That's like hiring a lawyer to sue your own business.

According to a board member, the FBI, at the request of the hospital, did a preliminary investigation and found nothing to pursue with anyone at the hospital. Considering that the board knows that only bad decisions were made and nothing fraudulent occurred, shouldn't the board be concerned only with salvaging the losses incurred and making sure it doesn't happen again?

Instead, a few individuals seem to be stuck on who should get the blame for the mistake. From the day it happened, Lambert has openly talked to the public about the issue. He's admitted that there were poor decisions made. We have long had an answer as to what happened with the MRI. Let's move one.

The hospital, in recent years, has improved. Their financial picture is better, their ER department has been enhanced, they've created a new clinic. You wouldn't know it from listening to a board meeting, but things are better at the hospital and they're moving toward even further improvements.

Unfortunately, in my opinion, this board and the hospital cannot move forward with such internal and external bickering. It is an embarrassment to the workers at the hospital and an embarrassment to our community.

But above all, it hurts the image of the hospital. A bad image can drive people away and shut down a business and I don't think anyone in Borger wants to think about life without a hospital again."

HIRE THE PUBLISHER'S WIFE AND CONTROL THE PRESS

The CEO's circulated Memo among hospital employees on November 10, 2000 announced that Ruth Rucker will join us on November 20, 2000, as the Director of Marketing. Ruth will only be here half time as she shares her time with Borger's News-Herald. Ruth's nine years of newspaper and advertising experience will assist us as she works to improve both our external marketing to the public and our internal communications to our employees, physicians and Board. Ruth is married with two small children.

It's interesting to note that Ruth Rucker became financially supported by both the newspaper and the hospital while living with her husband Ron Rucker, publisher of the newspaper. Wouldn't any intelligent person perceive this arrangement as a conflict of interest? How could there not have been joint financial benefits derived from Golden Plains for the Tucker family?

Ruth Rucker's employment with Golden Plains was announced 3 days following the board meeting. Ron Rucker's article in support of Norm Lambert ran 4 days after his wife, Ruth Rucker, was hired at the hospital. Who in their right mind wouldn't think that it appeared the hospital bought influence on the newspaper? What better way to control public opinion in a small town? Isn't freedom of speech lost whenever media can be manipulated?

RESPONSES TO NEWS-HERALD PUBLISHER

Pat Cleveland responded to Ron Rucker's article shortly thereafter through a letter to the editor that read:

"For the integrity of your newspaper, it is imperative that you retract the outright lie and slander you wrote about me (Pat Cleveland) and the citizen's Petition involving the purchase of the MRI machine in your November 11 to 12, 2000 editorial. I emphatically deny having anything to do with that Petition until it was presented to me on November

7, 2000 at the hospital board meeting. A slander on any member of the hospital board is a reflection on the entire board and there are very good and special citizens on our hospital board."—Sincerely, Pat Cleveland.

Frank Smith, longtime community leader in Borger was furious about the "nepotism" connection between the newspaper and the hospital. He contacted the newspaper corporate office in Alabama to complain about the publisher. In response, here is the letter Rucker wrote to Frank Smith on November 21, 2000.

Frank,

I have heard from our corporate offices in Alabama that you were unhappy with my opinion of the hospital board meetings. It is your right as a member of this community to voice that opinion.

However, I was disappointed that you felt the need to go about it the way you did. You are always welcome to write an article or a letter to the editor and voice that opinion. In addition, my door is always open and I'm always available on the phone to hear anyone's concern. I would have appreciated the chance to talk to you about the matter before you attempted to go "above me." Such actions generally do not solve problems.

I hope that in the future you will proceed differently with your complaints.

Best regards,
Ron Rucker
Publisher

John Curnutt responded to Rucker's allegations toward Pat Cleveland by submitting an opinion article to the publisher. It read:

On November 7, 2000, I John Curnutt presented a petition to the hospital board, with no less than 1,041 signatures, this is five times the number of voters in the last hospital board election. The intent of the petition was to request a forensic audit. At that time I stated openly and emphatically that I took full responsibility for the petition. I drafted the petition and had it checked by my attorney to insure it was legally correct. I then circulated the petition with the help of several friends, none of which had anything to do with the hospital or it's board of directors.

In fact, I especially and intentionally made the decision to take no help getting signatures from anyone who works for the hospital or the board of directors.

For the publisher to blame anyone on the hospital board is a gross misuse of his power as the publisher of the paper. To accuse any present board member smacks of yellow journalism.

The fact that Mrs. Rucker (the publisher's wife) has been hired by Norm Lambert, the administrator at the hospital as the Communications/Public Relations Director, Prior to his (publisher's) Sunday editorial leads me to question the publisher's credibility.

For the record, I, John Curnutt started, circulated, collected, tabulated and presented it to the board. The very idea that the signatures on the petition were called into question is ludicrous and is a slap in the face of anyone who signed it.

Mrs. Cleveland, President of the Golden Plains Community Hospital Board is doing what I consider to be a very difficult job and taking on matters that are not popular. Mrs. Cleveland has the support of the community as shown by the 1,041 number of concerned citizens that signed the petition. Mrs. Cleveland and the Board of GPCH should view that petition of 1,041 signatures as a clear mandate by the people to authorize a forensic audit and or investigation by the new law firm retained by the board.

In conclusion, if the board fails to act in what we the undersigned consider to be the logical conclusion to this matter, I will present this petition to the appropriate Local, State, or Federal authorities. This issue will not go away, even if it does make certain people uncomfortable.

John Curnutt's letter was censored by the News Herald Publisher and never printed. Rucker wrote Curnutt a very defensive letter and asked him to change his letter if he wanted it published. Curnutt refused to change his letter, therefore it was never seen in the News Herald.

The board never acted in behalf of the 1,041 citizens. John Curnutt was right, the issue did not go away. People in Hutchinson County do not forget. Golden Plains Community Hospital was approaching its 911 and the people would voice their disapproval. Injustice has a long memory.

KEN CRAIN RESIGNS FROM THE BOARD

In September, Ken Cain resigned from the hospital board and moved to Canyon, Texas. The hospital CEO recommended Mark Hedley to the County Commissioners for appointment on the board and got his wish.

Months following Crain's departure a disturbing news report in the Borger News Herald surfaced.

The headline on the April 4, 2001 front page read, **Crain pleads guilty to booster club theft**

"Jana Leigh Crain, 37, of Canyon, pled guilty to felony theft of monies Wednesday from the Gateway Elementary School Booster Club in Borger."

Jana Leigh Crain was the treasurer for the Gateway School Booster Club with her husband as co-treasurer between June 1, 1999, and May 31, 2000. When she left the treasurer's position, other club members asked her, "to turn over the club's financial records." She replied that, "They were lost" and later testified under oath, "They were thrown away."

District Attorney, Clay Ballman told club members they would need to review bank records and collect other documents. They proceeded to get the records from Amarillo

National Bank of Borger. They found several checks written to Cain payable to herself with the notation "reimbursement."

In court with Judge John Lagrone presiding, Jana Crain pled guilty to stealing money between $1,500 and $20,000. Her attorney presented a cashier's check for $19,500 and Mrs. Crain received two years probation.

While looking in the case files numbered cause 8668 at the County Courthouse, I found an anonymous typewritten letter and a clipping of the Jana Crain article from the Borger News Herald. The envelope had been postmarked from Amarillo, Texas.

The letter read: *"It is always nice to see that some folks have the right friends in the right places. I wonder how many people could steal $19,000 and get just two years probation. Not Many!!*

And where is the co-treasurer of the Booster Club? I am sure he did not know this was happening. We would not want to endanger his job at the bank—would we? By the way, was he not the chairman of the finance committee at our hospital, where we are only missing a million or so? But, again, he had nothing to do with that either—did he?

CHAPTER THIRTEEN

THE JERRY WAGGONER FOUNDATION AND FRITCH CLINIC

In Frank Smith's records there is a folder full of documents relating to the Jerry Waggoner Foundation dating back to April, 1991 when the foundation was organized. It was established as a non-profit corporation in honor of Jerry Waggoner who was the first president of the board of trustees when the hospital district was formed in 1989. The foundation's purpose was to award scholarships supporting persons in health care related careers.

Frank Smith had served as a foundation board member since its inception. Smith was elected president in January 1996, shortly after Lambert was hired as CEO at Golden Plains. During this time Lambert began to pressure Smith into signing a check from the foundation to build a Clinic in Fritch, Texas. Smith refused Lambert because the funds were set aside for scholarships and not for construction. In the rift that ensued, Frank Smith finally resigned and delivered the foundation records and checkbook to Lambert.

This event and others involving Lambert's frivolous management mishaps motivated Frank Smith's crusade to get rid of the hospital CEO. Regrettably, Frank Smith passed away before the task could be finished.

THE INGRAMS

This opinion article from the May 3, 2001 News-Herald impressed me because of the passion, intelligence and concern it expressed about the hospital.

Dear Editor:

What makes a company have employee retention problems, employee trust issues and employee instability? Your editorial on 4-29 suggested the reason was the "Snipping and Bickering" between the board and administration. As former employees of GPCH with forty years combined service, we disagree.

Could the reason be:

Non-adherence of Policy and Procedures.

— Giving bonuses to select departments, leaving others to find out through the "Grapevine".
— Rehiring employees who have been terminated for less than optimal performance.

- Preferential treatment of employees who are "friends" with managers and administration.
- Overlooking long time, qualified and experienced employees for job openings, instead giving them to outside, less qualified candidatesNeglecting concerns and problems on the employee level. Offering little or no benefits.—Giving raises to select employees while a hospital wide wage freeze was in progress.
- Evaluation techniques that allow only for mediocre reviews, minimizing pay incentives.
- Uneven pay scales.
- Inconsistent discipline practices.
- Hiring of department managers with little or no experience dealing with employee relations and departmental operations.
- Consistent under staffing, creating a decline in patient care.
- Extreme spending practices by administration and mid-management, eliminating the availability of funds for possible employee incentives.

These conditions create employee instability and moral problems for which the leadership . . . the administrator and assistant administrator are directly responsible for.

It is 100% appropriate for the Board to expect accountability for these and other pertinent issues. We applaud the efforts by the Board and we all should expect every effort by them to demand accountability for your tax dollars, and insure the optimal performance of this hospital.

While there are many excellent employees at GPCH, their optimal potential is stifled through a network of inconsistency and negativity caused by Administration and mid-management, NOT the Board.

Never in our years at GPCH have we witnessed an Administration so successfully responsible for dividing the Medical Staff, Employees, and Board of Directors. This continued behavior can only have negative consequences.

We chose to leave GPCH, not because we had nothing more to offer, but because GPCH had nothing more to offer us.

Sharon and Ken Ingram

I wanted to find out more about the Ingrams and I was able contact Sharon Ingram in New Mexico for an interview.

"Borger was our hometown. We were both born and raised there. My great grandfather was Justice of the Peace back in the hoodlum days when they would tie people up to the hitching rails out in front of the bars. I have a lot of history there with my family and it was emotionally painful about having to leave there.

We felt passionate about our work but we had to leave because we took a stand against what we saw was wrong. We expressed our views and met a lot of opposition with the Administration in the hospital. We were pretty quickly labeled as troublemakers.

When we moved to Raton, New Mexico and started working at the hospital, the administrator there was contacted by the administrator at Golden Plains. That's the reason the Doctors lawsuit ended up in Federal court was because Lambert called across state lines to the administrator in Raton and told him derogatory statements claiming we were trouble makers in an attempt to interfere with our jobs.

These people forgot about what Golden Plains was all about. It was about taking care of patients in an economical efficient way. When all that changed, I could no longer be a part of it. Conviction of knowing what it right and what is wrong. But, in Hutchinson County I'm not sure if the good guys will ever win.

The first year Lambert was there (1996) he presented me the CEO AWARD SPECIAL RECONITION AWARD and it says in grateful appreciation of outstanding and dedicated service to the patients, hospital staff, medical staff and board of directors presented to Sharon Igram, RN from Golden Plains Community Hospital.

How did I go from receiving the first CEO RECOGNION AWARD to being on Lambert's hit list? It was because I stood up for what is right and expressed my opinions. All of a sudden, I wasn't worth anything.

Mr. Lambert was not from that community and did not have a vested interest. We were good employees with a vested interest in the hospital. We were always looking for new things to bring in. Ken brought in so many things for the respiratory department. We weren't alone. There were a lot of good people in that hospital, but one by one got deterred about what there jobs really were.

I was out of high school for 16 years before going to college for my nursing degree. That's all I wanted to do was work in that hospital. I really did care about that hospital. To me it was like a slogan, "That's my hospital."

After ending the conversation and hanging up the phone, I wondered how many people in Hutchinson County can proudly say, "That's my hospital".

CITIZEN'S GROUP MEET WITH DISTRICT ATTORNEY

A concerned and frustrated citizen's group went to meet with District Attorney, Clay Ballman. They wanted to know if he could do something about the hospital's financial affairs, it's "bonus" programs and other issues. The group consisted of Frank Smith, John Curnutt, Past Board President—Pat Cleveland, Dr. Elston, Dr. Galagado, Dr. Quiros, and Dr. Sangalang.

It was in this meeting that the District Attorney stated that executive sessions are mistakenly considered confidential but there are no laws that mandate a requirement of confidentiality. This is what the hospital attorney Leon Mitchell had told Jerry Strecker and other hospital board members to silence them about the child pornography.

Dr. Strecker was shocked when he learned this. Was the hospital attorney ignorant of the law or had he blatantly deceived Strecker and others? He couldn't believe his ears and asked Ballman to clarify his statement. It's unimaginable how Dr. Strecker felt when the truth was revealed.

As a family counselor, he had experienced the feelings of adult patients who were victimized as children by sexual predators. He understood how the horrific experience robbed childhood's and wrecked lives. He knew that a person addicted to child pornography was a potential sexual predator of children. He became outraged by the deceit that allowed the hospital Chief Financial Officer to freely leave Hutchinson County where he could continue his pervasive acts in another community.

It was then and there that the District Attorney was asked to begin an immediate investigation to see if these victimized children could finally be protected.

CHAPTER FOURTEEN

CHILD PORNOGRAPHY EXPOSED TO PUBLIC

On May 8, 2001, sensational headlines blasted across newspapers in the Texas Panhandle. The secret told in a closed executive meeting in June 2000 to Dr. Jerry Strecker became public knowledge. Following is the article from the Amarillo Globe News.

FBI to investigate possible porn charges
By Ricky George

BORGER—The 84th District Attorney's Office and possibly the Federal Bureau of Investigation will investigate potential child pornography charges against a former employee of Golden Plains Community Hospital in Borger.

District Attorney Clay Ballman said that about two months ago he met with about 10 Hutchinson County residents who were concerned about how the hospital was being run.

"During the initial meeting, they mentioned there was child pornography discovered in January of 2000," Ballman said.

Ballman said he contacted the hospital district's attorney, who confirmed that a hospital employee was found with some child pornography at the hospital.

"The material was taken by hospital district attorney, was sealed and the employee was terminated," Ballman said. Ballman declined to identify the former employee.

At Ballman's request, the attorney turned the material over to the Borger Police Department.

"There were about six depiction's of nudity involving children and two of these involved sexual contact between an adult and a child," he said. "We concluded there was a violation under state law."

Possession of child pornography is listed as a second-degree felony, according to Texas statutes. A second-degree felony is punishable by a prison term from two to 20 years and /or a fine up to $10,000.

Borger police are trying to find the former employee, Ballman said. "Our office would like to arrange to interview this person and get this person's side of the story, but we can't find this person," he said.

Because the material may be from the Internet, the DA's office contacted the FBI in Amarillo, Ballman said. The FBI agreed to examine the material to decide whether they would investigate possible federal charges.

The DA's office has the former employee's computer from the hospital in case the FBI wants the computer's hard drive examined for any other pornographic images. "It's an isolated incident," Ballman said.

In a Borger News-Herald article it was reported that hospital attorney, Leon Mitchell had contacted Charlie Keys with the Borger Police Department.

Keys recalled the conversation with Mitchell in January or February of last year, saying "he said he had a possible pornography situation. He contacted me a few days later and said the matter had been resolved."

Keys said it must have been a miscommunication between the hospital's attorney and authorities. "The phrase 'pornography' was used. I was not aware that it was child pornography."

Possession of child pornography from the Internet is considered a third-degree federal felony and is punishable by a prison term from two to ten years, plus a fine up to $10,000.

Mitchell and Lambert both said the Chairman of the hospital board was notified immediately and other board members were informed on an individual basis. *(According to Pat Cleveland, board member at that time, she was not immediately notified. She had to threaten going to the State Hospital Association in order to get the truth.)*

District Attorney Clay Ballman said there is no law that requires employers to report such instances. He also said the hospital did what it thought was right and *"their intent was good."*

How in the world could Clay Ballman say, "Their intent was good?" How can the intent be good whenever there is an attempt to cover up child pornography? Good kind things for those in power and unkind things for innocent children!

DR. STRECKER APPEALS TO THE COUNTY COMMISSIONERS

On May 14, 2001, Jerry Strecker went to address the Hutchinson County Commissioners Court about the problems at Golden Plains Hospital. Unabashedly, Judge Jack Worsham and the four County Commissioners would only allow him to read the first and last page. By this time Dr. Strecker had already been smeared, demeaned and ridiculed in the community. Strecker was not a member in good standing in the Rotary or in the good ol' boys club in Hutchinson County. His freedom of speech throttled down that day in the Commissioner's Courtroom.

This is the first time Dr. Strecker's entire story is presented the County Commissioners and the people in Hutchinson County.

Dear citizens of Hutchinson County,

My name is Jerry Strecker. I am a present member of the Golden Plains Community Hospital board of directors. I was elected one year ago, and I have two years to serve on my term of office. I intend to resign in the very near future when I deem it appropriate. I cannot in conscience remain as a member of a group that I consider to he dysfunctional involving complicity in a system of power politics which I consider to be improper and an unethical—and in which I will no longer take part

.For those of you who do not know me, I have lived in Hutchinson County for approximately 10 years. I have my doctoral degree in Marriage and Family Counseling. I am licensed and work full-time as a counselor in Borger. I was asked to run for the board of Golden Plains Community Hospital representing the Fritch community and I believed that I would have something to contribute. I care deeply about the spiritual, physical and mental health of people and families, and I see Golden Plains Community Hospital has such a positive asset in serving our citizenry.

But even as a professional who has worked over 30 years in helping individuals and groups work through serious problems, I was totally unprepared for the mess I found and the absolute frustration I have felt for months, in trying to deal effectively with the issues we, the board have encountered.

I want to share with you something of what I'm talking about, and ask you to consider over the past year's time whether you have been receiving a balanced viewpoint of what has actually happened at the administrative level in Golden Plains Community Hospital.

POINT 1

Did you know that the CEO of Golden Plains Community Hospital hired the past editor's wife of the News Herald, as his publicity director. When at least two citizens wrote a letter to the News-Herald asking the question whether this constitutes a possible conflict of interest in fair reporting, he refused to publish these letters and in writing he threaten one person with a liable suit for even suggesting it.

Meanwhile, the paper began a continued series of articles praising the leadership of our CEO and insinuating in its reporting and actually stating in its editorial opinions that certain board members were to be discounted for the negative attitudes.

To this day, no one from the News-Herald ever contacted me to see if there might be even an inkling justification for my "negativity". But, it is just a coincidence that our CEO has channeled hundreds and hundreds of dollars into an advertising pocket of the News-Herald paid for by Golden Plains Community Hospital to advertise the practice of our new doctors in Borger. Wouldn't it have been nice, if the News-Herald is truly trying to be fair-minded and objective, that it would have freely disclosed any possible conflicts of interest and would interview all the board members to get a balanced reporting of facts? And now isn't it interesting for the first time in over 40 years, our paper has come at endorsing one political candidate over another who just happens to be the one our CEO is supporting?

POINT 2

On at least two or more occasions, our CEO has told and re-told the News-Herald, what he claims is a full disclosure story on the purchase of an MRI machine in the fall of 1999. According to his story, his mistake was in trusting too much of his own Chief Financial Officer who he himself had hired and it was this officer who led him astray.

Recently, I have found out that a number of employees already knew of this CFO's reputation because he was dismissed from the hospital in Dumas for serious violations while on the job. I've long believed that one of the most stupid things in the world is to trust an untrustworthy person. To do so is to invite disaster, that this is what our CEO claims he did and continued to do long after he was already receiving serious complaints about his (CFO's)behavior at our hospital.

Let me paint this picture and little different color. What if you had a teenage son to had a "trusted friend" who talked your son into going along with him in buying a car. Now it would be one thing, if they bought this car out of their own bank account, but instead they used your bank account. On top of all this, you find out afterwards that this salesman was so clever in describing this car, that he was able to jack up its market value from $3,000 to $6,000 and then sell it to them site unseen as with a full payment prior to delivery. And finally, you find out that when some knowledgeable people learned of this possible purchase, they offered to your son to go, free of charge and inspect this car to see if it was really what it was reported to be, and your son refused their offer. Then, low and behold, when the car arrived, it was a piece of junk that didn't even work.

I assume even you would be terribly angry at such a salesman for being so deceptive and even went to cuss out your son's "trusted friend" for his stupidity. But how would you go about holding your own son accountable for spending your money in a way that seems so irresponsible.

Now it would be one thing, if our incident involved a no-brainier of a teenage son, in our case it is a well-paid professional, our CEO, who made each of these choices. How are we to hold him accountable for his stewardship of hospital funds? Both ethically and legally, there is an important distinction to be made when someone claims he did not know any better. The distinction is this: between "innocent" and ignorance and "culpable" ignorance. Children are often innocent in their ignorance: we don't expect them to know better when they do some things. But guess what happens to one of us if we try to claim we did not know what the speed limit was, our how fast we were driving when a cop catches as going 85 on a 70 miles per hour road. That's culpable ignorance. You might, even declare your teenage son ignorant but innocent in such a car scam as I described, but I don't care how much our CEO claims he did not know what was happening, I believe it is his expected duty to follow normal accepted purchasing procedures for such an expensive item. And when he did not follow what I consider even a minimal level of accepted business practice, I believe he must be held accountable. In this case, I cannot see that any ignorance can be excused for less than full culpability and responsibility.

So how was our CEO held accountable? His performance evaluation for the year 1999 in which this first happened was judged by the Board to meet the standard of excellence, and our CEO was awarded a sizable bonus. This year, we did better. They were able to get a majority vote of the board to deny him a bonus for excellence, but he still received a standard pay raise. So for now, his total accountability for this huge loss of money for a hospital has been the loss of one year's bonus. He has not even received a written reprimand in his personnel file. Our discipline policy mandates immediate termination for employees who commit certain Level three offenses that don't even approach the gravity of the situation. They would be fired on the spot; he received a pay raise.

Some of us thought he should have been fired on the spot but the majority of the Board rules. The others of us began to see the accusations and ridicule of meetings and in the paper of being negative and aggressive in our attitudes toward our CEO.

POINT 3

And now I need to share the part that I have agonized over the most. It was announced very quietly in January, 2000, that a little over a year ago, the CFO of Golden Plains community hospital had resigned and moved on, being granted a month's "severance pay" supposedly for his excellence of service.

I was not yet a member of the board and my own assumption was that this was the price a "trusted friend" was forced to pay for his part of the MRI debacle. And ever since then, it seems to be that he was blamed and become the "fall guy" for this whole episode. It's even been suggested that this CFO and a salesman in the MRI were in cahoots and part of a fraud conspiracy. Part of what has puzzled me is that this person would choose to remain totally silent in defense of all these accusations. One possibility is that he is totally guilty as charged, and only wants to run and hide.

But there is another possibility for his silence, and it may never be able to be proven in a court of law or anyplace else. But at least I believe that you people deserve to know this part of an untold chapter. The real reason the CFO was forced to resign is that he was using its hospital computer, on hospital time, to search and receive off the Internet graphic child pornography. Supposedly with legal counsel, our CEO made the decision to seal this evidence and put in a locked file in the hospital.

Personally, I was horrified at this information. Far, far too often another brave but desperate person, comes to my office finally to reveal horrible wounds and tortured memories of having been sexually abused. My first question was whether any of this information was turned over to proper authorities to investigate whether this child or children (I had never seen actual pictures) were still being abused and tortured for profit of sick perverts. I found out that nothing had been done; that the real priority was in protecting the public image of Golden Plains Community Hospital, and this superseded any consideration regarding the welfare of innocent children.

Mr. Commissioners, I have lived at this horrendous secret for approximately nine months. I may need to explain why I didn't speak out long before now. The very heart of my professional counseling is to *hold myself to the very highest level of confidentiality*. To betray the trust of what ever anyone tells me in confidentiality is to betray myself and sometimes this means holding dark secrets, and only in the most limited circumstances am I ever allowed to write off confidentiality. One such circumstance, is when I receive confidential information, or even suspicion, that a child is being abused, then I am bound to report, what I know to the proper authorities under penalty of losing my license.

But in my orientation as a board member, which was given by our CEO, I was led to believe that the legal confidentiality levels required within our executive meetings of the board were even a higher level than my own profession in and under no conditions was I allowed to speak of information received there. The majority of the board chose to leave things as they were, I did not ever imagine that I would feel paralyzed in my efforts to help innocent children, but it happened. And it was awful!

Finally, a couple of months ago, several concerned and frustrated citizens asked me to go with them as a member of the board to talk to our District Attorney, whether they, or he, could do something about our hospital's financial affairs, it's "bonus" programs, that they saw as unfair, and other issues. It was in the midst of this meeting, that our District Attorney stated that executive sessions are considered confidential but there are not laws as I know that mandate a requirement of confidentiality as I had been misled to believe. I almost fell off my chair and I asked him very specifically to clarify his statement so that I definitely understood what he was saying. He stated the same, using the Fritch city council as a parallel example and what had once happened there. It was then and there that I shared what I knew about this child pornography incident, and ask him to begin an immediate investigation to see if these victimized children could finally be protected.

I then asked him to further investigate whether he could find that this whole deal was a way to get our past CFO to take the heat for an MRI fiasco, for which he was only partially responsible; and in exchange, he (CFO) would not be charged for a possible federal crime for which he could end up in prison because the evidence lay hidden in our hospital unreported to the authorities. Wouldn't any rational person suspect this might be a way to shut someone up permanently.

Again, I don't know if sealing this evidence and holding it under lock had anything to do with some sort of blackmail. But wouldn't a reasonable person wonder if they're just might be more than one motivation for handling child pornography in such a manner and especially after giving the perpetrator a month's severance pay for "resigning" under such circumstances.

Maybe our District Attorney will find a perfect logical answer for each question, but I believe as a Board member, I at least needed to ask the hard questions.

POINT 4

I want to give one example that is pertinent to my perception that our CEO is manipulative, far less than honest, and by purposely withholding information causes the board to be reactive to crisis instead of pro-active in planning.

I was appointed by our board president to be an interim chairperson for a new hospital. I was to prepare some information for our board regarding the standards and processes used by other cities to build a new hospital and other recommendations from Texas Hospital Association to do such planning in a legitimate way.

The information and the process that was suggested basically involved at least a two-year careful assessment of the future community needs and the state of our present hospital. It was stressed, this needed strong community involvement; openness in communication; and careful, respectful building of the consensus of public opinion, whether to continue to put money into our present hospital or to build a totally new hospital.

Also, I was asked to consult with board members of Frank Phillips College to see how they have so successfully planned, organized and implemented their new building program. I reported what I knew at our January, 2001 meeting. In February and March, I recommend expanding this interim committee to a larger group, including administrative people, Board and Medical staff representation and various citizens. The Board referred this to the Education Committee of Golden Plains Community Hospital for review, other suggestions and approval. This they did. Then I contacted the individual people to see if they would serve on this committee. All this time my assumption was that we were looking at a two-year period of planning and discerning what was the right thing to do it for the Hutchinson County Hospital District.

Meanwhile, our CEO had a different plan, without ever once having spoken to me about my research or my reports and recommendations to the Board. The night I did recommend a list of names, suddenly he introduced another list. At that moment, I thought it was strange that he had never before suggested ever one name when everyone knew I was trying to form such a committee.

Then in closed session, our CEO revealed a very professionally organized presentation, with pictures and graphics and statistics . . . including a very helpful presentation by our head of maintenance for Golden Plains demonstrating that terrible conditions present in several of the older sections. None of this was new information to them, but never once had anything ever been shared with us in a Board meeting. And certainly, I had not been included in any of this, even though I were supposedly representing the Board in precisely trying to design a fair and reasonable way to proceed.

All of a sudden our hospital is in a crisis. We were carefully instructed not to share what we had learned, and instead he was to make is carefully orchestrated presentation to send civics groups, etc . . . demonstrating the terrible status or hospital, which I tend to believe, and the absolute need for an election in the fall of 2001 to double the level of hospital taxes, to fund the building and a new hospital. And this was a political strategy suggested. If we carefully control publicity and not stir up too much interest, especially opposition, then likely only 30% of you, the citizens would care enough to vote anyway. So, all that is needed is approximately 16% of the people to vote in favor of a secretly concocted plan. I'm not saying it is the wrong plan; it may be just what we need, but I consider it a horrible way to treat the citizens of our district, and I consider it highly unethical for the board and our CEO to proceed in such a manner.

Now let me tie this back into the context in which all this was happening, which may or may not be connected. First, this was precisely in the midst of the time when our board was obviously split in our valuation of the CEO and the board unanimously decided to have a retreat to help us come to some resolution. The person who had selected to direct this retreat gave us some basic principles of operation, one being; "When the board cannot trust the CEO, then they must depart with the CEO."

No wonder some withdrew to make sure we never had this retreat. And no wonder our CEO knew it was time to create a whole new crisis by suddenly revealing that terrible condition of Golden Plains Community Hospital and the urgency to build a new facility. How could we depart with our CEO and be leaderless at such a critical time?

Second, in late January, 2001, our CEO received pages and pages of legal documents from Phillips Petroleum Corporation, laying out their plan to begin approximately $35 million in the construction at their refinery. The construction was scheduled to begin in the middle of April, 2001. They were seeking a one hundred percent tax abatement on this project, which would amount to huge savings to them over a seven year period, especially if the tax base for a new hospital would have doubled.

The board was given these documents for the first time at our April 6th meeting and Phillips was scheduled to begin construction on April 13th. At that point, I thought our retreat was still scheduled. I made a motion to table this item so it could be reviewed by hospital attorney.

My motion died for lack of a second to the motion. I wanted at least to delay and decision until we had gone into a closed session so that I could voice my objections. Is it ethical to insist that our elderly citizens on a closed income will be required to pay full taxes, especially if they become doubled, and we give Phillips Corporation a free ride.

But since I did not know this item was coming out, it was not covered in closed session, so it could not become a topic of discussion there.

I did note that the last of the documents was dated January 29, 2001 and I did ask to whom the documents were sent and why only now at this late hour were they presented to us. (We could have reviewed and discussed them at both our February and March meetings.) Our CEO sheepishly admitted he had them all the time. He stated that previous boards had automatically approved such tax abatements, and he thought we would do that, so there was no need for us to have had such information at an earlier time.

What our CEO did not say, but what he absolutely knew that makes this year very different, is his plan to try to get everyone else's hospital taxes doubled before the year is out.

I cannot say, he purposely sold us out to Phillips. Phillips Petroleum Corporation has been an outstanding and long time supporter, including taxes, for Borger and Hutchinson County. I can say it was less than forthright, and his choices definitely forced the Board to arrive at the conclusion that he obviously wanted in the first place.

POINT 5

By last January, 2001, the Board completed its evaluation of our CEO and it became undeniably obvious that the board was totally fractured and divided on many issues, but especially on our viewpoints of our CEO. We recognized we needed outside help if we were ever going to function effectively again. The Board made the unanimous decision to have a retreat, to be held by an outside expert. Mr. Stephen Henley, was selected because he is an attorney and served as a CEO in several large hospitals, and now teaches in Oklahoma, and has his own consulting firm that specializes in helping hospital boards. He came in March to interview each of us individually along with the CEO, and some other top administrative staff members, to get a feel for the issues involved and prepare a retreat format. A majority of the board voted to schedule a retreat in the first or second weekend after Easter. It was at this retreat than I intended to lay out these and several other issues of which I'm still concerned. Very quickly, individual Board members let it be known that they will not participate until finally, Mr. Henley himself suggested we cancel it for lack of commitment . . . that it would be a waste of time and money if some key people refused to participate. I felt like a board decision had gotten sabotaged by a few, and I felt angry and manipulated.

I hung onto a last straw hope when the Board scheduled our next regular meeting for May 1, 2001. I believed then, that we will would be having this final meeting of what was our present Board, and I was determined to have a very open and frank discussion in executive session in which I intended to propose that either our CEO be allowed to resign or be terminated immediately. I don't know if the proposal would have passed or not, but at least I wanted it to be on the open record exactly what each Board member stands in regard to their non-support of our CEO and his administrative decisions.

Then one board member chose to call three other Board members and convinced them that this meeting should be boycotted, and all four called in and said they would not be present, which blocked the other three of us from forming a quorum, and so this meeting too was canceled. I was left was only one choice of shutting my mouth or going public.

What specifically am I asking of you, our Commissioners Court? Number one by far, I am asking for whatever moral support or legal powers you have to help us, apparently a very small minority on the Board but a huge majority of our long time resident physicians of Borger, and for other concerned citizens for whom I believe I am speaking, to help us save Golden Plains Community Hospital

As long and maybe tedious as my statement has been, I know have only scratched the surface. In our annual audit of 1999, our hospital showed a profit of over $1,300,000 and in our audit for 2000, we show the deficit of over $700,000. We were given supposed reasons and excuses, but the facts are that we changed our financial position at the right of $2 million in one year's time, and already for this year 2001 of over 700,000 in additional deficit spending.

Something is failing miserably and it has to be stopped and be corrected, if it is not already too late. I don't know whom to hold accountable except us, as a Board, and our only hired employee, the CEO.

I know that one Board representative is up for re-nomination by this court in the very near future. I'm not asking you to accept my statement as the truth, but I'm begging you to seek the truth by asking the necessary hard questions that I have tried to raise, and other citizens are trying to raise, and that you as County Commissioners may have.

Meanwhile, I am asking this much, that you do not take action on re-appointing the Court's representative until you have sufficient answers to these questions, and know clearly where your representative stands in these issues. I've heard that our District

Judge can order a forensic audit of the hospital. If this is so, I would hope that you would support and even encourage such an option. I know our District Attorney is now investigating the whole child pornography incident and possible cover up involved. I hope as a Court, you would offer your full support for a quick, fair and thorough investigation of all aspects of the situation as our County can provide, both legally and ethically.

Finally, if you as a Court, find validity to my assertions of corrupted leadership at the administrator level at Golden Plains Community Hospital, I would hope you invoke a recall election of every present Board member, including myself, to re-establish public credibility in Golden Plains Community Hospital.

I offer these only as beginning options. I'm sure you are far better equipped for your own vantage point as Commissioners to do what is needed. I necessarily pray for your help; please don't let us down.

I thank you and God bless you.

Jerry Strecker

ANTI CHILD PORNOGRAPHY ANNOUNCEMENT

The MED (Medical Executive Committee), consisting of Dr. Holland, Dr. Sangalang, Dr. Trirogoff, Dr. Quiros, Dr. C.P. Quiros and Dr. Elston, felt strongly about protecting their professional integrity as doctors. They had no alternative but to announce to the community that they had no knowledge of the Child Pornography at Golden Plains Community Hospital.

On Wednesday, May 30, 2001, the doctors placed a paid advertisement in the Borger News-Herald stating:

THE MEDICAL EXECUTIVE COMMITTEE OF GOLDEN PLAINS COMMUNITY HOSPITAL WISHES TO MAKE THIS FORMAL STATEMENT FOR THE PURPOSE OF NOTIFYING THE PUBLIC THAT THE MEDICAL EXECUTIVE COMMITTEE WAS NEVER INFORMED OF THE CHILD PORNOGRAPHY ISSUE BY THE HOSPITAL ADMINISTRATOR. AS MEMBERS OF THE MEDICAL EXECUTIVE COMMITTEE— WE ARE EMBARRASSED, OFFENDED AND ASHAMED OF THE CHILD PORNOGRAPHY AND WE WANT THE PUBLIC TO KNOW OUR FEELINGS.
Paid by the Medical Executive Committee, 503 W. 1st Street

By morally and ethically placing this ad in the Borger News Herald, these doctors would never be rewarded with "good kind things" from the hospital administrator, board members, hospital attorney and others in Hutchinson County. This "Christian" community was led astray and rewarded these people with ridicule, smears and rumors of shame.

DR. JERRY STRECKER RESIGNS

Finally in absolute frustration, Dr. Strecker submitted this resignation letter to the hospital board and to the Borger-News Herald that ran on Thursday, December 20, 2001.

Dear Hospital Board Members:

I write this letter with great regret and disappointment, however the actions of this board and the administration of Golden Plains Community Hospital under the leadership of Norm Lambert, leave me no alternative.

I was elected by my community to represent their interests. I was not elected to participate in a campaign of defamation against members of the medical staff, nor to rubber stamp actions of a board and administration that, in my opinion, are questionable and unethical at best.

During my short tenure I have observed members of the board and the administration engage in behavior which I consider unethical, defamatory and malicious. The agenda being pursued is secretive and not in the best interest of the community of Golden Plains Community Hospital, however it is evident that the interests of the board and administration lie elsewhere.

Mismanagement of the hospital has caused it to suffer great economic losses. I witnessed as a political strategy was devised and board members instructed to implement it, in order to deny the public full knowledge of the issues. I have sought information which has been denied. Attempts to honorably carry out my fiduciary duties have met with interference or subterfuge. I have now, with full knowledge and support of the administration, also become a target of the defamatory and punitive campaign, which includes filing a false report of professional and ethical violations concerning unnamed individuals against me.

In brief, as much as I was honored by the people of Hutchinson County who placed their trust and confidence in my integrity and character in order to represent them, I cannot continue in good conscience, to serve on a board which I believe has amply proven its corrupt intent and means. To do otherwise would be a disservice to those citizens who honored me with their faith.

Regretfully,
Dr. Jerry Strecker

DOCTORS FILE FEDERAL LAWSUITS

When the Medical Executive Committee placed the ad notifying the public of the child pornography, they became targets of the hospital's administration. Following a year of turmoil, on June 4, 2002, a Civil Action Lawsuit was filed in U.S. District Court in Amarillo, Texas.

The plaintiffs were Dr. Gerry Holland, DO, Ms. Cynthia Lagrone, Dr. Romero B. Sangalang, MD, Dr. Jerry Strecker, PhD, Dr. Gloria Trirogoff, MD, Dr. Ed Quiros, MD and Dr. C.P. Quiros, MD.

The listed defendants were Mr. Norman Lambert, CEO Golden Plains Community Hospital and individually, Dr. Otoniel Huertas, Dr. Jessee Perales, Dr. Brett Simmons, Dr. Wally Mann, Dr. John A. Ribeiro, Dr. Basil A. Yuounis, Dr. Vic Maza, Dr. Bard Rogers, Dr. Carmen Purl, Ms. Kathy O'Keefe, Members of the Board of Golden Plains Community Hospital, Mark Headley, John Ribeiro, Connie Freriks, Tom Zeni, Joe Frank Wheeler, Paul Rullman, and Norm Lambert individually.

The following specific allegations were made in the documents filed as Plaintiffs Original Complaint:

DEFAMATION: Defendants committed Common Law Defamation, Slander, Libel, and Business Disparagement in that:

a. On or about June 5, 2001, Defendants Huertas, Mann, Perales, Purl, Riberio, Rogers, Simmons, Maza and Younis sent a letter to the Board, in which they accused the members of the MEC (Medical Executive Committee) of conspiring to exclude new doctors, and of working contrary to the welfare of their patients. A summary of the letter was published in the Borger News Herald on or about June, 8 2001.

b. On or about July 27, 2001, some or all of the Defendants caused an article to appear in the Borger News Herald with a headline reading "Sangalang Guilty of Malpractice.". However, jury found some negligence and no damages. The ruling was a take nothing judgment.

c. On or about September 4, 2001, Defendant O'Keefe, an employee of Golden Plains Community Hospital, filed a complaint with the Texas Department of Health claiming that an individual who's name she did not know had accused Dr. Strecker of being a "pervert". Ms. O'Keefe also said that two (2) other women had reported similar incidents, but did not state the name of the other purportedly accusing women. She published this information orally to third parties. No disciplinary action was taken by the Department of Health after duly investigating the allegations.

d. On or about September 12, 2001, Defendant Lambert told the Board of Directors of the Hospital that Dr. Holland had committed acts which constituted abandonment of her patients on the previous weekend. However, Holland had had no patients at the Hospital on the weekend in question.

e. On or about October of 2001, Defendant Lambert published defamatory statements accusing Plaintiff Trirogoff of refusing to treat a patient in an emergency, and of breaching a valid contract with the Hospital. These accusations were false. The incident referred to was not an emergency, and the contract referred to had expired over ten (10) years before.

f.   On or about January 17, 2002, shortly after the other charge was dismissed by the Texas Department of Health, Defendant O'Keefe induced another individual to make a complaint of sexual impropriety against Dr. Strecker.

The document continues on with allegations explaining that the Peer Review process on unresolved cases and questionable circumstances was previously reviewed by doctors other than the attending physician until it was arbitrarily changed in January 2002. The change shifted peer review responsibility to the hospital, defendant doctors and staff. The claim was that the change was made to harass Plaintiffs. Holland had two files peer reviewed, Ed Quiros had four files reviewed, Trirogoff had two files reviewed and Sangalang had seven files reviewed. During the same period of time few of Defendant doctors have had their files peer-reviewed, despite multiple reported allegations of serious medical occurrences on their parts.

The document also states WRONGFUL DISCHARGE in behalf of plaintiff Cynthia Lagrone who was employed four years as the hospital's risk manager and compliance officer. She had an exemplary employee record. She was unknowingly involved in concealing child pornography when Norm Lambert brought Lagrone a sealed envelope with instructions to leave it sealed and keep it in a safe place.

It wasn't until 14 months later on May 8, 2002 when an article published in the newspaper exposing the child pornography that Lagrone realized that the envelope she had been given contained the child pornography.

The following day, Lagrone contacted the Texas Nurses Association for advice concerning her duties and potential liability. She then informed Elsa Borden, Lambert's assistant, and Chief Operation Officer, and the MEC about this, and her intent to cooperate in any criminal investigation of the matter. On or about six days later, May 15, 2001, LaGrone was told that the position of Quality Risk Manager had been eliminated.

The document goes on to state that:

a.   LaGrone was terminated in retaliation for her refusal to perform an illegal act for which she could be held liable by hiding evidence and by knowingly possessing child pornography.
b.   In addition to this claim brought under the narrow scope of Sabine Pilot, LaGrone has completed the administrative process and timely filed a charge of Discrimination and retaliation with the EEOC.

Note: Records show that Lagrone received a $10,000 a year raise on February 2001, only three months prior to her termination. Was the cost of Lagrone's integrity the loss of her job? Were "good kind things" done to Cynthia Lagrone?

In the Thursday, June 27, 2002 Amarillo Globe-News, a headline read; SUITS ACCUSE BORGER HOSPITAL. In this article Norm Lambert was quoted as saying, "We believe they're frivolous lawsuits that have no basis, and we deny all the allegations." Leon Mitchell, hospital attorney was quoted saying, "The hospital is going to vigorously defend this. This case is without any merit and we're looking forward to our day in court."

On numerous occasions throughout the trial, the attorneys for the defendants tried to get the lawsuit thrown out as being "frivolous".* The Federal Judge rejected that tactic every single time.

The trial went on for months. The plaintiffs were asking for eight million dollars which was the estimated damages suffered as verified by expert witnesses. If the plaintiffs had won, the hospital would have most likely been closed because GPCH did not have that much insurance.

These plaintiffs were not lawyers, they were doctors who had taken oaths to care for their patients. They became frustrated with the time spent in court because it was taking a toll on their private practices. Rather than going forward, the plaintiffs settled for $240,000.

They had hoped this was a wake up call for the hospital board and changes in management would occur.

---

*   *Can child pornography ever be dismissed as frivolous? Child pornography goes beyond the bounds of decency, and is regarded as atrocious and utterly intolerable in a civilized community.*

CAMPAIGN TO DEFEAT THE HOSPITAL BOND.

August 2004 to September 11, 2004

CHAPTER FIFETEEN

FINANCING THE CAMPAIGN

I could afford to start a campaign, but would need additional advertising dollars to buy enough media to compete against Invest in Yourself. My task was to find business owners and others who would contribute against the bond election. It sounded easy but I found out differently.

The first retail business owner I met with apologetically said, "I don't give a damn about helping that hospital management get their hands on more money to waste. But, I can't afford to take sides." He was afraid of repercussions. Upon leaving I shook his hand and he looked me directly in the eye and said, "Sorry I can't help. Just give 'em Hell!"

Meeting with another business owner got me the opposite response. He became quick tempered to say, "I'm definitely for the hospital." I looked square at him and responded, "Well, I'm definitely against it." Finally, after further debate, we agreed to disagree and I left his office.

The next business owner had some advice for me. "If you want to go somewhere in this town you need a bankruptcy." I thought it was a joke until she went on to tell stories of men who came from the down and out more than once to become pillars of the community.

It became clear that going to retail businesses wasn't the way to go. What I needed was help from independent business. People who weren't controlled by what some call the "Click" in Borger. I picked up the phone and made a call and left a message.

MISSISSIPPI COMES TO BORGER

It was about eight in the evening when the phone ring. I ran downstairs to pick it up and on the line was Garrett Spradling. He said, "I read about the committee you formed. We're meeting tomorrow night with the group from Mississippi. Brandi Hannon found them on the Internet. They'll be here at our offices at seven. Can you attend?" After asking a few questions, I said, "See you there."

Wednesday evening I walked into Spradling Oil's conference room. There was Garrett, Garry Hannon and his wife Brandi with a group of other people I had never met. I was introduced to everyone including Dr. Bob Corkern, Ray Shoemaker and Missy Hutton with Health Care Engineers from Batesville, Mississippi.

Dr. Corkern stood before the group and began to tell about Tri-lakes Hospital. He was wearing a shirt and tie with a starched white doctor's lab coat. His boyish features and reddish hair made him look much younger for a man in his early forties. A friendly smile and a natural air of confidence combined with a soft down to earth Mississippi drawl put everyone at ease.

Dr. Corkern said, "Batesville hospital is jointly owned by the city and county. A 25 million dollar bond was passed and a new hospital was built in 2000. The new building didn't solve the past problems of administrative malfeasance and disenfranchising doctors. The hospital ended up in bankruptcy, the community was broken up and friendships were destroyed. I feel and understand what is happening in Borger."

He continued, "I was the doctor over the emergency room and was still on speaking terms with all the other doctors. We met and I asked the doctors to agree on one thing that would make a difference and I would take it to the board. Finally, everyone agreed the one thing needed was a new administrator."

I met with the board members and told them the administrator needed to go or all the doctors were leaving. "You can't have a hospital without doctors. All the doctors in a tent makes more of a hospital than a beautiful new building without doctors."

Reluctantly, the board agreed and they wanted me to run the hospital. I accepted and my first goal was to put doctors' first . . . give them what they need to do their jobs and keep them satisfied. Without doctors you cannot provide trusted service to the people. And service to the people is the number one goal in managing a hospital."

While watching and listening to Dr. Corkern I thought, "That makes sense. Another doctor can identify with other doctors better than a manager who isn't a doctor. Dr. Corkern was down to earth . . . warm and open. The CEO of Golden Plains style was aloof . . . cold and smug. The old adage "Walk a mile in another man's shoes" made sense.

The next thing Dr. Corkern said, "We were able to turn the hospital around within 6 months. There was enough profit to pay off the back bond payments and then make our current obligations."

Everyone in the room reacted to this statement and Garry Hannon asked "Would you repeat that?"

After repeating himself, Dr. Corkern introduced Missy Hutton, Director of Nurses and Ray Shoemaker, Financial Officer. Both of these people were equally impressive as they spoke and finished off the meeting.

The next day, Thursday, August 19, the three Tri-Lakes people with Garry Hannon were pictured on the front page of the local paper meeting with David Brandon, President of the Board and Norm Lambert.

I wondered if the Teflon administrator was sweating during the meeting?

THURSDAY NIGHT TOWN MEETING

Over 250 locals filled the auditorium at the Borger Middle School. The attendance was far greater than previous IIY town hall meetings where a majority in the audience were hospital employees and their family members. Unlike the IIY town hall meetings, this wasn't a planned canned presentation with prepared answers to questions.

Standing outside the building, I saw Norm Lambert arrive followed by Nancy Young, newspaper editor, into the entrance of the building. Leon Mitchell, Dr. Boyd and others supporting the hospital bond filtered through the audience.

Brandi Hannon started the meeting and told how she had searched for alternatives on the Internet and found Dr. Corkern's group from Batesville, Mississippi. Dr. Corkern was introduced and he shared how similar their circumstances were a few years ago. He shared the same story I had heard in the meeting the previous evening.

The audience was passionate in questioning and answering. There wasn't a time limit placed on anyone to control their comments. This was an open meeting where citizens could express themselves freely.

Someone asked if it made sense to spend 3 million dollars to tear down the old hospital building. It was almost moronic when three hospital employees stood up and chanted, "We don't want a crack house across from the High School."

Dr. Corkern addressed the question by saying, "We are using our old building in Batesville for senior services and it's full. In my opinion, it would be a mistake to tear down the old GPCH building because it can be used for overflow when a successful new hospital is built."

This isn't what the Invest in Yourself supporters wanted to hear. A few grimaced IIY members were shaking eggs off their faces. How dare anyone go against their plans!

The meeting became very lively and even heated at one point. Roy Haley was standing up asking a question, when he abruptly stopped to address the hospital attorney near the front of the auditorium. Haley said loudly, "Leon Mitchell this is no laughing matter. Turn around here and look at me Leon. This isn't a laughing matter!!!

When the meeting ended, a spouse of an IIY committee member verbally attacked me and I received "Go to Hell" stares from some others.

WHAT HAPPENED TO THE REST OF THE STORY?

Dr. Corkern's comments on the old building never saw the light of day in the front page article in the Friday paper. The half page coverage of the meeting under the byline, Nancy Young, editor, ended with (More on the Thursday meeting will appear on Sunday.)

The rest of the story never appeared on Sunday or on any other day.

The editor's Sunday front page story was about the beginning history of the hospital and was the first installment of a *six-part* series concerning the upcoming bond election. The lowly attended Invest in Yourself town meeting held the same time, Thursday, in Stinnett, got a three part front page coverage on Friday, Sunday, and Monday.

Also in the Sunday paper, a $1000 paid full page ad with signatures of members and supporters, ran for Invest in Yourself.

Remembering the past history with publisher Rucker, I wondered if this was the start of media diversion and denial? Was the newspaper being influenced by advertising dollars? Was the editor, a IIY member, biased?

My hat went off to Mr. Larry Lyons when I read his opinion letter in the following Wednesday paper. He was compelled to write and express some very important points made by the folks from Mississippi at last Thursday's meeting at Borger Middle School. He felt the whole story was not clearly represented in the News-Herald story covering the meeting.

"They (Dr. Corkern's group) were successful in making the hospital profitable, and are now expanding services including the addition of over 100 employees. Their hospital had problems before their bond issue, and the new building didn't solve them." Lyons continues to cover information omitted by the editor.

Thank you Mr. Lyons. In small towns, more people will buy a newspaper to read opinion articles than front page articles written by an editor.

CREATING THE AD CAMPAIGN

There was no time to waste in planning, producing and launching an advertising attack. I developed a web site picturing the prefabricated Doctors Building and listed information from the documents to educate voters. I also created newspaper ads.

The first ad appeared on Friday, August 20, 2004. The copy read: VOTE NO SEPTEMBER 11 . . . Get the facts. Click on www.VoteNo911.com . . . Paid for by Citizens Who Care About Hutchinson County. The size was small, only one column by three inches. The plan was to run it every day until the election. A quarter page ad was scheduled to run the following Wednesday.

Invest in Yourself had a huge advantage. They were well organized and launched their campaign on June 1st. There had been articles nearly every day throughout July. They had man power and speakers lined up to present to every club and organization in the county. They had infiltrated schools, churches and city councils in the county. They had raised over 13 thousand dollars. They had corporate contributions in addition to individual contributions including $1000 each from Norm Lambert, Leon Mitchell, and David Brandon.

Citizens Who Care About Hutchinson County was formed overnight and was scarce on time, money and man power. I called a business associate and friend in Dallas. Don was born in Borger but his family left when he was a baby. I said, "Don, I've got my hands full here," and I filled him in on the background story of the hospital. I feel like I'm surrounded."

After listening, he said, "Don't worry. You're a panther in the middle of a bunch of house cats." I smiled at his attempt to console me and knew my next step was to form an alliance with Borger Betterment Committee because our goals were similar.

WATCH YOUR BACK

Tuesday at noon, I walked into Dakes Restaurant for the weekly Rotary meeting knowing that County Commissioner Judge Jack Worsham, Conny Moore, Norm Lambert,

Paul Anderson and others supporting the hospital would be there. I was determined to stick it out in Rotary in spite of the swollen toes and bruised egos going through the buffet line. An air of uneasiness filled the room throughout the meeting. I imagined there were members present who had for years conformed to established peer pressure in disdained silence.

When the meeting ended, a fellow member stopped me in the parking lot and said, "I agree in what you're doing. The hospital administration is the problem. You need to watch your back. People have shown up missing in this county." I told him how much I appreciated his concern but I didn't think there was anything to worry about.

While driving home, the wheels in my brain were churning over the sadness of people living in fear. After all, this was just a small town, it wasn't Cook County. Then, Johnny Baker came to mind.

A couple of days later another prominent businessman told me to watch my back. I hoped he was joking when he said, "I'd rather walk behind you instead of in front of you."

At first I didn't take it seriously, but as the months progressed and the more I heard the comment "watch your back," the more it concerned me. A doctor called my home one evening and told my mother that I needed to watch my back during their conversation. There were phone calls in the evening where when I answered, "Hello", the party on the other end would hang up. I decided to call in a relative who works at the FBI in Dallas. When I explained what was being said he told me, "You need to prepare a sworn statement where you list all those involved and deliver it to the FBI Office in Amarillo." A few days later, I received an e-mail with the name of a contact in Amarillo.

LETTERS TO THE EDITOR

The rest of the week of August 23rd was fairly calm. There were 6 hospital opinion articles in the Thursday newspaper. Mr. Tom Reynolds wrote about homeowners being overtaxed and in conclusion said, "If our hospital manager can't run the current hospital, then what would he do with a new one? Articles by Phyllis Pfister and Susan Quezada were in agreement that a new hospital wouldn't solve the problems.

The most interesting article was from Dr. Bret A. Simmons in support of the new hospital. Dr. Simmons had left Borger after being recruited during the Larry Langley era. The special concessions awarded to Dr. Simmons by Lambert's administration had created disparagement among other doctors.

The Borger Rural Health Clinic was the property of the Hospital District. The practice at property was essentially sold to Simmons for a negligible amount. It's reported that the practice was sold to Simmons for $6000. Some other doctors in the community felt discriminated against because they were not offered an opportunity to purchase the practice.

Was this legal? Was this discrimination? Why wasn't the Rural Clinic practice put up for bid? Wasn't it the fiduciary responsibility of the hospital board and the administration to get the highest price? Did the hospital administration, the hospital board and the commissioner's court act like they owned the practice? These people serve as stewards of the Hospital District that is owned and supported by the tax dollars of the citizens in Hutchinson County? Were the citizens in Hutchinson County best interests served or were they short changed?

Simmons goes on in his opinion article by saying he was concerned about the "long-term well being of the community". How sincere is this coming from a short-term doctor added to a long list of doctors who left after receiving generous recruiting packages? Simmons stated his reasons for leaving as "being purely personal and family related."

What is the value of the clinic and who owns it today?

There were two "against" opinion articles in the Friday paper. Gary Gibbs submitted an entertaining viewpoint stating that, "We've lost retail stores. We've lost lumber yards. We've lost entertainment. We've lost countless small businesses. I'm a 45 year resident of this county. I've seen it. It's a good thing oil and chemical venues are located outside the control of our "community leaders" or else Borger would be a ghost town. A new hospital building will not heal a dying town. Neither will taxing the residents to oblivion."

Then in another paragraph, he says, "Even better, put some vending machines inside the aluminum dome that dispense some of those $30 Band-Aids and $20 aspirin and call it good. That would at least make a profit."

Joe Mihm said, "I attended a meeting and asked Mr. Lambert if the hospital was paying their bills on time. He said they had several bills that were 90 to 120 days past due. I was surprised by his apparent lack of concern about it. A few days later, I saw that Golden Plains Hospital had sponsored some of the T-shirts for a local charity fund-raiser.

It's odd that that the hospital is behind on paying bills, but still able to donate money. I try to pay what I owe before donating money. To me this looks like another indicator of fiscal mismanagement."

PREACHERS: HOSPITAL NEEDED

The August 27, Friday evening headline cast two of Borger's leading pastors into the hospital fray. The two pastors have a combined church membership of 2,500 people. That's a lot of potential votes!

The story explained how the two pastors (Reverend Steve Fields, pastor of the First Baptist Church, and Reverend Richard Robbins pastor of Grace Fellowship Church) were at the IIY meeting to voice their views concerning a new assisted living center and nursing facility. Fields gave a power point presentation on behalf of the committee and shared what got him involved in the nursing project.

A senior adult minister at First Baptist approached Norm Lambert saying, "First Baptist would like to see if we could secure some sort of assisted living/independent living/ nursing home care in Hutchinson County.

Fields said, "Baptist Community Services contacted Norm Lambert independently of us." Fields said that the need for health care in the county was not only important from a financial standpoint, but also from a humane standpoint. He went on to express there was a need to investigate the market.

Fields said people were saying that, "If we're going to take Jesus seriously, we're going to address the needs of hurting people." He added that there's also a need of helping people with compassion when they're hurting."

The initial feasibility study was partially funded by both First Baptist Church and Grace Fellowship Church. Each pastor offered $7,500 to aid in a $25,000 BCS Feasibility Study to analyze the potential of assisted home facilities coming to Borger.

Pastor Richard Robbins said, "He (Conny Moore) said First Baptist was going to raise $15,000 to do this." I didn't know exactly what the Lord wanted us to do, but I said, "We'll give $7,500 to Baptist Community Services just to do the survey to see *if* it would be feasible.

Glenn Hollins spoke on behalf of Baptist Community Services about the possibility of a new assisted living facility. He said he would not be sure when the feasibility study would be finished, but *it appeared* that the census demand was high enough that people would stay in the community *if* the facilities were to be built, and that the county could support an assisted living facility and nursing home.

However, Hollins reiterated that adequate medical facilities had to be built before Baptist Community Services would commit to the project.

Did Conny Moore, Chairman of Invest in Yourself, Chamber of Commerce President, Pharmacist at Golden Plains Community Hospital and a Deacon at First Baptist, politically involve the church into influencing senior citizens to vote for a hospital bond? When this article appeared 15 days before the election, the feasibility study wasn't completed. Was this all pie in the sky? Was the reiteration that "adequate medical facilities had to be built before BCS would commit to the project" a big carrot being dangled in front of senior citizens? Was this another "fear of loss" sales tactic.

The results of the feasibility study never surfaced on the front page of the News Herald in the following 15 days leading up to the election on September 11th.

Reading the news article caused me to recall seeing Pastor Steve Fields listed on the IIY speaking schedule. I pulled out the schedule and found his name. He was scheduled to present the IIY slide presentation on June 28, 2004, to the County Commissioners. Out of the four commissioners, only R.D. Corneilson publicly endorsed Invest in Yourself.

This "Letter to the Editor" was written after reading "Preachers: Hospital Needed."

Immediate Release to News-Herald
Separation of Church and State?

Looking through the scheduled speaking meetings organized by Invest in Yourself, there is one speaker and one meeting that stands out from all others. This meeting was scheduled on June 28, 2004 at 11:00 a.m. at the Hutchinson County Courthouse. The presenter was Steve Fields, pastor of the First Baptist Church of Borger, Texas. The audience was the four county commissioners representing Hutchinson County. These commissioners are responsible for appointing three members of the Board of Trustees in the Hospital District.

Pastor Fields was not a member of Invest in Yourself Committee, so why and how was he convinced to present one side of a $25 million dollar bond issue to the commissioners? Why didn't someone on the committee make the presentation to the commissioners? Was the pastor mislead and wrongly drawn into using the house of worship as a perceived means to convince the commissioners to publicly endorse the bond issue? Why didn't the one minister, Paul Anderson, who served on the Invest in Yourself Committee and donated $100 on May 5, 2004 make the presentation to the commissioners? Dr. Anderson participated in many of the presentations, town hall meetings and answered questions on the radio in behalf of Invest in Yourself.

The only commissioner to endorse the bond proposal was R.D. Cornelison, who on May 12th donated $200 to Invest in Yourself. The other three chose to stay away from it.

The IRS takes seriously, provisions of federal tax law forbidding partisan politicking by tax exempt groups, including religious organizations. The IRS provides clear guidance on this issue. Clergy should examine those simple guidelines and then obey them. It's in everyone's best interest.

Reviewing the letter, I had second thoughts about e-mailing it to the News-Herald. Since Pastor Fields had only been a minister at First Baptist for two years, maybe he was naively recruited into Invest in Yourself like I was. Maybe he didn't know about the involvement of child pornography in the past history of the hospital. Why wouldn't he have faith in his Deacons who were leaders on the IIY Committee?

This letter stayed in computer memory and was never sent to the paper.

WEEKEND NEWS HEATS UP

Things started heating up on the weekend of August 28-29. Leon Mitchell received front page headlines from comments he made at a town hall meeting at Borger High School.

Lambert addressed a question from someone about a Citizens Who Care About Hutchinson County ad. Lambert is quoted, "I hope everyone is very clear what the magnitude of the tax increase really is. Some of the literature being distributed in the last few days is trying to scare voters into believing your tax increase is going to be 150 percent. You can calculate for yourself what your taxes are going to go up. Your tax is not going to go up as much as some people would like you to believe."

My phone rang and John Curnutt on the line said, "They can't do simple math. Lambert has a defective calculator that he used for that Doctor's building and that worthless MRI."

The first time John called me, I first thought it was a prank call because of his speech pattern. A tragic head on collision with a drunk driver has confined him to a wheel chair for the past 31 years. In a short time I developed a great respect for John. He has more guts, more determination and intelligence than most physically normal people I have met in my life.

In the same newspaper, a full page IIY ad was placed in response to our a quarter page ad. The headline read; "Attention Voters: Don't Be Misled—Learn the Truth. The Citizens Who Care About Hutchinson County has made the following claims:" The ad proceeded to list and counter all the information point by point. I was pleased to see this ad. The competition was spending three times the money on a full page "defensive" ad and reiterating the points made in our smaller ad.

We never ran the quarter page ad again. The IIY full page ran twice

OVER MILLION DOLLARS PAST DUE

Earlier in the week in a meeting with BBC and Garrett Spradling, he handed over GPCH financial printouts acquired through open documents request. Garrett said, "take a look at this" while pointing out numbers to me. I said, "That's a lot of red for anyone's eyes! Do you think the public knows this?" Spradling said, "No!"

In the same weekend edition, I broke the news in the Letters to the Editor column. In a normal city, this news would have made the front page, but not in Hutchinson County.

"As of last week, the financial printouts from GPCH shows $501,638 is 90 days past due and another $682,394 payable up to 90 days. That's $1,184,032 due to creditors and suppliers.

Any good businessman facing these financial burdens would have started months ago trimming all unnecessary expenses in order to get out of the red."

The article continued to list a $3000 expense to a charity, Lambert's salary plus bonuses up to $20,000 a year and ended with, "I ask the citizens of Hutchinson County . . . why in the world would anyone vote yes to move this administration into a new $25 million dollar facility? Voting against isn't really saying no to a hospital; it's for changing the administration."

When word of the hospital's debt got out to the barber and beauty shops, the street talk started to buzz:

"That hospital is sinking like the Titanic." "Who in their right mind would invest in a new ship and put the same Captain in charge?" "No banker will loan them 25 million, and they think taxpayers are stupid enough to bail them out."

INFORM SENIOR CITIZENS

The Citizen's ad in the weekend edition targeted the senior citizens.

"THERE ARE 3,672 OVER 65 SENIOR CITIZENS LIVING IN HUTCHINSON COUNTY. MANY LIVE ON FIXED INCOMES. HOW CAN THEY AFFORD A 150% TAX INCREASE

TO PAY FOR A NEW $25 MILLION HOSPITAL? IT'S YOUR HOMETOWN-VOTE NO-SEPTEMBER 11.

We felt the IIY committee was out of touch with seniors who couldn't afford a tax increase. Affluent people were on the committee. There was no one on the committee who was living on a fixed retirement income.

A tax increase would have been a disaster for many seniors and a burden on others. During lunch at Onions Restaurant, I set in a booth with a Phillips' retiree who lived near the Country Club. He said, "I'm retired, have a nice home and live on my investments. The interest on bank accounts is nearly zip and the cost of gasoline and everything else is going up. I really can't afford $300 dollars a year increase in taxes to pay for a new hospital. I don't want to help pay to build a new building for a hospital I don't trust."

CHAPTER SIXTEEN

THE TWELVE DAYS OF WAR

DAY ONE . . . Monday, August 30, 2004

I felt jaded going into the Borger News-Herald and seeing an INVEST IN YOURSELF BANNER across the bottom of the counter. This morning, I sent a complaint letter to the Texas Ethics Commission regarding the editor of the News-Herald and the Eagle Press being members of the IIY committee.

We lose our free speech whenever media can be bought off by advertisers. Media that is not embedded provides checks and balances of government.

"Local group travels to Mississippi to see hospital," was the headline on the evening paper.

Garrett Spradling, Garry Hannon, Brandi Hannon Chuck Litteral representing the BBC and hospital president David Brandon traveled to Batesville, Mississippi to tour Tri-Lakes hospital. Garry Hannon said, "Brandon as the lone representative for the hospital district and IIY, was receptive to the BBC, saying he was taking their concerns into consideration."

Hannon went on to say, "I believe that CEO Norm Lambert should resign from Golden Plains Community Hospital. Norm has been there eight years, and in those years, we have not moved forward. There's division among the doctors and that is a red flag that's against moving forward. We've got to step back, re-group and get the problems solved. Step one is change administration."

Chuck Litteral said, "We don't want to close the hospital. The main thing I want citizens in Hutchinson County to know is that yes, they can have a new hospital, but we don't have to have a tax. There is another option. The folks in Mississippi have that option for us. All we have to do is say yes."

"Their strategic plan is second to none," he said. "If a hospital is going to make money, the CEO needs to be a person who knows doctors. Without doctors, you don't have a hospital and without a manager who can talk to a doctor, who would be another doctor, then you really don't have any good communication."

Litteral went on to say, "Tri-Lakes would furnish a Doctor/CEO."

In the Letters to the Editor, I made a counter attack against Lambert's spin on the tax increase and the "Don't be mislead" advertisement.

"There's a lot of humor and sadness in the Full Page Ad that Invest in Yourself placed in the weekend edition of the Borger News Herald. First it is not a claim; it is the truth that when there is 10 cents per $100 tax and when 15 cents is added to make 25 cents that equals a 150% tax increase in Hospital District taxes. This elementary math is taught in the Borger schools. Could it be elementary reasons the hospital has fired, resigned or hired, however you want to say it, 4 Chief Financial Officers in the last 4 years?"

"When I was on the IIY committee, the prefab doctors building was never mentioned in any of the meetings. Now when it is brought to their attention, the spin in the ad states . . . THE BUILDING CAN BE MOVED TO THE NEW MEDICAL CENTER SITE AND THUS SAVE TAXPAYER'S MONEY. Does this mean that the 20,000 square foot Doctor's Building has been taken out of their plan ?"

Consider the people who are leading IIY . . . what they claim, what they are saying and how they change what they say to meet the situation. Then consider the possibility of a bankrupt medical facility down the road. What would that do to the economy?"

Looking back at the Board Meeting notes from October 5, 1999, it's stated that, *"When a new hospital is built, the building can be moved."*

Why did the CEO forget this convincing benefit, presented 4 years earlier to the board? Did the administrator expect the public to forget about the prefab building? Was the plan to sweep this "cracker box embarrassment" under the rug with bulldozers in the proposed 3 million dollar demolition?

DAY TWO . . . Tuesday, August 31, 2004

My day started out when Dad walked down the stairway and saw the curtains drawn open. "I want those damn curtains closed right now! I've told you before, I don't want my carpet faded. If you can't mind what I say, you can get the . . . out of my house!"

Although the carpet had been faded for years, I pulled the curtains to and tried my best to calm him down. He had forgotten that months ago we agreed that if I placed a rug in front of the glass sliding doors, it would be all right to open the curtains. At the time I told him, "When the drapes are open, I don't need lights and can save on electricity." I knew his miserly mind would agree if it meant saving money.

It was shocking and sad that was he was cussing, ranting and raving. He would go into a rampage every morning and evening. I had bought and read *36 HOUR DAY* about Dementia and Alzheimer's disease. My mother and I were getting desperate in finding ways to live with him. God help our blood pressures!

He mumbled more obscenities while slamming the door on his way out.

Later, everything got brighter when I stopped by the Phillips Building and picked up another $2,500 contribution at the receptionist desk. This would be the final ammunition needed to buy newspaper, television, and radio advertising. The attack was on and reinforcements had arrived!

I stopped by Spradling Oil to look at campaign signs. Garry Hannon called me the previous evening. "Glenn, we're going to start putting up over 200 signs in the morning." I said, "That's great news because it really adds to all the other 'against' advertising."

On the front page of the evening paper, Garry Hannon was pictured placing a vote "against" sign in a yard with caption under the photo, "Campaign signs are visible throughout the county regarding the upcoming bond election. Early voting began Wednesday in the upcoming bond election."

A board member's wife submitted a letter to the editor asking that seniors vote for the bond in support of the assisted living facility. *THE BIG IF!*

DAY THREE . . . Wednesday, September 1, 2004

After seeing Leon Mitchell's weekend article on the front page, I approached the publisher Michael Wright.

"Michael, you know we're spending thousands of dollars in a campaign against the hospital bond. IIY is on the front page every week with a town meeting or some other story. It's just not fair and we need equal time. I'll write the story and all you need do is put it on the front page."

There were no invitations for "opposition" presentations in front of clubs, churches, schools or any other organization. The Rotary Club and the Chamber of Commerce where I was a member, had several Invest in Yourself presenters and these two organizations never offered us the opportunity to present our side of the issue. Any rational person would suspect the Chamber of Commerce was controlled by its president Conny Moore, Norm Lambert and others who served on the board of directors.

The silent opposition in the Rotary and Chamber couldn't afford to speak out. It wasn't good business to be outspoken. It was reminiscent of belonging to High School clubs run by peer pressure.

Finally, the newspaper placed a Citizens Who Care About Hutchinson County article on the front page. The article was titled "It's about the forgotten taxpayers," stating the goal of Citizen's Who Care About Hutchinson County is to work together where each citizen may prosper and benefit from an inspired community life based on a shared vision for all citizens and not only a few who decide for others.

The story went on to cover all the issues of the hospital management.

"Mr. Lambert fails to inform taxpayers the Invest in Yourself Committee has plans to increase the taxes through another bond election for the schools. I'm sure Mr. Lambert didn't want to scare them by informing them of this. Lambert and his committee prefer only to scare taxpayers for their own benefits with statements like, 'If this isn't voted for, the hospital will close,' etc. The shame of everything is that tax dollars are the only way to fund school improvements. There are other choices that would not increase taxes or need Mr. Lambert as an administrator. Scary, aren't they?"

"I hope it is clear that Mr. Lambert and others need the taxpayers to bail out the hospital. I say that the taxpayer's revenue should not be taken for granted and spent carelessly. Taxpayers should have these questions to ask Mr. Lambert. Have you ever decreased your salary as other prudent corporate executives do in times of financial crisis? On the ballot it states that the funds can be used for general hospital purpose. Does that mean paying off current and past debts? Can we trust you to manage 25 million dollars? I'll bet this question really scares most taxpayers!"

I applauded the Letter to the Editor from John F. Holland, a former Director of Maintenance at Golden Plains who called it like he saw it. His excerpts stated:

"I would like to make a tour throughout the hospital with our County Commissioners and show them they are going to sit in silence and let this extravaganza of a deal by the hospital administrator and a few do-gooders do good for themselves and not the county taxpayers. The group of deceivers are playing trickery with the help of a consulting firm at the expense of Hutchinson County taxpayers.

The eleven areas of renovation that Mr. Moore and his cronies called the 10 problem areas for renovation (in the old building) is nothing but a bunch of BS.

I can assure the people of Hutchinson County, through the eyes of our County Commission that the administrator, Mr. Norman Lambert, has worked more on this project of getting a new hospital and making false promises to our new doctors than he has at administration of your hospital.

The administrator and departments throughout the hospital are put through a very strict inspection of documentation and condition of equipment and handling of equipment. In other words, the building and its condition and all departments have to meet very strict rules and regulations. I have kept up with the he accreditation of this building and the way it has been operated ever since I left working there in 1980. By the way, this building was plumbed with hot and cold domestic PVC piping throughout the whole building.* The contract was given to Mr. Gene Penington of Stinnett, a master plumber and a very hard working gentleman. The contract, as I recall, was between $1.5 and $2 million by the time it was completed. This is a false statement #1, made by Mr. Moore and the group of deceivers. I was also in the heating, air conditioning and refrigeration business for 20 years. The heating and air conditioning has been kept up with tip-top equipment and is presently in excellent condition and not very old, which is false statement #2. Shall I go on Mr. Moore and Mr. Lambert?

The County Commission needs to question the real condition of this wonderful hospital and make the hospital board and Mr. Lambert explain how it passes the strict inspections of the Joint Commission of Accreditation in order to qualify for Medicare and Medicaid payments by the Federal Government."

---

* The Invest in Yourself "Top 10 Reasons" sheet states, the plumbing and electrical systems are 67 years old and continue to deteriorate. God bless gripy old men!

Note: Mr. Holland continues to make a case that over 100 million in county dollars have been invested in the hospital that the deceivers are wanting to throw away. He closes his article in saying:

"I am 72 years old and have lived in Borger 62 years. I think it's a sad day when some of our local preacher's bring God into this extravaganza deal to try to get people to vote for a bunch of falsehoods and promises that will cause nothing but a bad debt and no hospital in the future after the doctors leave and it goes broke.

We will not close this Golden Plains Hospital. The people who built it and own it will not let it be closed. Vote NO DEAL!

By the way, I'm not a radical or a nut, just a gripy old man who doesn't like my tax dollars wasted.

Sincerely, John Holland

GUEST COLUMNS

Two side by side Guest Columns featured David Brandon, President of the Hospital Board of Directors and Garrett Spradling, President of Borger Betterment Committee. Their viewpoints come after their trip to Batesville, Mississippi.

GARRETT SPRADLING'S COLUMN

Garrett Spradling told the background story of Tri-Lakes Hospital following the construction of a new hospital with a $25 million bond and nearing bankruptcy when Dr. Corkern was appointed as CEO.

"The new CEO wasted no time and within 6 months had increased revenue and profit enough to pay off the back bond payments and then meet current obligations. The Tri-Lakes facility is a site to be seen. What they have managed to do in one year is nothing short of amazing.

A year after the new CEO and his staff had taken over; the average census of the hospital is 55. The hospital is FULL. If that was not enough, they opened the old hospital for special services, and it too is now full. The hospital now needs to expand with the construction of new facilities.

Had the Board not changed leadership, the Medical Center of Batesville would be paying off the debt. We should learn from other's mistakes. A new facility will not solve the problems. It can improve our health care, but only if the problems are fixed first.

The Tri-Lakes group is completely sold on Borger. They are so optimistic that on our way out they laid a proposal on the table. The proposal was, "What would you say if we came to Borger and built a hospital for you with no cost to you?" Could you imagine; a new hospital without having to raise taxes to pay for it? And to take away some of your concerns, I asked about making sure that they would not close the hospital and leave the community. I said that we do not want a hospital that would be sold every year either. The group answered that we could come to an agreement on that before we ever started construction. We can have a private hospital and still have control."

The article concluded by comparing numbers between Tri-Lakes and Golden Plains. The administrator salary at Tri-Lakes was listed at $99,000 compared to Norm Lambert's salary of $140,000. Tri-Lakes has an average profit in 2003 of $1,235,000 compared to $590,000 at Golden Plains.

In 2003, the GPCH board awarded Norm Lambert a $20,000 bonus.

DAVID BRANDON'S COLUMN

In his first paragraph he promotes the nursing home and assisted living facilities that Baptist Community Services "has stated they will likely build in Borger *if* there is proper medical care available to support their customers' needs. This would be a six to twelve million dollar investment and employ about 150 individuals, a tremendously positive impact to Hutchinson County's social and economic well-being."

"We could lose the opportunity for the nursing home and assisted living investment by Baptist Community Services. That is a tremendous risk. On the other hand, if we approve the bond, we can still consider the Tri-Lakes proposal with adequate time to study and investigate and still have plan B ready on the shelf."

NOTE: This was another "fear of loss" sales technique. When considering how well planned and detailed the Invest in Yourself plan was, how blue sky was it to promote a nursing home and assisted living facility on promises that it would be built if the feasibility study passed and if the bond was passed and if the hospital was built? The "BIG IF" and "FEAR OF LOSS" were used as tactics to convince seniors and other taxpayers to vote "for".

David Brandon is a Borger native and a retired engineer from Phillips Petroleum. Two generations of his family have been members of the First Baptist Church. David was serving as president of the school board and the hospital board. I'm sure that Brandon's intent was to do "good kind things for others" by serving "free" on both boards. My impression of Brandon is that he is a man with strict morals. He has no bankruptcies or other blemishes on record.

It's only natural he would serve on boards with fellow church members. Was Brandon perceived by the administration as the perfect front man and yes-man to lead the hospital board? Was he non-thinking about leading a board in forwarding a hospital administration that attempted to cover up child pornography and enacted unkind things upon others? Was he blind to the negative public perception of hypocrisy by aligning the child pornography aurora of the hospital district with a school district of children?*

---

*   *Following the May,2005 School Board election, Brandon stepped down as president for non-disclosed reasons.*

PHONE CALL FROM BORGER NURSING HOME

When I answered my phone that evening, I heard the voice on the other end of the line say, "Mr. Baxter, I'm a nurse at the Borger Nursing Home. It makes me mad hearing Connie Moore say there's no long term assisted care facilities in Borger for seniors. We're licensed for 120 beds and fill an average of 65. If we're not full, and another nursing home went out of business, why is there a need here for Baptist Community Services to build an assisted living facility?

I answered her by saying, "The assisted nursing facility goes with the "sales package". With no feasibility study completed, it's just blue sky to convince seniors to vote for the hospital bond. Moore's concept of the new facility would probably not be affordable for most seniors in Borger. It would be a facility that he and affluent others could afford."

She continued, "Wealthy seniors go to Amarillo to be within walking distance of shopping and there are more cultural activities." I replied, "That's a good point."

"Mr. Baxter, keep up the good work and keep the pressure on."

Hanging up the phone, I wondered if the feasibility study would be completed before election day.

DAY FOUR . . . Thursday, September 2, 2004

Roy Haley called today. He said, "I think everything's turning in our favor. When I used to drive my car around town, people would give me a frown and a one finger wave. Now they're waving normally and smiling. I parked my car in the back of the house last night and a neighbor called and asked, 'Where's your car Roy? Why aren't you parking it in front where everyone can see it.' I told him I would from now on."

John Curnutt's van came to mind. He had Dave paint the sides, "NO WAY NORM" and "J.C. WILL VOTE NO TO 150% TAX INCREASE." John said he thought folks at Walmart would think the J.C. stood for Jesus Christ. He said, "It was my way of fighting back at the churches getting involved in politics in favor of that hospital."

Our grass root's movement was gaining momentum. Invest in Yourself had fancy painted billboards and we had hand painted vehicles. The BBC were towing big "VOTE AGAINST" signs on trailers around town.

Spradling Oil offices are in the same bank building as Leon Mitchell's law firm. The Spradlings had posted "Against" signs in the entrance of the building. When Mitchell saw the signs, he removed them and complained to the Bank. When the word got to Charlotte Spradling that the bank wouldn't allow the signs, she got madder and meaner than a roughneck. She yanked all of Spradling Oil's money out of the bank. The next morning there was a trailer with a 4 foot by 8 foot sign parked across the street from the entrance to the bank. God bless that woman!

The evening Letter the Editor page was overflowing with opinion articles. Deanna Austin of Fritch wrote, "My husband and I are not inclined to go to the lions den to vote so we will wait until September 11, and vote at the library. So, if you are as uncomfortable as we are with the hospital administration having control of your vote, please join us on September 11. This is not a vote for or against a new hospital. It is a vote for or against the current administration."

Joe Mihm was quizzing the timing of GPCH picnic, "It looks like I wrote my letter about the T-shirts a little early. Had I known about the Community Appreciation Picnic being "hosted" by the hospital (paid for with tax dollars)? I'd have mentioned it too. It looks like more of a "Borger for a Vote" picnic.

I wonder if they'll bring a couple of ballot boxes to the park. If it is really an appreciation picnic, having it after the vote sure would have looked more appropriate. I would much rather have the five or so dollars they'll spend per person on burgers taken off my taxes!"

This event was listed in the Invest in Yourself Campaign Timeline. Enticement with hamburgers was a planned marketing tactic. I was told that a few people stopped by the park to eat a hamburger before voting against the hospital!

Loyd Gooch wrote about the 150 percent tax increase, "My Okie education tells me that is an increase of 150 percent. Please vote against the bond issue and tax increase for the sake of us on fixed incomes."

Chuck Litteral wrote, "BBC wants a hospital; not additional tax. People, we can do this. We don't have to be mad at each other. We shouldn't hold grudges. We should come together and just make it happen. Please open your mind and be receptive to a different idea."

The Citizen's half page ad on that day read; DON'T LET SPIN DOCTORS MISLEAD YOU. The Blame Game brought to you by the GPCH Administration of Spin. Blame the Doctors—Blame the Patients—Blame the Vendors—Blame the Numbers—Blame the Building—Blame the Citizens. Are you fed up with them playing games with your tax dollars? Maybe it's time you really show your appreciation by voting Against on September 11th. "See your tax dollars in use online at www.voteno911.com" was at the bottom of every ad. The goal was to drive people to the web site to view the prefab Doctor's building and read more information.

DAY FIVE . . . Friday, September 3, 2004

I went to the News Herald to personally hand a full page ad to Micheal Wright, publisher. My plan was to insert the ad titled "TO TELL THE TRUTH" as the last full page before the day of the election. I wanted people to see the child pornography documents.

The first letter titled "Some local doctors favor bond election" was submitted by all of the Administration's supportive doctors.

"Lawyer outlines reasons to vote for election" was submitted by Leon Mitchell, hospital attorney. He states that if the bond issue is not passed the community will suffer a loss of $200,000 in the generous offer of eleven acres.

That's a bit of an exaggeration when the land is listed with Hutchinson County Appraisal District at $121,500. According to City engineers the acreage is in a flood *plain and the developer abandoned a townhouse project when the city wouldn't pay for the excavation. After reading this, who would trust the other reasons outlined by the hospital's attorney?*

"Courtney say building needs to be replaced," was submitted by Danny Courtney, hospital director of engineering, debates John Holland's Letter to the Editor. *Remember Courtney's quote about the Prefabricated Doctors Building in GPCH meeting notes dated October 5, 1999 . . . "My perspective of viewing the building was very positive on the overall workmanship and materials that went into the building. The modular building is structurally sound." Does Courtney have a mechanical engineering degree or other similar degree? What is his expertise?*

"Urges vote for new medical center," submitted by Bart Boren, IIY committee member, asks everyone to vote for the bond, then trust the board of trustees to do the right thing with management, etc.

The citizen's in the county were not that gullible! The board supported toxic management and there were no guarantees that passing a 25 million dollar bond would change anything.

DAY SIX . . . Weekend, September 4-5, 2004

It was relaxing in Santa Fe, New Mexico on a week end getaway. I called back to Borger to get the news from the paper. It was no surprise that Norm Lambert, Invest in Yourself and others were attacking me in the News-Herald Letters to the Editor.

Norm Lambert wrote, "There is a small group of people who are now trying to influence this bond election with scare tactics, mud slinging, misinformation and down right lies. They have tried other tactics in the past to promote their self-interest and have failed. Now they have influenced others to speak out for them in order not to be seen. You are being confused by misrepresentation of numbers related to the cost of the bond issue, numbers related to the operation of the hospital, events that happened years ago, events that never happened as being told and personal attacks against individuals who have made very honest and skillful efforts to work for the good of everyone."

Does the CEO believe he speaks from the heart of an administrator of good kind things for others?

"Now we see the ugly side of our community. You now have a choice: you can let the ugly side continue to show or you can vote for improved quality health care, economic growth and a stronger future."

Lambert's statement is grossly exaggerated and sadly deplorable. The truth can be ugly. Didn't the ugly side of the community show up with the attempted cover up of child pornography in January 2000. What's uglier than allowing an alleged sexual predator freedom to prey on children? Didn't Norm Lambert hire Larry Langley at GPCH?

"Some very self-motivated people would have you vote for their irrational views by voting "Against" this brighter future. I don't think I am just naïve; I think Hutchinson County voters are smart enough to make the right decision."

Lambert's disinformation comments on "irrational views" insulted the majority of voters in the county. The eyes of the silent majority were opening to see the CEO's irrational management style. Finally, I could agree with Lambert on one thing. The voters in Hutchinson County were smart enough to make the right decision.

The Invest in Yourself committee really stepped in it, as they say in Texas, when they tried to bush whack and discredit Citizens Who Care About Hutchinson County with in a 13 question Op Ed article. Questions one through four attacked the credibility of Citizens Who Care About Hutchinson County.

Question 4 wanted to know if I was the only committee member as though that would violate some constitutional law. The fact that I wrote every ad, every OP Ed article, every television commercial and every radio commercial violated no law. There wasn't a membership cost and people would call me all the time to be counted on the committee. It must have been frustration not to be able to use character assassination to smear and negate my civil rights.

Question 5 was; "Why is Charlotte Spradling this committee's only acknowledged financial advisor?"

This was an outright fabrication. Charlotte Spradling never contributed a dollar. The man in cowboy boots who didn't care about the past city manager was the main contributor. When the committee report of contributors was filed at the County Clerks Office, it became public information. I'd like to have seen the look on Lambert's and other faces when they found out it wasn't Charlotte Spradling. It was OHM who didn't want his and other people's taxes going up.

Questions six through eight really intrigued me. The questions were: (6) Are not political action committees required by law to register with the Texas Ethics Commission or at least with the local governing body that they represent a political action group for or against? (7) Why is the "Citizens Who Care About Hutchinson County" committee not registered with the Hospital District? (8) Have they broken the law?

They must have had sugar plums and prickly pears dancing in their heads thinking someone just might get thrown in the County Jail?. They thought they had NIGYSOB'd (Now I got you, you S.O.B.) us.

I did file with the Texas Ethics Commission and with the Hutchinson County Clerk's office because I didn't want to walk in the hospital to file, just like the voters who didn't want to walk in to "early" vote. How frivolous was it to ask, "Have they broken the law?", when in their ranks were those who conspired in the get away of a child pornography predator?

The IIY continued grasping for straws with their other questions. They were on the defensive and desperate to smear others and me. If there was a "Borger Inquirer" rag, they would have plastered me on the front cover.

The letters to the Editor continued with an opinion from Bard Rogers, one of Lambert's supportive doctors. In my opinion, the last letter was written by a woman salaried and cowed by the hospital administration to smear me. It was a lame filler for the rest of the page. The entire Letters to the Editor page was 100% pro hospital.

Was this a tactic to dominate the Op Ed page in the final days up to the election?

DAY SEVEN . . . Monday, September 6, 2004 . . . News-Herald Suppresses Truth Ad

Michael Wright called me and said the newspaper could not run the "To Tell The Truth" ad. Angry and frustrated, I told him I would take out the documents and put them on the web site. He said, "If you'll make those changes, we'll run the ad."

The Letter to the Editors had one column against the hospital bond and 4 columns for the bond issue. The page was dominated in favor of the bond issue.

On this day, Mr. Harry P. Johnson stated the problem was the administration and went to say, "Clean out the existing administration including the board of directors and county commissioners. The new hospital board should hire a new administrator, someone with a proven track record, and then let him run the hospital."

A man with the same last name as a woman employed in the administration, expressed what I thought was a convoluted view of things while attacking Citizens Who Care About Hutchinson County. He ended his opinion with "All of this does make me especially thankful of one thing. That God the Father is ultimately in control of all things. I find rest in the fact that His perfect plan is far better than any that we could devise on our own."

I agreed with this probable spouse that God the Father was in control. I believed he would provide good kind things for the majority of hometown folks by defeating the bond issue."

Hospital Board Member, Jock Lee stated "Rumors are flying. People are calling other people names. People are telling half truths. Others are telling outright lies." Then he continued with the same old sales rhetoric and ended with, "get back to the important issue of caring for people in our community. We need to do that."

Was Mr. Lee sincere in wanting good kind things for others?

DAY EIGHT . . . Tuesday, September 7, 2004

Garrett Spradling placed a full page color Case Study on the Batesville Hospital. Headline read: Vote "Against" and tell the Board you want better options for a better tomorrow. The ad reiterated the Tri-Lakes success story and stated, "I can tell you that the Tri-Lakes group is completely sold on the Medical Future of Borger. They are so optimistic that on our way out they laid a proposal on the table. The proposal was, "What would you say if we came to Borger and built a hospital for you with no cost to you?" Could you imagine; a new hospital and leave the community. I said that we do not want a hospital that would be sold every year either. The group answered that we could come to an agreement on that before we ever started construction. We can have a private hospital and still have control."

Here was a new hospital being offered 4 days before the election that would not cost the taxpayer one dime. This would put the administrator and some others to the test. Would they embrace a new hospital for the community if the bond election was defeated? Or were these power addicted, greedy individuals who would not easily relinquish control of a hospital owned by the taxpayers?

I would have loved to have been a fly on the wall and seen the faces when they read the ad.

A quarter page Citizen's ad was placed in the newspaper with the headline: **VOTE YES AND HAVE YOUR HEAD EXAMINED.**

Letters to the Editor had only one letter in favor of the hospital.

DAY NINE . . . Wednesday, September 8, 2004 . . . Censors Truth Ad

The phone rang early in the morning. It was Michael Wright, publisher of the News Herald. He said, "Glenn, I'm calling to let you know we cannot run the full page "To Tell the Truth" ad. Corporate will not allow it." I replied, "What in the hell are you talking about? Isn't this a late notice? I took out all the documents and put them on the web site as we agreed." Michael replied, "I can refund your money on the ad." I was fuming when I said, "Keep the money! Just run the "WHO ARE THE REAL CITIZENS IN HUTCHINSON COUNTY" ad!

I hung up the phone and thought, "I had just gotten a real taste of censorship of free press and freedom of speech in Hutchinson County. As an American citizen, I refuse to wear blinders, ear plugs and duct tape across my mouth in fear of those who would try to suppress first amendment rights. The election was only a few days away and no one would be able to stop the invisible duct tape coming off thousands of mouths throughout the county in the form of a silent vote."

That evening, the front page of the newspaper announced, "RECORD NUMBER OF EARLY VOTES" . . . Denette Ehrlich, Hutchinson County Hospital District administrative assistant, said this morning that 1,699 Hutchinson County voters cast ballots during the early voting. Ehrlich said, "4000 ballots were ordered for the election and an additional 2,000 ballots were ordered this morning."

Recalling the CEO's past political sneak attack strategy, reported by ex board member Jerry Strecker in May 2001, I imagined the CEO sweating over this heavy voter turnout.

The headline in the Citizen's full page ad in the evening paper read, "As of August 12th GPCH Financial Printouts show $501,638 past due for 90 days and $682,394 due to creditors up to 90 days. That's $1,184,032 in debt. This pulled out all the stops and frontally attacked financial irresponsibility of the hospital administration.

In the Letters to the Editor, Jeff Brain, The Mayor of Borger, wrote, "the past mayor went to the City Manager and mandated that city employees come to the council room. I did ask our acting City Manager to invite the employees to attend the council meeting to hear the IIY presentation. Their attendance at the meeting was not mandated."

The word mandate was written in the ad when city employees called me to complain. Several teachers also called to complain about the IIY presentation in the High School Auditorium. Both groups felt this unusual request "pressured" them to attend and there was no equal time for the other side.

Was it just an oversight in not getting an invitation from the Mayor and his fellowship? Citizen's Who Care About Hutchinson County were never asked to make a presentation where city employees could attend. Where was the democratic spirit of the Mayor and City Council? Was it unheard of to expect equal representation and equal rights in Hutchinson County?

DAY TEN . . . Thursday, September 9, 2004

Spent a restless night and got out of bed still thinking how wrong it was for the newspaper to refuse to run the ad. I wondered if the corporate office really called the shots in sinking the ad.

Tomorrow would be the last day of advertising and I was looking forward to seeing 3 new ads with the headlines, "Voting For is like Trusting The Captain & Crew of the Titanic to Navigate a New $25 Million Cruise Ship," "Tax the Needy to Feed the Greedy," and "Let's Rock Their Boat Tomorrow on September 11 by Voting Against". The "To tell the Truth" was suppressed but another full page ad would be in its place. It was almost over except for the voting.

The headline, "WHO ARE THE REAL CITIZENS OF HUTCHINSON COUNTY," was the full page ad of the day.

The Invest in Yourself Ad defending the 150 percent tax increase was down to half page. It looked as if their campaign was losing steam and they were running out of dollars.

In the Letters to the Editor: Eddie Hall spoke up to say, "The whole problem falls directly on Norm's shoulders. He is responsible. He has to take the blame. He is the one making the BIG BUCKS. You can change the CFO all you want, but the problem isn't fixed until the CEO is changed.

As far as the mud slinging is concerned, I don't believe it's mud slinging if it is the truth. I believe Mr. Baxter has done his homework. Everything he has printed and said in meetings seems to be very factual to me. He may seem like a radical because he has a different view. But anytime a major change is taking place anywhere, then you see all different views.

Just because you have a different idea doesn't make you a radical."

They could call me a radical, a troublemaker or worse. I could live with it if that's what it took to help seniors from being taxed into oblivion, eliminate toxic management and get better choices for health care in my hometown.

DAY ELEVEN . . . Friday, September 10, 2004

The front page of the News-Herald boldly announced, HOSPITAL ELECTION TO BE SATURDAY. Heavy voter turnout is expected in what has become probably the most controversial election in the history of Hutchinson County."

The contributions and expenditures were listed on the front page on each political action committee that were filed through the Texas Ethics Commission in Austin, Texas and with the taxing entity conducting the election. The total contribution made to the Citizens Who Care About Hutchinson County was $6,400 and the total contributions made to Invest in Yourself was $12,309.60.

The listed expenditures for Citizens Who Care About Hutchinson County listed $4,649.76 expenditure with the News-Herald. Shockingly, there were no Invest in Yourself expenditures listed for newspaper ads in the News-Herald? Why? Who paid for all the newspaper ads?

As an "unenlightened" IIY committee member, I developed the web site and didn't charge a dime for it? By definition of the law, this expenditure should have been listed as an "in kind" donation. It wasn't!

Who paid several thousand dollars for the newspaper ads? WAS THE LAW BROKEN?

The last Invest in Yourself ad was another half page defensive ad trying to convince voters that it wasn't a 150 percent tax increase. In the Letters to the Editor, Mr. R.L. Boyd said, "He was voting no on the hospital." He gave an example on how to figure the tax increase and concluded, "Any way you slice it, that is a tax increase of 150 percent."

He wasn't buying the hospital's spin on math. The next day, the final figures would be counted in votes. The hospital Administration wouldn't be able to spin those. It would be win or lose.

DAY TWELVE . . . September 11, 2004

I was looking forward to sleeping in late on Saturday morning. A phone call got me out of bed earlier than planned. Throughout the day others called saying there was a heavy turn out at the polls. I planned to drive my mother to Borger Middle School where we would vote that afternoon.

We walked to my pickup truck where I placed a step stool at the passenger side to help Mom get into the truck. Dad previously went into a full scale rage about me driving her in her car. His elder rages were all about control and manipulation. He didn't want her to leave the house and buy anything. She was unable to drive her Cadillac and it was easier to drive my pickup rather than confronting him. It made me angry every time I saw my mother suffering from osteoporosis, wearing a pain patch 24/7 and resorting to riding in a pickup.

It wasn't right, but there was no one else to stand with me against my Dad. My sister and brother-in-law depended on my father for their financial livelihood. When it really came down to siding with my mother, they would look the other way. Lifetime habits were hard to break. They were trapped, blinded and in denial of a lifetime habit of dysfunctional behavior.

Dad made all the decisions and called all the shots. The wind would blow his way and he controlled his family with a tight fist. Tragically, the tendons controlling his fist were weakening and reasoning was leaving his mind.

The most frustrating feeling was to love my Dad and feel helpless in reasoning with him

It was peaceful walking with my Mother into the Middle School to place our votes on that Saturday afternoon, September 11, 2004. I thought of 911 in New York City and how horrible it was see how some people violently terrorize others and take lives with no remorse. Then, I thought how others are psychologically terrorized in ways that gradually takes freedom, integrity and pride away from souls.

More than any other time in my life, I realized how precious and powerful the silent vote can be. We cast our votes "AGAINST"!

ELECTION RETURNS . . . THE WAKE AT SUPTHENS

I spent the evening at Spradling Oil offices waiting with others for the campaign results. Finally, the phone rang and it was a reporter from the News-Herald. Our side had won by a landslide. Cheering rose from the offices and Garry Hannon was the first to the phone. He told the reporter, "We are very pleased with the results. Now we can move forward, with the hospital board's approval, with a plan that won't be a burden on the citizens of Hutchinson County. I just think the voters were not asked their opinion about this spur of the moment proposal. They said they have been working on this plan for 10 years, but you would think they would have wanted to get the opinions of the people who make the final decision, before proceeding with their plan. In a IYY meeting, I asked if they had a plan B, and Leon Mitchell said, we don't need a plan B. That was a mistake because everything needs a backup plan."

Garry went on to say that Tri-Lakes were willing to invest millions into the community and that there is a good plan that will work if the hospital board is willing to listen.

The phone was handed to me and I said, "I believe the voters of the county exercised their right to vote in the democratic process and things can begin to go forward in a new direction. It's a great victory for the voters of Hutchinson County."

The News-Herald was delivered late that night. On the front cover was a full color picture of the pre-planned victory party at Sutphens. Helium filled balloons floated up from tables among a banquet room crowded with IIY supporters. Many of them were wearing yellow Invest in Yourself shirts and in the middle of it all stood Mr. Lambert with his arms crossed. It looked like a celebration party. The cut line under the photo said, "Invest in Yourself members gathered Saturday night to receive results of the $25 million bond election to construct a new medical facility. The measure was defeated."

My phone rang, it was John Curnutt. He asked, "Have you seen front page of the News-Herald?" I said, "Yes, they got better coverage in losing, bitching, moaning and whining than we got by winning." John replied, "I'll bet they were really peeved off when it rained on their party. The photo in the paper looked like a WAKE AT SUTPHENS!"

The County Judge, the Commissioner's Court and the District Attorney had ignored the 1,041 signatures on the petition requesting a forensic audit. The District Attorney's office had looked the other way and did nothing about making an investigation. The court of public opinion in Hutchinson County scored a victory on September 11, 2004.

CHAPTER SEVENTEEN

THREATENING E-MAIL FROM A SORE LOOSER

All day Sunday, I felt elated over the victory and the beginning of a wake up call for changes in the community. My elation ended when I read my e-mail on www.voteno911.com. The e-mail arrived after the election at 1:28 Sunday morning from one of the administration's surrogates.

From: feedback@wsm.ezsitedesigner.com
To: gb@voteno911.com Cc: Date: Sunday, September 12, 2004
Subject: Visitor Feedback from Your Web site
Comments: Now that the bond issue has failed, this community is faced with the prospect of soon having no hospital. Time is running out on the grandfather clauses which have allowed the facility to remain open. Since you were adamant in your belief that the bond should fail, I think it's reasonable for this community to assume you have a plan to prevent us from losing our health care.

When will your Master Plan be revealed? I hope it's very soon, because we will soon be a county in crisis, thanks in part, to your efforts. I expect you'll find that any plan you have will be difficult to put into action, because you have no credibility or respect from anyone in this town involved in health care, or any business, for that matter.

Do you know who believes in you? People who don't care enough to educate themselves and who are so short-sighted they can't even think one year into their future. You're the blind leading the blind.

How many "websites" do you think you're going to sell to these people? It's ironic that you talk about "preachers with no business sense." You are a "business man" who has just turned every potential customer in a town against him! The people who actually think you have any worth have no use for your "business" services.

Do you think others are going to support you financially? They got what they wanted from you, and now your name is destroyed. So, congratulations, I have seen the pain your vile acts and lies have caused, and it's horrible.

I think it's your turn to be on defense for a change. So, announce your plan. I will make it my personal mission to criticize, ridicule, and belittle it. Then, I will attack your personal character, as you have done to so many. I will find out every ugly detail I can. I will publicly announce every questionable business decision you have ever made. And if I get some of my facts wrong, well that's just what happens in a smear campaign, as you well know. I'm ready and waiting, Glenn.

Throughout the campaign, I had received numerous e-mails from this address and there was no way to respond. Some of the e-mail said things like f—you, you're a liberal ass hole and so forth. The unusual thing was that one e-mail actually gave me information that was helpful. It must have come from a disgruntled employee. I suspected the e-mail originated in the hospital or a doctor's office.

As I read the e-mail a second time, several things stuck out. Did the sentence, *"People who don't care enough to educate themselves and who are so short-sighted they can't even think one year into their future,"* aptly describe how some in this group arrogantly view the majority of people in the county.

The threat of boycotting my business was the perfect example of how a group of mental terrorists can control others in the community through threats and character assassination.

The sentence, "I will make it my personal mission to criticize, ridicule, and belittle . . ." exactly described "unkind things" the hospital administration had done to others who did not agree with its tactics.

DEMOCRATIC VICTORY 68% VOTE AGAINST

The Invest in Yourself Committee, hospital administration and board of director's were soundly beaten. A majority of citizens in the county, the owners of the hospital had spoken. They did not trust the hospital administration and who could blame them. The hate e-mail convinced me these others were not giving up even after losing a campaign where the cards were overwhelmingly stacked in their favor.

Sunday evening sitting at my computer composing a victory story, I imagined it would take the tenacity of a pit bull to make changes in this administration. Like a snow ball in hell, I knew there was no chance this release would make it on the front page of the News-Herald.*

Immediate Release
September 12, 2004

On Saturday, September 11, the citizens of Hutchinson County gained a democratic victory in defeating the hospital bond election by a voter turnout of 68% against verses 32%. The Citizens Who Care About Hutchinson County presented a track record of mismanagement and failure of the hospital administrator to be accountable for the past and present financial problems including attempts to control, intimidate and alienate Doctors, Board Members, and other employees.

---

*   *I was right, the release was published in the Letters to the Editor column.*

The Invest In Yourself supporters lost. They failed in thinking they could sell voters on placing management and services with a bad reputation into a new hospital and expect different results. They failed in thinking that a few on a committee could decide what is best for the majority. They failed being in touch and having empathy with the 3,672 seniors over 65 and others who work hard everyday to make ends meet.

Even in their defeat, they make excuses. On the front page of the weekend Borger News-Herald, the administration is quoted as saying; "the people in the county had received considerable misinformation and confusion during the campaign." They still don't get it! In all the past newspaper articles including the $615,000 MRI disaster with 1,040 citizen signatures on a petition, it was never said, "We made a bad decision." In a past news article, the administrator makes the comment that anyone could make a mistake in buying a bad refrigerator. Don't you think that's taking taxpayer's dollars lightly? Blame everything and everyone except the administration.

A prominent IIY member stated, "The IIY will still be available to find a solution." They still don't get it. Why would the 68% of people who voted against the IIY plan want the same committee to be involved in another solution? Why would voters trust them after IIY tried to steam roll a single option, cast in concrete proposal over the citizens in the county? Maybe they wrote somewhere in the IIY plan, on pages 7 through 11 saying, "If so ever our plan fails, quickly become flexible . . . ask voters to forgive and trust us?"

What the IIY supporters need to know is that the Citizens Who Care About Hutchinson County has a plan. Our next steps are to create a petition that calls for (1) the immediate resignation of the hospital administrator, (2) the immediate resignation of the Board of Trustees including an inquiry into liability toward fiduciary irresponsibility, and (3) a Forensic Audit of GPCH.

And last, but not least, is to form an interim board of trustees and a citizen's committee to research and present other choices for health care in Hutchinson County that will meet the needs of all citizens without placing a tax burden on seniors and others who cannot afford it. There are 3,581 citizens who voted against and others who will qualify to help with our plan. I want to thank everyone for voting against and I encourage all of you to call to sign up today.

Glenn Baxter
Citizens Who Care About Hutchinson County

What had become a standard operating pattern at Golden Plains was wrong. Others had tried to set things straight and now it was my turn and I wasn't turning loose. I was damned and determined to see it through. These people were blind to their own corruption and righteousness.

The victory of voters was short lived and a war of words in the Letters to the Editor was about to begin.

A WAR OF WORDS

September 12, 2004 to Who Knows When

CHAPTER EIGHTEEN

THE FIRST BOARD MEETING

On Monday, I called Garry Hannon and talked about attending the hospital board meeting on Tuesday evening. He said Chuck Litteral was going with him. I said, "See you there," and hung up.

A crowd filled the boardroom. It consisted of hospital employees, nurses, people from the offices and family members. Judging from the hostile stares, we were surrounded and outnumbered by those in favor of the hospital. I recalled Pat Cleveland telling me about the "kangaroo court" style board meetings of the past. The pattern was repeating itself before my eyes.

David Brandon, chairman of the board spoke, "We recognize that the public has spoken, and the implication of that voice and vote cannot be ignored."

I considered that to be a fair and logical statement as I raised my hand to address the Board. Looking at the seven board members, I said, "The Citizens Who Care About Hutchinson County want to bring the pharmacy management agreement to the attention of the Board of Directors. This agreement is signed between Norm Lambert and Conny Moore for $140,000 a year. Mr. Moore had alluded early in the political campaign that he had no conflict of interest. Mr. Moore is receiving checks of over $5000 at his home address."

"That is not a conflict of interest," Brandon said. "He is providing a service for those fees, services of greater value than what those fees pay. He has covered the pharmacy since he took over, seven days a week, 24 hours a day. You try to get any other pharmacist to do that for $140,000 a year and you're barking up the impossible tree. It is not a conflict of interest. He's providing a service."

I replied, "I disagree with that because I was told by someone on the board (I meant to say the IYY committee) that Moore was providing services for free and not under a contract."

I was referring to Reverend Paul Anderson who told me that Conny Moore was semi-retired and did a lot of good things for the community. He inferred that Mr. Moore wasn't involved in a conflict of interest because the money wasn't important to him.

In the August newspaper article, why didn't Conny Moore just come clean and say, "I have a contract for $140,000 per year as the pharmacist at Golden Plains." In his defense, Mr. Moore did say in the article that, "It would be much better if people would get the true facts before they make public statements."

I was taking his advice and digging for the facts. An open document request letter had produced his pharmacy agreement. After getting this information and releasing it to the paper, GPCH administration sent a letter to the Texas Attorney General's office to attempt blocking the second open document request. I wasn't through digging for more facts that would eventually enlighten Dr. Paul Anderson and the rest of the community.

The meeting was closed when David Brandon said, "The Tri-Lakes group from Batesville, Mississippi will be coming in sometime during the next few weeks to make a presentation and would also be looking at other investment possibilities."

"I think we are certainly obligated to do that, and to do that in good faith. The citizens have spoken and we cannot tell from the vote whether or not the majority want a new hospital. We can certainly tell from the vote the citizens do not want to pay for one. We will try to find either a way to make this operation profitable and be able to raise revenue bonds, or have private investment come in here and get us a new hospital before this one has to be shut down."

The president and some other board members were still looking the other way and in denial of the real problem at Golden Plains.

Rising to leave, I felt like Custer surrounded by a hostile tribe of hospital employees. One approached me and said, "You ought to be ashamed of yourself." I responded, "Thanks for your opinion, but I'm very proud of myself and a majority that voted "against"!

I walked outside and under the building canopy with Garry Hannon and Chuck Litteral. I saw Dixie Howard approach Garry Hannon.

She asked, "Why are you trying to destroy the hospital and undermine everything that has been done?"

Garry responded, "I'll be glad to visit with you." As he began explaining the other side of the story, a Nurse Kiljoy jumped into the conversation. She started screaming and yelling up close to Garry's face.

He told her to "get out of my face or there will be some consequence." She responded, "What are you going to do? Hit me?" Garry said, "No I'm not going to get physical. But, we'll get this matter stopped. You will get out of my face!"

Just then, I saw Norm Lambert and Elsa Borden, COO, coming out the door and standing behind Garry . . .

When Garry turned around there was Norm with a smug smile from ear to ear. He was quite amused that one of his employees wearing scrubs with her GPCH identification card was screaming and yelling at a private citizen. Lambert did nothing to stop it. He stood there watching it go on until Elsa Borden said, "You need to leave or you're going to jail!"

Garry responded, "No I'm not. I'm the one getting verbally abused. I'm a taxpayer. This is public property and I'm not leaving until I'm ready."

The next thing I saw was two Borger Police Officers drive up. In the next couple of minutes, Don Rice the photographer for the News-Herald pulled up and got out of his car.

Lambert and Borden looked at the Officers and said, "We want these people removed from the property."

I immediately thought they're trying to set up a photo and story for the newspaper. I walked over and spoke to the Officers. "I don't know what this guy Lambert is up to. This is frivolous. We have done nothing." One Officer said, "Don't worry, it's okay." I think the Officer was in disbelief over the call.

Later, when the three of us left, Garry said, "That was bogus, a set up deal from the get go."

My mind flashed back to the horror stories the Doctors and others had told me about the administration smear tactics. This was my first hand experience of the administrator's management ruse in using surrogates against those who disagree with him. They were wrong to call the police and involve the City of Borger in their vendetta. This time the administrations' actions failed in getting the media to report it.

GETTING THE FACTS STRAIGHT

The first thing Wednesday morning, I called the pharmacist preceding Conny Moore at Golden Plains. His name is Ken Roark and he is the pharmacist at the hospital in Snyder, Texas. Here's his story:

"The hospital Chief Operating Officer, Elsa Borden, told me I couldn't leave beyond 30 miles 24/7 of Golden Plains unless I had another pharmacist. I said it wasn't acceptable because I've got grand kids more than 30 miles away. At that time, Conny Moore was my backup pharmacist and COO Borden questioned his ability. The COO said he wasn't capable of taking my place, but six months later Conny had the pharmacy. I had more hospital experience than he did, but we both are certified with the State Board of Pharmacy. It really bothered me that I had to leave and be four hours away from my mother with leukemia. If I had been able to stay in Borger, I could have spent more time with her before she passed away."

Ken Roark was member of Keeler Baptist Church. Later, I found out that the Pastor, Dr. Paul Anderson, and some other church members went before the GPCH hospital board with an appeal to keep Ken Roark in Borger.

FRAME IT, HANG IT, SEE IT COLLECT DUST!

Who was this Chief Operating Officer acting as the CEO's strong arm and what were her qualifications? I rummaged through the boxes of documents and found her resume. It read that she had a Bachelor's and a Master's degree from the University of Oklahoma and a doctorate degree from Century University.

I knew nothing of this institution so I searched Google to find www.centuryuniversity.edu. First of all, the "university" is only licensed in New Mexico. Secondly, the web site states

that, "Individuals with no college background or less than two years of college can obtain a triple degree program by paying $8,099."
WHAT A DEAL!!!

CONFLICT OF INTEREST

I e-mailed this release to the News-Herald. Of course it didn't make the front page but it was printed in Letters to the Editor.

In the Tuesday Sept. 14, 2004 News Herald story covering outcry of denial of conflict of interest from some members of the GPCH Board concerning Mr. Moore's pharmacy management agreement, I would like to enlighten the readers, taxpayers, and others in the county to consider the following information concerning conflict of interest.

According to the MHA-Trustee Resource Center, the following is stated under the heading "Conflict of Interest Policy" . . . applies to lay professionals (such as bankers, lawyers, accountants, and real estate brokers) who do business with and provide advice and counsel to the hospital, to physician entrepreneurs, and to major vendors who do business with the hospital. Issues that may not have been perceived to be a conflict-of-interest in the past, present significantly conflict of interest today, and many of them are not well handled. Failure to maintain this conflict of interest policy is grounds for removal from the board.

Other sources on conflict of interest state the following: "Individuals who are business partners, blood relatives, or very close friends with individuals who have the types of conflict of interest identified above. *A conflict of interest occurs when an individual has a stake in both sides of any transaction or contemplated transaction.*

Mr. Moore is and was contracted with Golden Plains Community Hospital at the time of serving on the Invest In Yourself Committee. The attorney for GPCH was also serving on the committee who was receiving legal fees from the hospital. I'm not sure if these two gentlemen are close friends with the administrator. It appears that it would not have been in their best financial interest to recommend a private or other health care management solution to the citizens of Hutchinson County. It may have placed at risk their stakes in the contracts each have with GPCH.

PETITION TO REMOVE THE ADMINISTRATION
AND A FORENSIC AUDIT

The next board meeting was a month away. The plan was to get a petition signed for the removal of the hospital administration and the board of directors and a forensic audit. We met with the Borger Betterment Committee and put together a list of individuals who would circulate the petition. We would start the petition, present it at the next board meeting and ask the board, "How many names will it take for you to act? No action was taken on 1,041 names . . . How many names will it take you to act?"

The petition read,

Come now the citizens and taxpayers of Hutchinson County who respectively demand the following: That on September 11, 2004, a mandate by the voters has required that the Golden Plains Community Hospital be completely re-constituted for the Public Good.

Therefore, the undersigned require:

— The current CEO, Norm Lambert, be removed and the administration assessed and revamped
— That a full forensic audit by an independently selected firm be conducted to determine any deficiencies or discrepancies
— That concurrently, consulting groups be engaged to pursue management of the GPCH facilities until such time as alternate facility plans can be fully implemented

I called an attorney friend in Dallas and filled him in what was happening in Hutchinson County and at Golden Plains Community Hospital. After talking with him at length, he brought up the RICO laws. He explained that the Racketeer Influenced and Corrupt Organizations (RICO) Act could be used in Civil Lawsuits involving public corruption. It enables plaintiffs to sue for triple damages. Those found guilty can be fined up to $25,000 and/or sentenced to 20 years in prison. Crimes can be committed in a 10 year period where a pattern of cover-ups and conspiracies result in ill gotten gains.

More Internet research on RICO laws led me to find that for every John Gotti who is brought down by RICO, many abusive business owners and managers are also successfully prosecuted under this law. Among the private business owners prosecuted under RICO are a builder of oil platforms, a real estate developer and a hospital administrator. Moreover, RICO has also proved to be a potent weapon in public corruption cases. The government won convictions against five Macon, Georgia, police officers for accepting bribes to overlook state crimes and a Florida State judge accused of selling acquittals. (Press, Shannon, and Allissimmons 1979)

The question in my mind was, "Would the RICO ACT be applicable?"

CIRCULATING THE PETITION

In 20 days we had over 200 names on the petitions. I had gone door to door in one day and got 50 signatures. Only five people I talked with would not sign the petition. This meant there would be no problem getting as many signatures as needed to present to the board.

Almost every day leading up to the October board meeting there were opinion articles attacking Citizens Who Care About Hutchinson County. Many of the articles tried to justify Conny Moore's pharmacy contract. The authors of the articles would not identify that they were employed at the hospital or had some vested interest. I guess they thought they could fool the public. In each instance they were responded to and identified as one of the Administration's puppets.

I kept pounding away with the contract and the facts I'd received from open documents. I wrote humorous responses like: "Providing facts to citizens is not mudslinging. If you don't believe this, then maybe you and Mr. Moore should wear brown trousers so the mud doesn't show."

One person (a retired nurse) wrote to say, "Surprise me and everyone else and leave it alone. Let's see if you can be quiet for a change." My response was, "Your right . . . I can't be quiet when freedom of speech is at stake and taxpayer's money is abused. And I urge others not to be quiet. There is a hospital board meeting on October 5, 2004 at 6:30 PM. Every citizen in Hutchinson County has the right to attend and speak his or her opinions.

THE BOARD MEETING FROM HELL

There was standing room only in the board room. There were many more friendly faces there than at the previous board meeting. Hospital supporters were still in the majority. Early in the meeting, Rowena Hogan stood up to address the board about how she was dissatisfied with how things were being run. She ran into an argument with Leon Mitchell who reprimanded her and others for being out of order. She got angry and left the room.

There was extreme tension in the air when my turn arrived to address the seven members on the board. I stood up and shouts for me to sit down and other rude comments arose from the crowd. The hospital attorney said, nor did anything to calm things to order as he previously had done.

I ignored the heckling and proceed to read my prepared statement:

"The taxpayers of Hutchinson County have figured it out. Invest in Yourself now appears to be a mechanism promoted by all the usual suspects; business, managerial and legal, to convince the Citizens of Hutchinson County to vote for a 25 million dollar bond issue. These parties had a financial stake in the hospital through their contracts and relationships with the hospital. They may have violated conflict of interest and moral disclosure ethics. They acted in a self-serving manner by only presenting one option to the Citizens of Hutchinson County under the pretense that the new hospital would benefit everyone in the county on an equal basis.

There are those who may think that not getting caught telling a falsehood is the same as telling the truth. The Chairman of the IIY misled many people into thinking that he was not receiving income from the hospital and that he was acting only for the benefit of the community. This was found to be untrue. In fact, through open documents, this individual was receiving $142,000 in a Pharmacy Management Agreement. This is almost twice the amount of compensation paid to the previous pharmacists. This is excessive compensation and abuse of taxpayer dollars.

These individuals may have deceived the General Public by not revealing that the hospital was on the brink of bankruptcy. The apparent plan was to use portions of the bond money to bail the hospital out of debt. The ballot stated that the funds could be used for the "general purpose" needs of the hospital. It appeared that the intent was to continue supporting management that should be held accountable for the present financial condition of the hospital and a history of mismanagement at the expense of taxpayers.

They misled the general public by not revealing that 11 acres of land being considered as a site was in a flood plain. The owner previously sought to develop the land and sell tracts as town homes, but abandoned the plan when the City of Borger refused to bear the cost in correcting drainage problems with the land. The owners then offered the land as "free" to the Hospital District if they would build a new hospital on the property. It's been surmised that these owners would have received a favorable tax advantage. According to City of Borger engineers, this free land has an unknown cost to make it suitable for a new hospital or any other building.

The actors did not take into account nor did they survey all the existing owners of businesses surrounding the site of the present hospital. For years, these businesses have been supplying support services for the hospital and relying on the hospital for their business. Demolishing the hospital and moving to a new site would surely have damaged the business of these owners and decreased their property values. There was no respect for others and what they have built.

The IIY plan could have created an urban ghetto with more abandoned buildings in the community. These few individuals would have damaged the community at an estimated cost of three million dollars for asbestos abatement and demolition of the existing hospital facility. No real data or scientific information was presented to prove that these facilities cannot be viable properties.

The project to build a new Doctors Building to house 10 doctors adjacent to the "new hospital" seemed to be a tactic of the hospital management to create more conflict and separation in the Medical Staff by placing management's chosen doctors away from the others. The whole scheme appeared to be designed without regard to the impact on the Taxpayers in the County. The public trust has been severely damaged. The Board of Trustees and others could now incur joint and several liabilities. The possibility of RICO charges is being examined and a forensic audit is a must

I had the petitions with over 200 names in my briefcase and an example of a petition in my hand. I said to the board that I had over 200 signatures for removal of the administration and a forensic audit and I am handing you a blank petition to read. At that time I asked, "How many votes will it take you to act?"

Several of the board members began to vocally support and defend Lambert. I looked around the room and there were two cameras from Amarillo television stations and both newspapers recording the shouts and accusations from the crowd.

I reiterated that the 68 percent vote against the tax increase was because of the management. The September 11 bond election saw over 5,000 people in Hutchinson County voting on the issue. On Proposition One, the vote count was 1,755 for and 2,581 against. Proposition Two was 1,730 for and 3,581 against. How many signatures will it take for this board to take action on the petition.

Board member Glen Buckles spoke, "WE DON'T CARE HOW MANY SIGNATURES YOU BRING, WE DON'T HAVE TO ACT ON IT!"

I couldn't believe my ears. Was I standing in a meeting room in a small community in America or standing in a dictator's meeting in a third world country?

Jason Vance, hospital board member said, "We need to realize that this hospital gets about 34 percent of the local market. We had that 34 percent of the local market before we ever had a campaign to issue bonds to build a new hospital. That's not a good market share. The vote for the hospital was about the same as the percent of the market we get. That market share was split like that long before Glenn Baxter ever came along.

I have some issues about how he advertised against the bond issue. Glenn and I have talked about that. I don't believe that it was Glenn Baxter that slowed the vote against this hospital. If we believe that, if we think that, then we aren't looking at ourselves in the mirror very honestly.

We're never going to move forward," he said. "We've got to start looking, not blaming and moving forward in a positive manner. As a board member, I am committed to doing that."

Wow, I thought, Jason Vance isn't letting his ego get in the way. The man has integrity and like other past board members who spoke out with integrity, *Vance may become a target for Lambert just like Jerry Strecker.*

Lambert rose to speak, "Usually I defer my comments at this time, but given that a number of things have gone on over the last several weeks, I think it is true for me to make comments." He continued to spin rhetoric about his coming on staff 9 years ago and how he saw an opportunity for growth. "In 1982 the market share was 57 percent. In 1987, the market share dropped 38 percent, a decrease of 20 percentage points. I believed that I could take advantage of that opportunity. I think I've made a difference here at the hospital."

Hold it right there Mr. Lambert and let's do the math. If we subtract a decrease of 20 percentage points from 57 percent that equals a 37 percent market share when you arrived at Golden Plains. Jason Vance stated that the present market share is 34 percent. That's a decrease of 3 percent in the 9 years you've been administrator.

Lambert continued to compliment the hard work of the hospital Chief Operating/ Nursing Officer and the Chief Financial Officer. He conveniently forgot to mention the revolving door at GPCH where over 5 Chief Financial Officers have walked in and out of over the past 5 years. What's wrong with an administration that cannot keep a CFO?

Lambert defended Conny Moore's pharmacy agreement in saying, "The salary right now in the Panhandle for pharmacists is somewhere between $95,000 and $100,000 a year for just an 8 to 5 type job. When you put benefits on top of that, you're probably talking about $125,000."

I partially agreed with Lambert about the salary right in 2004 because I researched it on the Internet through www.rxsalary.com. Entering experience = 30 years Degree =

PharmD/PhD Position = Staff Pharmacist Function = Distribution/Dispensing Setting = Hospital-Rural-Location = TX Amarillo, Texas . . . computed an annual salary of $97,000.

Here's where Lambert gets deceptive by omitting information to lead the public astray by not comparing apples to apples.

— First of all, Lambert fabricates the "8 to 5 type job" because the $97,000 will get a pharmacist in Amarillo on call 24/7.

— Ken Roark was being paid $75,000 as GPCH pharmacist on call 24/7 five years ago when he was run off and replaced by Conny Moore with a then $120,000 contract. What was the going rate for a pharmacist then? Probably less than $97,000.

— And, why pay $45,000 more for a pharmacist to support a small rural hospital with a very low census count? Hospitals in Amarillo average an extremely high census count a day therefore the pharmacy stays busy filling prescriptions. Golden Plains averages an extremely low census count a day and therefore the pharmacist is not nearly as busy.

— This hefty contract for an entrepreneur like Mr. Moore gives him free time to make more money on other deals. He doesn't have to be at the hospital from 8 to 5 each day. He's on 24/7 call as needed.

— Finally, Lambert says, "you're probably talking $125,000." This still didn't account for the entire $142,000. That's another $18,000 frivolously spent on Mr. Moore for being a good ol' boy! Nice try Mr. Lambert, but it doesn't wash!

Lambert continued attacking Garry Hannon and me. He referred to the CCHS and the BBC in saying, "I could go on forever about the Citizens Who Care about Hutchinson County as a misnomer. The Borger Betterment Committee has several other names. Betterment is not one of them."

He continued in defense of his Administration to emphasize that the "against" vote was about people not wanting their taxes raised. He justified his $140,000 salary while evading that the administrator at Tri-Lakes was getting paid $90,000 to run a successful operation.

Incredibly he held up the blank copy of the petition and said, "You've (Baxter) alleged that the community voted on September 11 to have this administration removed, and yet you presented a blank petition to us tonight."

I tried to interrupt Lambert and reiterate what I had said earlier about having over 200 signatures, but was shut down by the board president. This obvious anti-free speech technique enabled the CEO to attack with an untruth and shut down the other side by not allowing them to respond. Did the CEO not hear 200 signatures or was he just a blatant deceiver with a bag of dirty tricks?

Leaving the meeting, I fully appreciated what past board president, Pat Cleveland, went through with Lambert and his cronies when she said, "That last year I would come home from a board meeting sick at my stomach. When there were 4 new members in there and there is hope that finally they may be a way to govern to save some money and not spend frivolously. But Lambert already had the new members sucked into his good old boy club. It was frustrating to see Jerry Strecker make a motion and no one would even second it."-Pat Cleveland

A NIGHTMARE CALLED "GOLDEN PLAINS IN WONDERLAND"

That evening on Channel 7 News at 10 showed the "WE DON'T HAVE TO ACT ON IT" comment from board member Glenn Buckles. Seeing again the audacity of this man caught on tape really angered me. How could anyone representing taxpayers make such a comment?

The next morning, I looked into the box of documents for anything that would give a board member the power to ignore those he is supposed to represent. I pulled the "HUTCHINSON COUNTY HOSPITAL DISTRICT BY-LAWS" to read.

> 2.2   The Board consist of seven directors. One elected from each county district and three appointed by the County Commissioner's Court.

> 3.6.2 **REMOVAL.** The President/Chief Executive Officer may be removed with or without cause, by two thirds majority vote (5 out of 7) of (all) the directors of the Board. Such removal shall be in accordance with any then existing management agreements.

It would take more than a majority vote to remove the CEO. Theoretically, if the CEO was in collusion with the Commissioner's Court then he could manipulate the three appointed members and remain in power regardless of a majority vote of the Board. Was this perverted democracy in action?

Then, I found in the enabling legislation that a majority of four out of seven board members could vote to sell the hospital. That was a revelation!

IT'S EASIER TO VOTE TO SELL THE HOSPITAL THAN TO FIRE THE CEO! I HAD NEVER HEARD OR READ ABOUT AN AMERICAN BUSINESS OR CORPORATION WHERE THE BOARD OF DIRECTORS PLACE THE CEO ABOVE THE WELFARE OF THE BUSINESS.

This was 360 degrees opposite of anything I had ever read in any newspaper, Wall Street Journal or any other business publication. The stories always cover the firing of CEO's by a majority vote of the board of directors before the business goes down the tubes. Often, the leadership of a new CEO will turn the business around. This was the case of Tri-Lakes.

Three rubber stamp board members could prevent Lambert's removal and snub their noses at the taxpayers and a majority of other board members. Any rational person could think of unlimited ways to manipulate 3 board members. People can be bought, threatened or blackmailed. This seemed irrational and insane. It came to mind a nightmare called, "Golden Plains in Wonderland."

Now I understood why Glen Buckles said, "We don't have to act on it!" Three board members could refuse a petition of 24,000 signatures (entire population of the county). ISN'T THIS HOW DICTATORS GOVERN?

MARGARET DUNHAM CALLS!

The phone rings the next day and Margaret Dunham is on the line. She and her husband Bill are members of Keeler Baptist Church and are fine people. Margaret is a retired English teacher and she was publisher of the newsletter for the Republican Women.

Margaret said, "I was so angry at what I experienced at the hospital board meeting. Leon Mitchell was biased in his comments and you shouldn't have been treated the way you were. I wrote an opinion letter and sent it to the editor. If Nancy Young doesn't publish it, we're going to picket the newspaper."

I thanked Margaret for her support and said, "I'll be on the watch for your letter and be standing by to carry a picket sign."

After waiting two weeks, Margaret Dunham's letter appeared in the newspaper on October 21, 2004.

DIDN'T LIKE GPCH MEETING!

Dear editor and Fellow Borgans,

Monday night, October 4, at the GPCH board meeting, I was totally unprepared for the raucous actions of the majority present!

Supposedly, this was a business meeting and should have been conducted as such. But, shortly, Leon Mitchell would severely lecture Rowena Hogan on just what conduct would be tolerated from her and the crowd; however, it became transparent that only those dissenting with the hospital administration would be chastised! Where was the "good fellow" when the majority of the crowd began hissing and booing when a speaker disagreed with the illustrious CEO and his cohorts?

Lawyer Mitchell just sat there like a mute. Why? Because clearly Norman Lambert had "encouraged" friends and employees (Mitchell is his hireling) to be his cheering squad. From assessing the group, a good guess is that at least two-thirds of the audience were hospital employees.

Amid the jeers, Glenn Baxter presented his petition. I was totally appalled at what followed. Mr. Lambert continued that Baxter had attacked people of the community. Then the CEO, who himself had charged Mr. Baxter of falsifying records, began a triad on the hospital pharmacy contract with Connie Moore.

As many of you know Ken Roark was a pharmacist here about three years ago. His salary was under $80,000, and his hours were 7/24 with instructions not to leave

Borger further than 29 miles. The administration ran off one good pharmacist! These facts can be checked!

Now Moore is drawing over $140,000. The administrator then as now was none other than Norm Lambert. Now who is distorting the facts, for he said a pharmacist couldn't be hired for less that $95,000.

Now, Mr. Lambert says he doesn't know why Glenn Baxter wants to change the administration! I might say that I don't know why myriad Borgans don't seek change . . . and now!

Do some math, Borgans! Our hospital doesn't have to carry a deficit! Borger is a small town; we don't need an administrator with a salary of over $140,000. Think of the savings.

Yes, our vote on September 11th was a mandate for change. We want change; we want a new administrator, not one who threatens that the Borger hospital is about to shut down. Yes, Lambert closed by saying, "I want to close by saying this is 2004. Don't let this . . . hospital close." Also, let me say that this hospital is needed here. When a person considers that over 55% of us Borgans are retired, we do indeed need this hospital.

I thank most of the board members for their efforts; they work without compensation, but there is one member who should not run for re-election—Glen Buckles who told us Monday night that he doesn't have to listen to any mandates or petitions no matter how many signatures are on it. Bad mistake if you want to stay on this board, Mr. Buckles.

About giving thanks, I salute you Mr. Glenn Baxter for all you have done for this community, and I hope you continue to work for Borger in spite of that degrading night. I say welcome home, Glenn. The population of Borger, for the most part, is a sweet, caring people!

Margaret Dunham, Borger

THE HOSPITAL ATTORNEY'S BEHAVIOR WAS NO SURPRISE

The attorney for the hospital has a pattern in supporting Norm Lambert. One previous example of the attorney supporting Lambert was in a letter his law firm composed and addressed to Lambert on June 26, 2000. The letter was used to suppress then board president, Pat Cleveland from discussing Lambert's record (management decisions that led to the losses upward toward one million dollars at Golden Plains) to new board members. According to Pat Cleveland, the letter was written to thwart an executive board closed meeting by referring to violations of the Open Meeting Act as being a misdemeanor punishable by a fine up to $500, confinement to county jail for not less than one month, or more than six months or both.

'Lambert had hand written on the envelope holding the letter, the following:

Pat Cleveland, President, HCHD Board . . . Please distribute a copy of the enclosed memo to each Board member at the start of the Executive Session. This is a memo from the hospital attorney marked "Attorney-Client Communication" and, therefore, should be distributed in the closed session.

I am unable to attend the meeting due to a prior engagement with several physicians at my house.

Thank you, Norm Lambert 6-26-2000.

Who should the attorney for GPCH represent? Should it be the administrator or the board? The administrator is only a hired position. Since the majority of the board members are elected directly by voters in the county and the district is supported by tax dollars, shouldn't the hospital attorney represent the citizens in the county? He is paid by tax dollars. And shouldn't the president of the hospital board represent the interest of the citizens of the county?

"There has always been a tremendous waste of money spent at that hospital. Once the CEO was putting up a room where sheet rocking was needed. It was a doctor's X-ray room. He came up with this price of $28,000 and we asked him about it. 'Why didn't you bring this to the board for approval?' The board members are supposed to be exercising our fiduciary duties. We were supposed to watch that money and it wasn't being watched. Lambert explained that he didn't have to take the estimate to the board because there are 3 or 4 different contractors. I was chairman of the board and asked him to give me an accounting of everything that was done. He did and it came to $8,000. I asked why he first said $28,000? He never gave me an answer and I have not gotten an answer to this day."— Pat Cleveland

Pat Cleveland was attempting to represent the citizens through questioning fiduciary responsibility of the Administration. She was unkindly smeared and ridiculed for her efforts.

NEWS-HERALD SUPPRESSES OPINIONS

All of Lambert's comments at the "meeting from hell" were featured on a front page article two days later on October 6. In the Letters to the Editor, the hospital's attorney's wife wrote, "One had to go to page two to read that the petition he presented to the hospital board had no names on it. Once again, Mr. Baxter received a lot of attention and his negative opinion received top billing. I am pleased that the new policy on letters to the editor allows only one letter per week from individuals."

These people were desperately reaching for straws. It was clearly stated in the paper for everyone to read, "He (Baxter) said he had over 200 names on the current petition, etc." How ironic was it that this letter was printed on the same day when Lambert's article was on the front page? Was this orchestrated? Did the newspaper instigate a one letter a week policy to shut me and Garry Hannon out of responding to the Administration puppets who did not identify themselves as being associated with the hospital.

Ms. Carmen Shopteese stated her opinion quite eloquently when she said, "I do not like the new letter policy. How dare you set rules that only allow the voices of the powers that be, have access to. I am sure this smacks of breaking the 1st Amendment. I want to hear what Mr. Baxter, or Mr. Hannon have to say, and you are caving in to the whining of Mr. Lambert, or Mr. Moore. I am considering contacting channel 7 to see if they are interested in the latest attempt to silence the public. You do not have the right, maybe a refresher course in journalism is called for at this point. News is not what a reporter had for lunch last week or her opinion on the price of rice. This is not NEWS, I want real news, town people are not stupid. Our rights are being stepped on and I'm sure you will hear about it."

CHAPTER NINETEEN

FREEDOM OF SPEECH SUPPRESSED

Out of frustration from the one letter per week policy, the following letter was submitted to the Borger-News Herald:

I have never experienced a city where the freedom of speech and press is controlled like it is in Borger, Texas. During the bond election, the Borger News Herald refused to run a full-page ad that presented the public documents relating to the child pornography scandal with the CFO at Golden Plains Community Hospital. There was nothing in the ad that asked the readers to vote one way or another. The ad only asked the readers to decide their vote by studying the documents. The Borger News-Herald refused to give a reason not to run the ad.

After disclosing the $142,000 Pharmacy Management Agreement signed between the hospital pharmacist and administrator, Golden Plains Community Hospital has blocked further open documents request by sending a letter to the Texas Attorney General's Office. What more do they have to hide?

According to Martin Fletcher Recruiting, a national recruiting service for hospitals, salaries for pharmacist in 2002 were $71,000 for low, $88,650 for average, and $120,000 for high. This means that $120,000 will pay for a pharmacist in large hospitals with high patient census in large cities. Federal law states that non-profits, tax-exempt organizations cannot operate to the benefit of any individual. Doesn't this appear to be an excessive financial benefit and abuse of taxpayer's dollars?

A week ago, The Borger News Herald announced that only one person or one organization would be able to have an opinion letter published each week. Does this seem like another attempt to control freedom of speech?

Those representing the hospital and the hospital board continue to use the words attack, and mudslinging as a means to diffuse facts that have been presented by citizen groups. These facts are based on records received from the hospital.

At the GPCH Board of Trustees meeting held on October 4, 2004 at Golden Plains Community Hospital, the question was asked about debts owed to vendors. Are there vendors who have placed the hospital on C.O.D. or any who are in the process of filing lawsuits? The response was "NO".

The next morning following the meeting, I received a call from The Heart Group in Amarillo. They were upset upon hearing this on the news and informed me that GPCH has owed them over $5000 since September 2003. They informed me they had notified by certified mail—a Hutchinson County Judge, Hospital Board President, Hospital Administrator, and others at the hospital to no avail. They further commented that if they were not paid by November 1, 2004, they planned to file a lawsuit*. According to them, this is the truth.

Glenn Baxter, Chairman
Citizens Who Care About Hutchinson County

PS I'm submitting this as my one opinion article per week to the Borger News-Herald. I can only hope that it is printed to inform citizens in Borger, Texas. If it is suppressed, I will submit it over a database to 20,000 press contacts across the U.S. I wonder if the ACLU would be interested in this story.

As expected, the News-Herald never printed the opinion article and when it was released on the Internet there were only two sources that picked it up. I became resigned in thinking that the national media considered small towns under the radar.

PAY YOUR BILLS TO STAY IN BUSINESS

On November 3, 2004, The Amarillo Heart Group copied me a letter sent to Mr. Lambert.

Dear Mr. Lambert,

We recently received the payment for the balance due on the indigent patient account in response to the letter of demand. I appreciate every effort you made to resolve this issue. I do hope that all future billing will be handled expeditiously as to avoid a re-occurrence of this negative situation.

All of the physicians in Amarillo Heart Group wish to continue a good working relationship and expect reimbursement within forty five (45) days of the statement date.

Sincerely,
Ron Welty, C.M.P.E.
Executive Director

County Judge Jack Worsham, board members and commissioners were also copied the letter. Who's telling the truth and who's misleading others?

The hospital owed a local pharmacist over $20,000 over 90 days. This was mentioned in an opinion article in addition to the hospital pharmacist currently getting two checks per month in excess of $10,000. When this local pharmacist was finally paid by GPCH, he stopped me on the street and said, "Thank you. You're better than any bill collector for hire!"

TRI-LAKES GROUP MEETS WITH PUBLIC

Thursday evening, October 6th, I went to the public meeting held by the Hutchinson County Board of Directors with Tri-Lakes. Both sides were well represented in the room that evening. The three people from Mississippi were there and Dr. Corkern rose to address the crowd. He stressed the need for public unity. He explained how crucial the doctors were to providing a full spectrum of care within a hospital. He said, "Our way of looking at this would involve joint venturing with physicians. He explained how important a sense of ownership was in keeping doctors. Dr. Corkern sat down and the two other people with him spoke.

When the meeting ended, I was standing next to Dr. Paul Anderson and listening to the questions he was asking Dr. Corkern. I could tell Brother Paul was impressed with what he saw and heard.

That evening, I typed out an opinion letter to e-mail to the News-Herald. This would be my "freedom of speech restricted" one opinion letter for the week.

TO: BORGER NEWS-HERALD 10-6-04

In their presentation last evening, the three people from Tri-Lakes made a very generous offer to invest 20 to 25 million dollars to build a new hospital in our community. These three people have an impressive track record in their rural community of Batesville, Mississippi. They are not takers. They are givers who realize it's best to inspire physicians, nurses and support staff to work as a team. Their business philosophy is to instill an attitude of the pride of ownership in everyone who works in their medical facility. They place physicians first because they realize that without them, there would be no hospital. Their success has come from sharing in their responsibilities in caring for patients.

The irony of their business philosophy is that it fits the motto of Citizens Who Care About Hutchinson County. "Goals for a unified community hospital that works toward a health care facility where each employee may hope to prosper and benefit from an inspired management. A community hospital based toward a shared vision for all employees, not only a few who decide for others."

Doctor Paul Anderson, minister at Keeler Baptist Church, was very impressed with these three people. He asked very pertinent questions for them to answer during the meeting. When I spoke to Brother Paul following the meeting, he seemed almost amazed by these three people and what they were offering our community. I commented to Brother Paul that these people seem like a "God send."

There are no accidents in life. God directs our journey. Brother Paul has heard me say this and that his bringing me into the Invest in Yourself committee was no accident.

My prayer at this time is for the board of trustees over the hospital. I pray they will set aside their egos and act in the best interest of the whole community. The community needs to unify. It's not about being righteous, because being right kills off love and understanding of others. It's about an opening for forgiveness and moving forward in their best interest of everyone involved. Everyone in the County needs and deserves an excellent medical facility. An offering has been placed on the table.

The next morning, I called Brother Paul to read the article for his approval before submitting it to the newspaper. It was a very emotional conversation. I hung up the phone and sent the e-mail.

The letter was censored and never published. I even called the Editor to complain to no avail.

Three days later, the newspaper printed a front page article covering the meeting. Tri-Lakes offer at the meeting to invest 20 to 25 million dollars to build a new hospital was conveniently omitted. The News-Herald may have censored the fact because is was downright embarrassing for those who had claimed Borger was under the radar for a private group to build a new facility.

This was a generous gift horse up to 25 million dollars looking right in the faces of Norm Lambert, Conny Moore, Leon Mitchell and the Board of Directors. Any idiot could see this was a much more generous offer than the 11 acres of free flood plain they were trying to pawn off on the community? It wouldn't cost the taxpayers one cent.

"Heaven Forbid" if for the good of the community, the administrator and others would risk relinquishing the money they mismanaged and sucked away from the taxpayers. Weren't these the same people proclaiming that the hospital will be closed if the bond issue fails? If that was true, the board didn't have time to analyze, re-analyze, and hire a consulting firm like Quorum to recommend actions to take? After all, I recalled seeing an expenditure to Quorum for over $200,000 and they claimed Borger was under the radar. How much more would it cost to be in the radar?

Brandi Hannon didn't charge a consulting fee to place Golden Plains in the radar of Tri-Lakes!

CACTUS THROAT

The phone rang on Thursday afternoon. On the line, a man's voice said, "Mr. Baxter, I've read about you in the newspaper and I have some information for you about that hospital. I asked his name and what information he had, but he said he was afraid to reveal it over the phone. After hearing "watch your back" for months, I was wary about this meeting. So, I told him we could meet in the lobby of the Phillips Building on Monday. There was safety in a public place. We agreed to meet at noon.

The following Monday, I arrived early at the Phillips Building. The receptionist said I could use the room to the right side of the receptionist desk.

Shortly thereafter, the man arrived and we shook hands, walked into the room and closed the door behind us.

He said, "I'll only take up a few minutes of your time. What I want to touch base with you about is that I see where you might get at some records, if the law allows it and they can't keep it from you. For years these folks have been selling children and its necessitates the use of the hospital to do this. There's going to be a paper trail that may let you get your foot in the door. Once you find this and you can ask questions like "what happened to this birth certificate?" Why isn't there a follow up of this child using this birth certificate entering a school?

There are many such birth certificates in use here in Hutchinson County. It's been going on for years. I don't know if they've quit this practice, but I do know it was going on up to 1968.

A great many of these people are in cahoots. I won't even ask who your associates are that allow you this ability to stand up and ask these questions you're asking.

Moreover, one other thing I want to lay on you. In the last few years, the offer has been made to these towns who have a high proportion of felony drug bust for a great deal of surveillance equipment. The kind of equipment that not only allows you to triangulate on a cell phone and to monitor that specific call and all incoming calls. When you come to the point where you want to keep something close to your vest, stay off that cell phone. I don't know if the city of Borger availed itself of this technology. I know for a fact that it was offered to them and they would have been stupid not to have done it.

You should try to find this book by Sonny Donaldson out of Conroe, Texas. Have you heard this talked about on the radio? A person has written a little nasty book talking about the city of Borger and about several murders that took place here. I don't know the name of the book but the radio station is willing to talk to you about it.

It would be worth your while to get a copy of this book because it talks about the people here involved in drugs, murders and other things.

I've led a sorry, miserable life that I should know things like this. I know some really sorry ass people and you are about to be undermining a portion of the system that operates what needs must be here to work. A friend in law enforcement and some of his associates tried to do something about this years ago and the Attorney General sent up an agent. The agent told them, I can't do anything for you because the very people I need to prosecute are also involved.

They have used the hospital before, not in the commission in crimes, but in covering up crimes in this town. They need that hospital, because it allows folks who may have died under conspicuous circumstances to be swept right under the rug and buried in the local cemetery. If you've lived here very long, you understand the system. They have a way to take care of individuals from the time they die until the time they're planted.

If you are successful at this, I will get in touch with you in the future. I know things about this place that people shouldn't know. There are some really bad people who operate in this town.

All I can tell you is to watch your back. Be careful what you say over an electronic mechanism. This is like a plum with this refinery here. A great deal of money flows through this town. My law enforcement friend and his associates tried to do something about the corruption here and failed. The state of Texas does not give a rats' ass about what goes on up here, because this might as well be the desert. There's not enough people here to make it worthwhile for a politician to stick his neck out to do anything about the corruption. We might as well be an island unto ourselves. They don't give a shit what goes on and neither does the Texas Attorney General's Office. They'll help you but they can't do anything about it, because all these people are in it together.

If you come up against anything you don't understand give me a call."

After departing, I thought over what was said. The story sounded far-fetched, unbelievable and disturbing. I wasn't concerned about the hospital back in 1968 because there was no Hospital District until 1989. All this sounded unreal! Was this an outrageous story coming from wild rumors and part facts? I couldn't discredit the entire story because of some irrational behavior I had observed that didn't make any sense.

This small Texas town was certainly under the radar and there was a pervasive attitude I couldn't quite put my finger on. There were individuals in prominent positions whom I trusted. They had warned me with the same three words, "Watch your back."

MEETING WITH THE FBI

I had heard those three words once too often. Looking through my notebook, I found the name and number of the FBI agent in Amarillo. I called his office, introduced myself and told him a relative with the FBI in Dallas had referred me to him. We scheduled a meeting and I prepared a sworn statement with a list of persons. I would take that to him along with some files and documents the following week.

OPERATION DENIAL

O what a tangled web we weave, when first we practice to deceive!
—Walter Scott

CHAPTER TWENTY

RESEARCH SURVEY SAYS ...

It was maddening to hear the hospital board of directors refuse to admit the number one problem. "IT'S THE ADMINISTRATOR" was one of the dominate messages in the "against" campaign and it was the talk on the street in every barber and beauty shop throughout the county. Were some of these individuals unbelievably out of touch? Maybe they drive to Amarillo to get their hair styled!

I had an idea and stopped by to share it with Garrett Spradling at the BBC. I said, "What's needed is an independent survey that shows why voters voted against the bond proposal." Garrett picked up on the idea right away. He said there were some other things he would like to find out and he would contact Texas Tech University to conduct the survey.

1995 STRATEGIC PLAN

While reading a 1995 strategic annual plan created under Lambert's regime, I was shocked to see the physicians in the community were segregated as being supportive and non-supportive. After all the talk of unity, why in the world would any manager or board approve such a plan.

I searched back to find a copy of Lambert's Employment Agreement. In my opinion, the agreement is weak in applying financial accountability toward Lambert's performance. The agreement requires more than a democratic majority of the board (5 out of 7 votes) to terminate Lambert. Three good ol' boy votes can perpetually cement the CEO as a hireling.

I looked under ARTICLE 4. TERMINATION to see what causes could the District could apply to terminate Lambert's Employment Agreement.

a. Materially breaches or materially neglects the duties that he is required to perform under the terms of this Agreement or the enabling legislation of the District only after written notice of such breach or neglect is presented to Lambert, Lambert has been given sixty (60) days to correct the breach or neglect and correction has not been made;

b. Materially violates rules covering his duties and performance;

c. Commits dishonest act towards the District, is convicted of a felony, or is convicted of a Class A misdemeanor criminal offense; or

d. Commits acts of moral turpitude

In the event this Agreement is terminated for cause, then the District shall have no obligations to pay.

Severance Benefits to Lambert.
Under ARTICLE. *DUTIES* OF LAMBERT, Section 3.2. Lambert shall be obligated to: I moved down to read item b. which states:

b.   Work with the Medical Staff and serve as the liaison between Medical Staff and the Board.

There is no "liaison" between the Medical Staff when Lambert shares no common respect and has no connections with nine (9) Doctors he and others in his administration label as non-supportive. Given that the nine non-supportive doctors are in the majority over the six supportive doctors should say volumes to the members of the hospital board. Whenever any manager or football coach fails to pull their team together and has dissension from the majority of players, isn't that a neglect of duties and cause of termination? Has the board ever given the CEO a written notice of 60 days to correct the problem or become terminated? The answer is NO!

BOARD MEMBERS DEFEND LAMBERT

I don't remember attending the next board meeting in November. Perhaps I chose to sit in a corner dispassionately to avoid the Administration's smear apparatus. The meeting was reported in the Wednesday, November 3, News-Herald, by Nancy Young, editor.

Garry Hannon with the BBC was enraged when Lambert referred to their group as a "loud, self-serving organization."

Garry Hannon said that the Borger Betterment Committee was spending money out of their own pockets, and they were not a loud, self-serving organization. Hannon said that the group would have results from a scientific poll in January, 2005, that was being done by Texas Tech University at a cost of $3500, being completely paid for by the BBC.

"It's going to address things like, 'What do you think of this administration?' 'What do you think of this hospital board?' 'How have they done their job?' 'Have they done it well?' "There's going to be all kinds of questions on there," Hannon said

He said he believed the hospital board would be surprised by the results, and would not get the support of the community with the administration acting the way they did in hospital board meetings.

"You're not going to get support from anyone. Once this goes out in the public, it's going to be detrimental to this hospital," Hannon said. "All I'm asking is, how long are we going to pussyfoot around and not take action with this administration? I'm asking each of you. How long?"

He said he believed the track record of the administration was terrible. He said enough was enough and it was time to take action.

"We want a hospital. How do we get there? Well, you've got to start with number one," Hannon said. "You've got to change your administration."

Board member Julia Barker spoke, "It's Norm Lambert that you want to get rid of. Why don't you just come out and say this to us? Why do you want to get rid of him? Prove to me why."

Hannon asked if it was normal for a hospital administrator to have a contract where it was almost easier to sell the hospital than it is to terminate him. He said, "It would take four votes to sell the hospital and five, with cause, to terminate the administrator."

"Why do you want to get rid of him?" Barker again asked.

Hannon asked if he had not already proved that to her. She said that he hadn't and that none of the other board members were convinced either. He asked her if this poll would be proof. She said, "it wouldn't and polls didn't mean anything to her."

"You people are going to have to quit being narrow minded," Hannon said. "Just open your eyes."

"We've got them open. That's why we're listening to all these other people," Barker said.

David Branden, board president, intervened and asked the two to calm their remarks to one another and went on to say that the poll was being conducted by a reputable organization. He said the board would have to pay attention to the information gained from the poll.

Board member Jason Vance said the board would be open to input from the community and he would not ignore a scientific poll from Texas Tech University that would give them information about the hospital and its board. "I'm interested in all that information," Vance said. "I don't have a problem with Texas Tech conducting a poll. It's certainly nothing that I fear."

Hannon said he had a copy of a personal excellence strategy plan that named doctors as being "supportive" or "non-supportive". He said the report named Borger doctors the hospital considered non-supportive.

"Do you think these doctors are going to step up and want to work with somebody, an administration that calls them non-supportive?" Hannon said.

Lambert said the report was made two months ago at a strategic planning meeting between physicians and board members, and that everyone agreed as to what went on that paper."

Hannon responded, "Let me tell you something. What are we going to do next? Are we going to have non-supporting and supportive bathrooms? I'm just tired of the no process."

"You're tired of not getting your way. That's your problem," Lambert said.

Board member (WE DON'T HAVE TO ACT) Glen Buckles came to the defense of Lambert by saying, "You're only screaming to get Lambert out of his position and had not brought them any positive feedback on the hospital moving forward. All you're screaming is for us to fire this man here. You've brought nothing positive as to what we're supposed to do in place of him or anything else."

Was Buckles blind? Wasn't he at the meeting where Tri-Lakes presented a proposal to build and manage a 25 million dollar hospital facility? What power did the administrator have over this board member? Hypnosis?

Dr. William Boyd was present at the meeting, and offered his views on the current hospital situation.

"What our community was subjected to over the last three months was not either factual in all cases. It was largely propaganda. It was a huge circus act really in the paper on a daily basis," Boyd said. "I'd like to say that our current medical staff is totally behind Norm. I don't think to a physician there's anybody who has any problems either with the way he's run his nursing staff or the quality of patient care he's provided. There has been historical issues in the past, but those are water under the bridge type of things and we've moved on from there.

"Norm has undergone some tremendous adversities in managing this hospital, largely, I would say totally, none of his doing. He didn't cause the rift in the physician community. That was an old guard versus new guard thing. It was totally brought upon by the physicians," Boyd said. "He did his best to operate under it and I think he did a great job. He's continued to, despite losing over half of our surgeries due to orthopedics who have to leave town for whatever reason, I'm mean, we're still in the black and doing okay, and we will continue to do okay, This is an opportunistic type of situation that we have here right now that this hospital was properly managed, but in this current situation, anybody would have a problem with it.

"I just think cooler heads need to prevail and you guys need to execute your judgment and don't overreact," Boyd said.

TAKE THIS "CIRCUS ACT" AND SHOVE IT!

What the Doctor said in the board meeting enraged me. I responded and this time my response was printed in the Letters to the Editor column.

November 4, 2004

We find Dr. William Boyd's views on the current hospital situation to be a tragic comedy. He is quoted in yesterday's News-Herald stating, "What our community was subjected to over the last three months was not either factual in all cases. It was largely propaganda. It was a huge circus act really in the paper on a daily basis."

We want to make it clear that what the community was subjected to was information retrieved from public documents and newspaper accounts. These documents were presented to inform the citizens of Hutchinson County about the management record at the hospital. In no way did these documents lie or attempt to deceive the general public. The process educated the voters. The $25 million bond issue was voted down because the voters were smart enough to realize that placing current management at GPCH into a new facility would be risking financial disaster for the community.

An interesting fact is that The Citizens Who Care About Hutchinson County spent less than one half the amount of advertising dollars in their "vote against" campaign than was spent by Invest In Yourself in their "vote for" campaign. The CCHC advertising campaign was produced and presented in less than 45 days. The Invest in Yourself Campaign was conceived and produced over 12 months. IYY had a tremendous advantage in presenting its case to the community. Why didn't they win the vote?

In our opinion, IIY presented propaganda. It was not revealed to taxpayers that the hospital needed the bond money to bail itself out of over one million dollars in debt to vendors and that the "generous free 11 acres" was a previously abandoned project by the Amarillo developer when the City of Borger refused to spend tax dollars to fix the flood problems on the property.

The Chairman of IIY publicly denied a conflict of interest in his pharmaceutical relationship with GPCH. Through a public record request, it was revealed that the IIY Chairman was receiving $142,000 annually in a Pharmacy Management Agreement signed between himself and Mr. Lambert. Interesting to note that the contract pays the pharmacist $2000 more than the administrator's salary. NOTE: According to a national recruiting firm, $120,000 is high for a pharmacist in a major market at a major hospital. The worth of a pharmacist in this market is $75,000. That's what the two previous pharmacists were being paid at GPCH. Section 4958 of the Internal Revenue Code, also known at the "excess benefit rules" states that "insiders" who receive "excess benefit" from transactions with a non-profit can be penalized at a penalty rate of 25% of whatever is found to be of excess. The IRS considers any "Unreasonable" Employee Compensation an excess benefit.

Dr. Boyd's statement that the process was a "huge circus act" insults the intelligence of every citizen in Hutchinson County. We have figured it out. We are aware of the misuse and mismanagement of taxpayer dollars by the current management. We are also aware that the board of directors of non-profit hospitals have a duty to care and a sworn fiduciary responsibly to the taxpayers. Dr. Boyd jesters only for those doctors the administrator compensates for their loyalty. Norm Lambert holds court over documenting doctors who he judges as being supportive and non-supportive. He has failed to work with the medical staff and serve as liaison between the Medical Staff and the Board. He has proven to be incapable of unifying all the doctors as a team.

A majority of citizens in the county do not trust the hospital administration. A 68% vote against was a mandate to terminate the present administrator. It's time for every member of the GPCH board to wake up and act in the best moral interest of the community.

How many times would this need to be repeated before these people would get it? The hospital administration lost the election. Why wouldn't they accept defeat? What was their payoff in their undying support of the CEO? It was time to "MAKE CHANGES THAT SUPPORT THE TAXPAYERS!"

JOCK LEE'S TOWN HALL MEETINGS

Things remained relatively quiet until the first week in December when Jock Lee made an announcement of a town meeting in Fritch, Texas. Veterinarian Jock Lee has his shop there and it's the precinct he represents as a hospital board member. Lee was one of the longest serving board members. He was elected to the board on May 2, 1993 and was defeated by Dr. Jerry Strecker in 1995. When Strecker was ridiculed and smeared into resigning in the middle of his term, Lee was re-appointed to fill the vacated seat.

In my opinion, Lee's track record is one of a staunch supporter of Norm Lambert. I suspected this had something to do with a "keep Norm" strategy. So, I decided to attend the meeting and see what was going on.

Only a hand full of people were in attendance. The majority in the room was filled with "pro administration" people. My idea of a town meeting was where several hundred people attended. Something like the meeting at the Borger Middle School held in August. This small number of people did not honestly represent a cross section of citizens in the county. If I had not called Dr. Jerry Strecker and two other people to attend, the comments in the newspaper would have been totally one-sided.

The News-Herald reported the meeting as a big deal by placing it on the front page in two installments. The reporter failed to mention the small number in attendance.

Jock Lee set the stage for the meeting by saying there were to be no negative comments toward the administration. This was to be a constructive, positive meeting.

My comments made were published in the News-Herald in support of a new medical facility that would provide an economic boom for Hutchinson County. These comments were based on what Tri-Lakes proposed. A new facility and new management that people could trust would support a 99 bed acute care facility.

Eck Spahich commented on the nursing/assisted living facility and said it would keep people from moving out of the county. Lee responded that there was a two year extension opportunity.

The telling paragraph in the article was, "Fritch Mayor Kevin Keener asked if a smaller facility with emergency care services and less beds would be viable option for the county. Dr. Lee said that a hospital facility was needed to back up an emergency room facility, and that it would be *a huge financial advantage if the hospital were to become a critical access facility.* He said changes would have to be made to qualify for that designation."

Had Lee tipped his hand? Would this huge financial advantage prove to be another link that connects to the whole pervasive scheme of things to keep the CEO? "Critical access facility" is limited to 25 beds. The county could support a larger 99 bed acute care facility that generates more patients, more income and more jobs. Was the huge financial advantage in favor of the administration or the citizens in the county?

In my professional opinion, Lee's town hall meeting was a tactic to lead the public astray. The News-Herald had omitted reporting the low attendance and all of Dr. Jerry Strecker's comments in the meeting.

Note: I did complain to the News-Herald about not reporting the low attendance.

DEMENTIA ESCALATES OUT OF CONTROL

On Wednesday, December 15th at 11:30 AM, I called my mother to check in. She said, "I want you to come and get me. I asked why and she said, "I'll tell you when you get here." When I arrived at the house, she was standing outside waiting. She said, "I called 911 because your Dad got angry when he got out of bed, walked into the living room and saw the curtains open. He threw a chair across the room."

Whenever, he got up around 10:30 to 11:00 each day, we closed the curtains before he saw them open. This morning they were open and he flew into a rage. She said that two officers arrived and talked with my Dad

I drove her to my sister's house. She stayed there while I drove to speak to the Chief of Police about what happened. I was in his office sometime after 1:00 PM talking with him, when his phone rang. It was Dad on the other line. When Chief Adams hung up from talking, he looked at me and asked if my Dad had Dementia?

I explained he had been diagnosed by a neurologist as having Alzheimer's disease and been told not to drive. I also brought up that my father had recently run a red light but denied it and had the ticket dismissed. Chief Adams said, "There were two witness that saw him run the light and that the ticket should not have been dismissed."

I went back to my sister's house and waited for her and my mother to return from Amarillo. Mother and I stayed there until about 10:30 and decided to go back home. When we arrived, Dad was already asleep and nothing occurred.

This was really a bad situation because I realized that Dad would hold a grudge. Sure enough, two days later he was taunting mother by hitting on the wall and saying, "Go ahead call them!" I walked upstairs as I heard him yelling at her saying, "Call the police again. I just don't give a damn. That's just the way it is. ARE YOU GOING TO CALL THE POLICE!"

At the top of the stairs, I looked at him and said, "If you get out of hand I may."

Turning to look at me he said, "I'm not out of hand, this is my house. I don't need your ass up here. I don't need your presence!"

"Why can't you be reasonable. Screaming and yelling isn't working," I said.

"I'm not screaming and yelling. You came up here and sat your ass down and you heard me. Get your ass back down stairs if you don't want to hear it. Anytime my wife calls up and cops on me that's a bunch of bullshit."

Mother went to her bedroom and I went down stairs to get away from him. I thought things were only going to get worse from this point. Five days later, Mother found out that Dad was at the Bank. I have never seen her more hurt and angry at the same time. He was trying to totally control her by taking all finances away. In the following two days, she had me take her to remove funds from savings, open her own checking account, and have her social security check deposited into the account each month. It was the first time in 60 years that she had a personal checking account.

The next day I drove her to see a local attorney who recommended a divorce attorney in Amarillo.

It's impossible to describe the agony of going through this situation with parents who you love. Mother was afraid to live alone with him because of past experiences and present explosive rages.

WITHOUT OPENNESS THE PUBLIC WILL LOSE CONFIDENCE IN ANY GOVERNMENT INSTITITION.

"ATTORNEY GENERAL: GPCH MUST PRODUCE RECORDS" screamed across the front page of the News-Herald on Tuesday, December 28, 2004. The headline was followed by a half page article explaining how the Texas Attorney General's Office had ruled against Golden Plains and in favor of Citizens Who Care About Hutchinson County.

The first open document record request we received on August 21, 2004, revealed the hospital pharmacist contract. Following the publishing of that information, GPCH Administration blocked the second open document request by sending a letter to the Texas Attorney General's office claiming "harassment".

Was this a concocted fictitious legal complaint to curb open records and free speech? I wondered if the hospital attorney wrote the letter in behalf of the Administration and if so, what was the cost to taxpayers in legal fees?

The letter effectively delayed records for 4 months and denied Citizens Who Care About Hutchinson County more information for possible use in the "against" campaign.

This wasn't the first time that Golden Plains under the leadership of Norm Lambert had resisted being open to the public and received adverse publicity.

On March 17, 1999, the front page of News-Herald reported HOSPITAL CHOOSES OPENNESS. The newspaper had challenged the hospital about a closed meeting and Lambert canceled an un-posted, closed finance and planning meeting after talking to Chairman Ken Crain. Lambert addressed the issue of having a closed meeting by saying, "We are not trying to break any law. There is no intent to hide anything."

In the same 1999 article, Jock Lee was quoted saying, "Trust is a big word. People should trust elected officials to do the job. We should take trust seriously."

The article also stated, "In January (1999), results of the community survey by Opinions Unlimited, Inc. were made public. According to the report, about ***one-third of the residents have a negative attitude toward GPCH.***"*

DID LAMBERT, LEE, MITCHELL AND OTHERS BELIEVE REPEATING SIMILAR BEHAVIOR FIVE YEARS LATER WOULD INCREASE PUBLIC TRUST? DIDN'T A FAMOUS PSYCHIATRIST SAY, "MANAGEMENT THAT REPEATS THE SAME MISTAKES WITH NEGATIVE RESULTS OVER AND OVER IS CALLED INSANE"?

It's was impossible for GPCH to buy a half page advertisement on the front page of the News-Herald to build a positive image. Management's letter to block our open document

---

*   *If the same survey was conducted today, would it show that two-thirds of residents have a negative attitude toward GPCH?*

request, effectively led to the same impact of a half page advertorial, negatively promoting the hospital. And when Lambert complained to the News-Herald that he was disappointed in the coverage, he inadvertently produced another half page negative advertorial for Golden Plains.

The Attorney General's Office said to Lambert's administration, "A governmental body may not refuse to comply with a request on the grounds of administrative inconvenience. Thus, we have no choice but to order you to release the requested information."

There are three reasons not to follow open government laws. Some try to hide information in violation of the law, some build barriers that make it difficult to get information, and some are ignorant or claim to be ignorant of what the law requires.

The News-Herald couldn't control news from the Texas Attorney General's Office. It was two days of Victory for the Citizens Who Care About Hutchinson County and two days of frustration for the hospital administrator and his good ol' boys.

HUTCHINSON COUNTY CRISIS CENTER

We entered the Safe Shelter while Dad was served with papers from the Sheriffs Department and remained there until we could safely return to the house. The Crisis Center did an outstanding job of counseling with Mother. It is a crucial service for women of all ages in Hutchinson County.

They explained that physical assaults may occur only once or occasionally but, they instill threat of future violent attacks and allow the abuser to take control of the woman's life and circumstances.

Dad had become a case study for elder abuse. He used power and control to intimidate, threaten, inflict economic abuse (taking away access to family income) making her ask for money, treating her like a servant and acting like master of the castle, putting her down, calling her names, humiliating her, isolating her by attempting to control what she did, whom she sees, and where she goes. He would deny and blame her by making light of the abuse and saying she was the cause. Their relationship needed counseling years ago and now with dementia leading to Alzheimer's it was dangerously going off the chart.

It wasn't a time to look the other way and deny the problem. My mother was at risk and I would do whatever it took to help keep her safe.

CHAPTER TWENTY ONE

SELL THE HOSPITAL???

Front page news broke on January 13, 2005. Sale of Golden Plains Community Hospital is under consideration. The board of directors is planning to solicit proposals to purchase and manage the existing hospital. The intention is to "then, in due time, to construct, own and operate a general acute care hospital in Hutchinson County," according to the Request for Proposal plan discussed during Monday night's HCHD board meeting.

Failure of the September bond election to build the new medical facility with tax dollars is the reason the board is considering the action.

A committee of board members has worked on the proposed RFP plan consisting of Jason Vance, Ed Davis and Dr. Jock Lee. CEO Norm Lambert and GPCH attorney Leon Mitchell were also consulted, said Board Chairman David Brandon.

The proposals will be sought from health care entities experienced in the operation of general acute care hospitals, and a company experienced in evaluating medical RFP's is under consideration to receive the proposals.

Brandon explained why the board is working to obtain proposals to replace the structure built originally in 1937. Plumbing and electrical problems at the facility have been major expenditures over the years.

"What brought us to this point is the failed bond issue—indicating for a large part— maybe not totally—that the vote was against additional taxes," said Brandon Wednesday afternoon. "Now, if we can't go to the taxpayers to get the capital funds needed to build the building, then what do we do? The hospital financials are not adequate to support revenue bonds to build a new hospital."

"So, one of the alternatives to get a new hospital built is to have somebody purchase the hospital with a firm commitment of building a new building with a 2-4 year time frame." He said.

We have other options that we are considering and moving forward on. One is the critical access hospital designation. That is a federal government program that will restrict the number of beds and average hours of stay in a rural situation," he said. He said that Medicare and the federal government will increase the reimbursement of Medicare, and said that it would increase the local hospital's income by about $500,000.

Brandon said the plan would effect the doctors because of the critical access status, but that several (supportive) doctors met with the board Tuesday night and are in favor of the plan.

THE REQUEST FOR PROPOSALS

Under the first point, minimum qualifications to respond, the following requirements are listed:

1. At least ten (10) years experience in the provision of hospital services.
2. Prior experience in a community hospital acquisition with resulting service enhancements and capital improvements to the acquired community hospital.
3. Average net patient revenues for the preceding three fiscal years of at least $50 million per year.
4. Total fund balances or net worth in the aggregate as of December 31, 2004, of at least $75 million as verified by a certified audit.
5. An exceptional record of community service and participation in those service areas in which its hospitals are operated.

The proposal says, "a respondent may request a waiver by the board of directors in respect to any requirement contained in this section. The grant of a waiver shall be solely in the discretion of the board of directors."

The RFP set very high standards and the two groups who were interested would have to apply for waivers. The amount of money (7-10 million) the board was requiring in escrow was unreasonably high. This wasn't the "Jewel of the Panhandle" in health care facilities for sale. It was a financially burdened hospital where less than a third of the market trusted its services.

KRISPY KREME THE CEO

We finally lucked out and got a Guest Column in the News-Herald on January 22-23 weekend edition in a response to the RFP.

It's great news that GPCH board of director's are moving forward with a request for proposals to privately owned groups to purchase and manage Golden Plains Community Hospital. Finally, the GPCH board may be acting in support of the taxpayers in the county.

Taxpayers spoke loudly on 9-11-2004 when the $25 million bond proposal was defeated by voters by a 2-1 margin. It's been debated whether the bond failed because of a record of mismanagement or because of taxes. The campaign against the bond educated voters about the past management failures' . . . decisions that have wasted hundreds of thousands of dollars, alienated physicians, and created mistrust of the hospital. Also, voters learned that there are approximately 3700 Seniors in Hutchinson County who would have been unnecessarily burdened with a tax increase.

I remember when "Invest in Yourself" held a town meeting at Borger High School and one of the board members addressed this question from a concerned citizen— "Has the hospital board looked into private enterprise to invest and build a new hospital where the taxpayers would not be burdened?" The board member's answer was, "We retain Quorum as our consultant and they have informed us that our community is under the radar."

Isn't it interesting how more effective the radar became when someone else switched it on. Now it's reported that 3 groups are interested in investing in our community. The plan at the last board meeting is to send out the request for proposals throughout the United States. One of the groups, Tri-Lakes was contacted by BBC and another, Blackhawk Healthcare, contacted me before contacting GPCH to make a presentation. I was most impressed by the presentation made by Tri-Lakes. They offered to build a new hospital and assisted living facility with 25 million dollars of their own money. They said they would sign a 20 year contract agreement not to sell. They have an impressive, successful track record in a rural community that matches the needs of our community. They place physicians first and provide them a percentage of ownership. The physicians work together as "owners." They are not manipulated or segregated by management as supportive and non-supportive doctors as identified by a document distributed by the present GPCH administration.

At the board meeting on Monday, January 10, 2005, it was reported that the hospital revenues are one million dollars down from the same reporting period last year. This financial condition was blamed on the season and the absence of flu cases. Patient volume has decreased and the tax revenue will end on January 31.

Lambert said that physician recruitment is a solution and used Dr. Ribero as an example of the income his surgeries brought into the hospital. How can the board members really buy this solution based on this administrator's past recruitment record?

How many doctors will the administrator need to recruit before the board sees that his management style is not working? There have been 8 doctors recruited who have left our community over the last 3-4 years. This is a tremendous cost to our community? Today, the local surgeons who stay here find it necessary to take their patients to Pampa and Dumas.

A motion was made and approved by the board for a $400,000 line of credit from Wells Fargo Bank. One of the members stated, "This is what businesses do." My response was that owners of businesses will cut their salaries in order to keep from laying off employees. The board said that administrative staff salaries have been decreased by 10%. The question I failed to ask and would like an answer to is; will administrative staff be reviewed for layoffs before other staff employees?

Will the administrator continue to state that in "no way" will he take a cut in his salary as stated in the board meeting on October 4, 2004. It would be a shame to lay off nursing and other staff. These people are the backbone of the hospital. They need and deserve their jobs.

Again, we would like to remind GPCH administration and its board of directors they are working for a non-profit organization supported by taxpayers. It's in the public good to inform everyone in the county about decisions made in open GPCH board meetings. We believe it's crucial for citizens to know whenever the hospital board makes a decision to borrow $400,000 as they did the Jan 10, 2005 meeting. We question if this places more financial burdens on the taxpayers to save a sinking ship.

We request good management decisions and quick actions. It concerns us when Mr. Lambert reports to the Amarillo Globe News on January 18 that, "It will take another two to three months to finalize request for proposal and 6 months before any concrete action."

It appears the board is continuing to allow Lambert's actions to determine the time frame. We hope this is not what is happening. As we now look at final options, are the board members now prepared to wait months for responses when during the bond issue, this same board talked about how the need was now? Can we really afford to waste almost another year?

In October 2004, a petition of 200 names to remove the administrator was presented to the GPCH board. The board was asked, "how many names will it take to act in support of the citizens". One board member's reply was that "we don't have to act on anything." We hope this attitude has changed. The majority of citizens in Hutchinson County do not want to continue wondering why the motives of some board members excuse poor management that continues to operate on excuses.

GPCH board members can learn what "businesses really do" by looking at some recent stories from the Wall Street Journal. Last week the board of directors of Krispy Kreme Donuts forced the CEO to resign. Following his resignation, their stock dramatically increased. The GPCH board can choose to learn from Krispy Kreme or they can continue to behave like the board of directors of an Enron. Your stockholders (68% majority of taxpayers in the county) are watching you.

LIVE FROM GOLDEN PLAINS . . . "BAGDAD BOB"

Almost 5 months following the bond election, Garry Hannon expressed his frustration in the Letters to the Editor in the Tuesday, January 25, 2005.

"In my last letter, I tried to be as polite and reserved as possible. With new information, however, I cannot keep from calling it as I see it. First, the Request for Proposal (RFP) Is complete. It is my opinion that Mr. Lambert and a few board members are holding up progress once again because they can't decide if they want to hire an outside firm, Stroudwater & Associates, to oversee the RFP process. When are they going to stand on their own two feet and do something for themselves. They have spent hundreds of thousand dollars to hire outside firms to do their jobs. What are we paying management to do?? Citizens, we are running out of time and money. At the last board meeting, the board approved a $400,000 line of credit, a loan, to keep this sinking ship afloat. Has this money already been accessed? If so, what for? What happens when this money runs out in 30 to 60 days? Answer: We are deeper in debt. It doesn't take a CEO or CFO to figure that out. Citizens, do you remember about 6 months ago that "time was of the essence", we need to pass the bond issue, our nursing home license will expire in

November . . . ? Isn't it odd that since the bond issue has failed, there is no rush. Are we going to take our time while the hospital goes deeper into debt?

There are private corporations interested in Hutchinson County. One of the corporations showing great interest is the group from Batesville, Mississippi who are currently operating Tri-Lakes Medical Center. I spoke to their COO, Ray Shoemaker last week. He called to tell me he was very excited that they had made another $500,000 bond payment and they had $1.2 million in operating cash. They took a struggling hospital on the verge of bankruptcy, and within 2 years have got things totally turned around. These numbers speak volumes—they know what they are doing.

Lastly, several hospital employees have called me and said they are beginning to see that they have been mislead throughout this whole situation with the hospital. Their hours are being cut. They are concerned for their jobs. Under the current management, I feel they have every reason to be concerned.

This hospital management reminds me of "Bagdad Bob" when he was assuring the Iraqi people that everything was OK while bombs fell all around them."

DISGRUNTLED EMPLOYEES

Reading about hospital employees reporting they were mislead throughout the whole situation at the hospital, I remembered this anonymous e-mail I received from AFRAID TO TELL

Subject: Reply to Newspaper in Small Texas Town Suppresses Truth about Child Pornography in Hospital
To: glennbaxter@horizonsouthwest.com

Dear Glenn Baxter,

I was a mid-level manager @ GPCH and was a victim of the bloody downsizing led by Norm Lambert in 1997. I thoroughly support your efforts and could help you with old information but am afraid to come forward. When I was terminated or what was fancifully called "laid-off" I lost my cool and told Lambert what I thought of him and his Gestapo techniques. He and his puppets immediately let loose a vicious campaign to ruin my reputation both professionally and personally. They succeeded professionally. I was planning on leaving the area within a month when he did me dirty so he could have saved himself the trouble but had to destroy me because we didn't like each other at all.

Since I left, I have had trouble getting a job because I cannot get a good reference at GPCH. He does not break the law by direct liable statements. Rather he says that he has nothing to say about "that person". That says it all. The message is given and I don't get the job. I have given up and haven't tried in years because of what he did to me personally. I cannot take legal action against him nor can I come forward without destroying my marriage and relationship with my family. His lies and ability to sway others to believe them are a constant dark cloud over my head.

INSIDER INFORMATION

I received a copy of a letter Norm Lambert had circulated throughout the hospital to employees. Employees were starting to worry about their jobs and distrust of the Administration was increasing. I responded through Letters to the Editor on January 26, 2005.

We have received a copy of a letter Mr. Lambert has written and distributed to employees at GPCH. It's important to share this letter and comments with concerned citizens in Hutchinson County. Citizens are the owners of this tax supported entity and they deserve an inside view of how the administrator is managing their property.

The CEO states in his first paragraph, "Media coverage of events at GPCH has gotten a little out of control lately, so this prompts me to write to you directly. First, let me apologize to you for not communicating better and sooner. I do believe we do need to communicate to our employees about what is going on at your hospital before you hear things through the rumor mill."

This paragraph brings up several questions. Is it true as reported in the January 10, 2004 board meeting that the hospital revenues are one million dollars down from the same reporting period last year? Is it true that the hospital board approved a $400,000 line of credit loan? Is it true that Lambert is not accountable for the financial condition of GPCH? Is it true that he has failed to work with the Medical Staff and serve as the liaison between all Medical Staff and the Board? Is it true that in the CEO's "strategic performance excellence" plan for GPCH segregated physicians by labeling them supportive and non-supportive of the hospital?

Is the rumor true that the CEO is looking for another job. It must be difficult finding a hospital in another small community that will pay $140,000 annually plus bonuses and benefits? Lambert's been at GPCH for 8 years. High performance CEO's at hospitals generally only stay for 3 years because head hunters hire them away at increased salaries and benefits.

The shareholders (taxpayers) would love to hear the CEO spin a story that explains how he can be the only CEO in America that is not accountable and cannot be forced to resign for financial negligence.

It's true that only 6 (supportive) physicians attended his meeting with the board to discuss a Critical Access Hospital proposal. A majority of 9 physicians did not attend the meeting. It appears that the majority of physicians do not support the CEO, or Critical Access Hospital because he labels them as non-supporters.

The letter to the employees goes on to state, "A Critical Access Hospital can only have 25 licensed beds. GPCH now has 99 licensed beds, but only operates 47 beds."

Why didn't the CEO communicate to the employees that only about 50 % of the them will be needed for a 25 bed facility. There will be layoffs. He doesn't communicate to the employees why his low performance as a CEO will not successfully fill all 99 beds. Is down sizing to a Critical Access Hospital a ploy to keep Lambert's salary and benefits? Is it a band aid for a sinking ship?

The offer is on the table to invest approximately $25 million in a hospital and assisted living center for our community. Tri Lakes has said it will invest the money and sign a contract with the Hospital District not to sell their new hospital for 20 years. (If they should fail, the county would get a new hospital.) A new hospital with a new administration would potentially attract 60,000 patients in the surrounding area. It would hire more employees. It would be a facility that could handle a major disaster from one of our local plant facilities.

If the GPCH board really wants to save jobs and prevent layoffs, please act quickly in the best interest of the community. I recall Mr. Lambert stating in an IIY meeting, that if someone would give the community $25 million, they would gladly take it. It's interesting how his thinking changes when he won't be in control.

EMPLOYEES SPEAK OUT

In the previous month, numerous employees came forward when they were terminated at Golden Plains. These are interviews with two of them:

Debbie Knight worked at the hospital pharmacist's pharmacy for eight years and at Golden Plains for two years. Francis Atwood was hired as the office manager at Golden Plains. Both were very candid in sharing information and their experiences.

Debbie: They hired a contractor to come in and she was supposed to help get caught up for the fiscal year end. I had all the commercial accounts. The VA people who would take forever to pay anyway, their paper you know is horrible. The contractor was hired to come in and do the old follow up so we could focus on everything we could collect electronically or was paid in ten days like Aetna and some of the bigger ones. And this contractor came in and within a month had gotten our office business manager, Francis (Atwood) fired. Larhonda had been there less than a year. They hired the marketing director's daughter and got rid of Larhonda. I knew I was next and they would have total control.

Question: What happened when you were laid off?

Debbie: I was traumatized. When I do a job I feel it's a reflection of me so I take it real seriously. And I was traumatized and I called her back and said nothing you said on that paper is factual. What are you doing? "Well, the CFO wanted you gone." So, I just finally said fine and so she said "I'll talk to human resources and go ahead and file your unemployment. I said I was going to file unemployment because there was no justification as far as I'm concerned for my termination because I had a work list. I had documentation for everything I'd done. So, I filed my unemployment and I get a letter back from unemployment saying they (GPCH) were fighting it and that I wasn't productive therefore I wasn't going to get unemployment. I thought no way so I appealed it and had a hearing.

Question: What happened to Francis Atwood?

Debbie: I don't know how she (contractor) got Francis out of there. Because Francis brought the contractor in here. Francis told me she knew this person when she worked in Spearman. She called and asked her to clean up for us so we could get it done by the end of the fiscal year. That's what she was supposed to be there for. Now, what she did to Francis I don't know because Francis called me after I got fired and said that they were training a girl to take my place for 3 weeks before they let me go.

She (Francis) had come to me and Larhonda and kept asking us what kind of records could we get because Larhonda was just like me. Everything we did we had paper for. We were big on CYA not because anybody was on us, just that I've always done that and Larhonda was the same way. And she (Francis) would come and say "What do you know about this account and why wasn't it written off?" The only time you're supposed to write one off is if we've messed up the billing. We made a big mistake or they've made it in surgery or whatever and it comes from the administration. She wanted to know why a few accounts were written off. We hadn't requested them and all we knew was that maybe she was looking into things.

Question: What do think of advertising expenditures?

Debbie: I mean you know, there were standard ads that doctors are pictured in each month and other than that when they were fighting for the hospital to stay here they would to do the little Golden Plains Talk. (Testimonial patients in favor of hospital) 95% of the people in there were either working for the hospital or married to someone working for the hospital or the son or daughter of someone who worked in the hospital. You know and after a while some of the people thought it was very nice but find someone who's not connected in some way. I thought it was a waste of money.

Question: I wonder how the hospital stays afloat?

Debbie: I don't know how they stay afloat. When I was doing billing we would go to meetings and they would say, it's because the business office isn't billing things out. So, I started way back last July, Carolyn when she posted everyday, she made a sheet that showed how much cash Maria got that was on accounts, how many commercial checks, how many Medicare checks, how many

Medicaid checks, on one sheet and I started keeping the totals because that was the solid money that we as a business office collected.

There had to be things they could have cut back on. You know having 6 nurses up there while we got one or two patients. To me that makes no sense, but what do I know?

Question: How does it run like that?

Debbie: I don't know, but my question was how much does it take, what dollar amount does it take to run this hospital. And I never got an answer. So once I started keeping those logs and I believe it made me a target. Because you don't ever question and that was one thing the CFO hated. He and I clashed from day one.

Question: Did you ask him that question?

Debbie: Yes, how much does it take and I asked him every time. Tell me so that maybe we can make a suggestion.

When they started changing and when they started changing people's jobs like Carolyn. You know she posted forever, then they take that away from her. You know they're taking the people who have the knowledge or just getting rid of them . . . that's not right. They can't all be stupid to the fact that that's not going to work. I find it hard to believe that it's going to work.

Response: You're a disgruntled employee now.

Debbie: Exactly, I'm just making it up. I'm not, and I do have documents that show what I did, what we did for months and how much we collected. They were going to file charges against me until they found out I was looking for a civil lawyer to file against them personally and against the hospital. I mean they have as far as I'm concerned in a town this small basically ruined my reputation as a respected employee. I did do my job and they didn't count on me taking my records this time. This time I had them because I took them home with me. I wasn't going to get caught there . . . and I knew things were going downhill.

Question: You supported IIY. Afterwards, what did you think of management?

Debbie: You're right and you've nailed it (management problem) When I was there I thought how can he know that management is the biggest problem? But it is!

You know when we were in it and when it started of course we knew there were problems and asked why are they picking on management. But then when you see things progressively happen and you get back you say oh man did they nail it.

Question: You have a CEO and you got all these CFO's and you find you can't keep one, isn't that a sign that things aren't running smoothly?

Debbie: In the two years that I was employed there we went through 4 business office managers. And there were times when we went without a business manager. They just couldn't find one. It was bizarre! Then there was one named Tom who was there for a total of two weeks.

Question: So when you left, what was the condition of things.

Debbie: It was bad. They've taken the people who have the expertise in one field and that's what they're good at and moved them. You know you can't be productive if you're doing something that's not familiar. You've got 5 people doing things that aren't familiar. When they started changing people's jobs like Carolyn. She posted forever and they take that away from her. They're taking the people who have the knowledge or just getting rid of them . . . that's not right. They can't all be stupid to the fact that it's not going to work. I find it hard to believe that it's going to work.

Francis Atwood's Account

"I had worked as the business manager in the hospital in Spearman, Texas. When I came to Golden Plains, Charles Powell was the CFO who hired me as the office manager. Then before long, he got so stressed over things that he resigned.

I was trained as a certified coder for hospital accounting. I had been through the office manager side and billing side of converting the hospital in Spearman into a Critical Access Hospital. It's a whole different ball game. I was and could have been more of an asset because GPCH was converting to CAH. But, I was abruptly fired.

They just up and fired me with no warning or anything. I didn't even meet the criteria for immediate termination and they didn't follow the normal process. I just said some stuff and they just didn't like what I said or questions I was asking.

Before I got there, Misty had never had anybody in the business office show her what the numbers meant she was entering. She didn't have the big picture. So when I went to her and said this is the big picture. We should be doing better than what these financial statements show because this is how much I see we have in payments, yet here what's showing in the General Ledger. Misty and I went to Norm and asked him what are these numbers. What are they tied to and where are they going. And, then all of a sudden BAM neither one of us are there.

I did a report because they were questioning why the Accounts Receivables was dropping. The girl before me was just writing things off the books. It wasn't being collected, nothing was being done. I asked, why are you writing this off and it's not on the Accounts Receivable. You're not going to write off another damn thing until we figure out where we are going to enter it in the books.

It took me six months to get everything caught up that she had written off. For over a year she was writing stuff off the accounts receivable and putting it a bad debt account. We were getting complaints that patients didn't receive a statement for two years. These people (patients) she was writing off never received anything.

It was a mess! I had to fix the computer system, fix the billing and all other things. Everything was set up on a cycle so it will be turned over to bad debt and everything will be written off by September. I put everything in a report to Norm.

Then, they wanted to bring Quorum in to spend more money on a business office analysis. Why are we going to spend more money with Quorum when we are all ready paying them $200,000 a year? Guess what Quorum's report said, the exact same thing I'd given to Lambert three weeks earlier. The guy who came in from Quorum said I was on the right track.

There were only so many hours in a day and only so much that you can clean up in one time. Why do they spend all the money with Quorum. I just don't understand it. This hospital pays out a tremendous amount of money in outside services. *Why was there a $200,000 contract for Quorum? Why are they paying them when there's an Administrator getting paid over $140,000?* I brought this up several times . . . what are we paying Quorum to do?

You can't fix an eight year problem in a year. When the end of September came, what I said should be done was done. We were in the right ledger accounts . . . you just can't write stuff off and put it somewhere and that's what was happening.

Lambert has been there long enough to where the hospital should be in better shape. In my opinion, his scapegoats have been the CFO turnover. Some of them may be gone because god knows what reason. I heard stories about Larry Langley and wondered why Norm hired him.

The employees know there is no loyalty given back to them from the hospital administration. I had busted my ass all year and there was light near the end of the tunnel. Then I got fired."

Who would disagree that these two ex employees describe inadequacies in record keeping, control weaknesses, waste, inefficiency, a turnover in office managers, turnover in CFO's and other experienced accounting employees?

CHAPTER TWENTY TWO

MOVE OVER AL PACINO: BLACKBALLED BY THE COUNTY COMMISSIONERS

I read in disbelief the headline and story on the front page of the News Herald on January 26, stating, COMMISSION APPROVES TWO, DISAPPROVES ONE TO THE HCHC.

The one in the headline was yours truly. The article stated that two people were approved and a third, Glenn Baxter was unanimously rejected by the commissioner's court. How did I rate front page coverage on such a silly thing as attempting to volunteer for a committee? I had not stolen anything or committed a crime. This wasn't a story about a METH BUST! News about Jana Crain's $20,000 embezzlement during the time her husband (appointed by the commissioner's court) served on the hospital board and was co-treasurer of the Gateway Booster Club did deserve front page news. THIS DID NOT!

I immediately wrote and e-mailed this response to the Letters to the Editor.

It's no surprise that the Hutchinson County Commissioners decided against approving me to the historical commission. It had slipped my mind that the Museum Director had mentioned he wanted me to serve on the commission. I'm not disappointed. It's no big deal. I will continue to support the museum.

Since the defeat of the bond issue, I've visited with three commissioners over the telephone. I asked for their input about GPCH and questioned their authority over the hospital district. In my opinion, they do not support the administration at GPCH. Their non-political stance in not publicly expressing their views is questionable. Maybe they think it's safer to say nothing when public servants can be hired and fired by voters at the polls. It would be political suicide to go against a 68% majority of the voters in the county!

The big deal is to be black balled by a few petty county commissioners. Voters in the county remember that R.D. Corneilson campaigned in support of the 25 million dollar hospital bond. He was the only commissioner who publicly endorsed INVEST IN YOURSELF. Many Senior Citizens who voted for Corneilson in the last county election were mad and have said they would not vote for him again. In fact, some of his fellow church members were upset about his parking a political sign on a trailer in front of the church on a Saturday during the IIY campaign. They felt their church should not be involved in a political campaign; unlike the First Baptist Church where the pastor made an Invest in Yourself sales pitch to the County Commissioner's Court in what appeared to be an effort to influence endorsements from all 4 Commissioners.

Judge Worsham's no vote is no surprise. He regularly attends the Rotary Club with his other cronies . . . Corneilson, Lambert, and Moore. As a former member, I can attest that each week these individuals stand up and recite the Rotarian's 4-WAY TEST . . . IS IT THE TRUTH, IS IT FAIR TO ALL CONCERNED, and so forth.

Today, the question is how many voters in Hutchinson County believe the truth was presented by Invest In Yourself and how many voters believe it would have been fair to all concerned?

The majority in the county spoke. Voters were not stupid. My resignation from Rotary speaks out that I despise hypocrisy, dishonesty and righteousness.

Eddie Whittington was absent. Red Isbell abstained from voting. Jerry Hefner's no vote surprised me. I respect him. I called him by telephone and he said he voted no because he felt I did not have time to serve. He is partially right! Thinking it over, it's best to stay focused on the hospital. The voters need to be informed whenever the board approves a $400,000 line of credit to keep the hospital open. It's a foolish attempt to keep Mr. Lambert afloat. Perhaps Mr. Hefner and other commissioners will do what is in the best interest of the county and appoint me to the hospital board of directors. My letter will be coming at the appropriate time!

After I called three of the County Commissioners, I called the editor to correct her article. She wrote, "The News Herald incorrectly reported in Wednesday's edition that Red Isbell voted against appointing Glenn Baxter. Isbell abstained on the vote while three other members on the commissioner's court voted against it. The remaining member was not at the meeting."

Some of the same good ol' boys who wouldn't allow Dr. Jerry Strecker to speak had finally found a way to strike against me.

A funny thing happened later that week while watching the movie "Dick Tracy". Al Pacino was playing Big Boy, the mob boss. He was seated at the head of a conference table with fellow members of his gang. He said, "We're going to take over this town. We all are going to start dressing like bankers and join the Rotary Club."

BORGER-NEWS HERALD GETS NEW PUBLISHER

In the January 26, edition a new Publisher L.W. McCall was announced. After reading the article I couldn't keep from wondering why the past Publisher, Michael Wright left and what shape the local news would take with the new Publisher.

"WE ARE NOTHING MORE THAN WELL-INTENTIONED PEOPLE!"

The above statement made by board member Jock Lee caught my eye in the middle of a front page article in the News-Herald on Friday January 28, 2005. How many people in the county would buy this statement? Where were the good intentions in paying the CFO severance pay and freedom to prey on other innocent children.

Lee had served on the board (without pay) as a "YES" man to Norm Lambert throughout the "Child Pornography" and every debacle that impacted the public trust. He served on the board when unkind things were done to others.

Now, he expects every citizen to forget his past history on the hospital board and accept him and others as well intentioned people who would only do good kind things for others. Why couldn't he see that Golden Plains had bankrupted their trust with the public in Hutchinson County?

The headline of the article was, "Lee answers questions about status of GPCH" and the story covered another town meeting led by the board member. This time, the newspaper reported a total of *only 7 people* including the media.

Now that's fair and honest reporting!

Again the Critical Access Hospital application and the reasons for GPCH applying for the status was covered in the meeting. Knowing the past history of Golden Plains, was Jock Lee spearheading the "critical access hospital" designation in an attempt to shape public opinion as a tactic to keep the CEO? Was a "Critical Access Hospital" going to be the salvation of the Teflon administrator?

I fired off the following "political humor" opinion letter that was never printed in the News-Herald. *Maybe the editor lacks a sense of humor.*

VET FROM FRITCH IS BARKING UP WRONG TREE

I would like to address Jock Lee's statement from the January 28, 2005 News Herald that a "committee composed of representatives of administration, medical staff and board members has been formed to address concerns of the medical staff . . . . the committee is attempting to get doctors together some time next week to discuss the concerns of physicians."

This is what I call unrealistic "dogged determination." Mr. Lee should know that he is barking up the wrong tree. He has a record as the strongest advocate and mouth piece for Norm Lambert since he has served on the board. He's been a sidekick to the administrator and supported him at almost every turn. There is no record of Mr. Lee disagreeing with "no blame" Norm when the administration has segregated doctors who do not agree with the administration tactics.

Mr. Lee says that we have to all pull together. He's 10 years too late with his "pull together" idea. No self respecting doctor who has dealt with "IT'S MY WAY OR THE HIGHWAY NORM" is going to believe this.

The number one problem with GPCH is the CEO. The solution is that he needs to go. Our community needs a replacement who respects and knows how to inspire doctors. We need high performance, quality health care from a hospital rather than low performance that operates in the red. Mr. Lee, if it's in your heart to sincerely serve your community and support a positive change toward the future, stop saying yes to the CEO. Show us that you really care!

SURVEY RESULTS REPORTED IN NEWS-HERALD

It was another victory for Citizens Who Care About Hutchinson County when the Texas Tech survey was printed on the front page of the News-Herald on the weekend of March 19-20, 2005. The survey showed the vote was 33.1 percent against management and 22.1 percent against a tax increase.

A follow up article in the next day's paper stated that 22.4 percent said their first choice was to sell the hospital with a long term contract in place. The favorable rating of the three citizen action committees were Citizens Who Care about Hutchinson County at 4.28, Borger Betterment Committee at 3.82, and Invest in Yourself at 3.71.

Remember the hospital pharmacist was quoted that he wished people would "get the facts" and now the facts were right in front of their faces. Now, would the board members act in support of the wishes of the majority of taxpayers?

This was an opportunity to release a victory statement to the News-Herald.

IMMEDIATE RELEASE March 23, 2005
SURVEY SAYS . . . POOR MANAGEMENT WAS THE NUMBER ONE REASON THE HOSPITAL BOND ISSUE WAS DEFEATED.

Shouldn't this have been the lead headline in the Borger News-Herald in the Weekend Edition?

Certainly, the majority of voters in the county have not forgotten when GPCH Board member Glenn Buckles proclaimed that the board "didn't have to act on anything" when it came to the management. His statement was recorded on television and in both area newspapers. Other board members proclaimed that the defeat had nothing to do with management. They stated that the bond issue was defeated because voters did not want a tax increase.

The Texas Tech Survey commissioned by the BBC revealed that 33.1 percent voted no because of the poor management record and 22.I percent voted no because of a tax increase. The BBC reported to me that when this survey was presented to the GPCH board, one of the board members claimed that The Citizens Who Care About Hutchinson County misinformed the public. As the Chairman of this committee, I have worked hard to be honest and outspoken in presenting information in past ads and opinion articles. It's no surprise to still hear a board member continue to use the word "MISINFORMED" as a tactic to continue support for Mr. Lambert.

Taxpayers in this county have not and do not appreciate the back room deals, secrecy and politics as usual in support of the inadequate leadership at GPCH. Open records request revealed that excessive benefits have been paid and are continuing to be paid in a contract to a pharmacist. After this was revealed, GPCH impeded open records and was ruled against by the Attorney General's Office. "Government officials are stewards of the public trust, and have a duty to be as transparent as possible in the way the public's business is conducted," quotes Texas Attorney General in Borger News Herald's Wednesday edition.

The majority of the public do not trust the stewardship at GPCH. It's time that the GPCH board puts the interest of taxpayers above their self-interest and place value on openness that gets to the truth. I invite any individual, GPCH board member or County Commissioner to contact me with what they claim is "misinformation." I will gladly schedule a meeting with them in a conference room and bring my documents that support the claims presented against the hospital management. I also request that the County Commissioners review with the Texas Attorney General's office legal methods of removing board members who refuse to act in the best interest of the taxpayers in Hutchinson County.

Garry Hannon attended the board meeting and he told me Jock Lee was the board member who said, Citizens Who Care About Hutchinson County misinformed the public. I politely omitted Lee's name from my opinion letter in saying he used the word "MISINFORMED". The letter flushed the Vet out like a bob white quail hunkered in the shade of an old Mesquite tree.

LEE ACCEPTING GLENN BAXTER'S INVITATION

Weekend Edition, March 26 and 27, 2005

Dear Editor:

I am happy to respond to the invitation of Glenn Baxter to meet with a hospital board member to discuss issues concerning the misinformation he has given to the residents of this county in regard to the hospital and its management.

I also feel it is a good idea to involve the County Commission in such a discussion. I have contacted Jerry Hefner to attend this meeting Glenn and I are to have. I've so far only talked to his answering machine but am fairly confident he would like to sit in on the discussion. If Jerry can't be present, I would invite one or more other commissioners and/ or the Judge Worsham to sit in.

I've also invited Nancy Young of the Borger News Herald to attend, if this is OK with Mr. Baxter. If Mr. Baxter wants to invite someone from the Attorney General's office to attend that would be fine with me.

I would answer Mr. Baxter's invitation in a way other than through the newspaper but I've seen this is his preferred medium. So here is my response:

I will expect to hear from you Mr. Baxter with the next week to establish a time and a place for our discussion. My daytime phone is—. My address is PO Box—. Or as you are accustomed, you may answer me through the press.

Jock D. Lee DVM
Board member Golden Plains Community Hospital

When I read Jock Lee's response, I called Dr. Ed Quiros and he agreed to attend any meeting with me. Dr. Quiros served on the hospital board in 1979 when the District was formed.

Dr. Quiros is respected by many people in the community as being one of the best surgeons in the area. He served as a board member when the Hospital District was formed in 1989. He is of Philippine descent, and was labeled as a "non-supportive" doctor in the 1995 GPCH Strategic Plan. In 2003, he and his wife, C.P. Quiros as non-supportive doctors admitted 600 patients to Golden Plains. Go figure! He has been loyal to the community for over 27 years.

Dr. Quiros and I agreed it would be a waste of time to go over things already decided in the campaign. But, if Lee wanted to go over documents like covering the Child Pornography, MRI, severance check, etc. there was no problem with those documents being in the newspaper.

I called Jock Lee on the phone and told him Dr. Quiros would join me in any meeting he wanted to set up. I also, told him it would be futile to go over anything already decided. Lee was to set up the meeting and call me back. I hung up the phone and imagined Lee would have a hard time getting County Commissioner Jerry Hefner to attend the meeting because of 68% majority vote against the hospital and the survey results against the administrator. Hefner would be coming up for re-election and a showing of support for the hospital administration would be a political hot potato!

Based on past experiences, my trust factor was bankrupt when it came to Jock Lee and the News-Herald. If the meeting was to be fairly covered, it would need media exposure outside of Borger, so I e-mailed the information to a reporter in Amarillo.

E-MAIL LETTER TO AMARILLO GLOBE NEWS

Dear Reporter:

I want to alert you to this release to the Borger News Herald. The word "misinformation" is used to defend the management at GPCH. For over thirty years in DFW, I was responsible for public relations and marketing for several major corporations. I am a professional in gathering information and presenting it to the public. Everything presented during the hospital bond election came from documents received from past board members, doctors, others, open records request and newspaper articles. I did not misinform the public about the management record at GPCH. There are those in the county who believe that public corruption has been occurring at GPCH over the past decade. There is certainly a record of misuse and mismanagement of public funds and a record of ignoring the general public (taxpayers). If this meeting is set, I would like you to attend.

TIRED OF WAITING . . . LETTER TO NANCY YOUNG

April 27, 2005

Dear Editor:

On March 26, 2005 Opinion page, Jock Lee (board member GPCH) wrote that he would be happy to meet and discuss issues concerning "misinformation" in regard to the hospital and its management. He also felt it would be a good idea to involve the county commission in such a discussion. He was going to invite Jerry Hefner to attend.

Two days following the article, I called Mr. Lee and accepted a meeting. One month has lapsed and I haven't heard from him. I've grown impatient. I am ready to sit down with Mr. Lee, Nancy Young of the Borger News Herald and all 4 county commissioners. I would also like to invite a reporter with the Amarillo Globe. I have documents they and the taxpayers in Hutchinson County deserve to know about.

I will expect to hear from Mr. Lee to schedule this meeting next week. I've patiently waited a month with no response.

Glenn Baxter

CHAPTER TWENTY THREE

GOING UNDERCOVER

The administration at Golden Plains did not know I has documents in hand on the Doctor's Building at 202 W. McGee. I had an estimate dated October 29, 1999 from PREFAB, Inc.*. presented a preliminary proposal by the Sales Coordinator with a floor plan that totals $498,191.

On December 5, 1999 another proposal was presented to the board in the amount of $498,191 for the building and an additional $129,331 for site development. This totals $627,522 and signed by the Sales Coordinator.

I requested all the documents on the building on my first document request. The document received was titled PRICING SCHEDULE and did not have a date on it. It totaled $563,208 and was signed by the Vice President and not the Sales Coordinator. Since the document had no date and is different from all other documents, one might suspect a call was made to the company to expedite the document in compliance with the open document request.

Following my first open document request, Golden Plains Community Hospital sent their letter to the Attorney General of Texas blocking me from further documents until a ruling could be made.

In the interim, Mr. Weldon Luginbyhl made an open document request and gave me documents that GPCH did not submit to me. This gave me reason not to trust open document request from GPCH. Luginbyhl received a copy of an invoice for $553,142 less $7,000 for a total of $546,142. This is $17,066 less than that what GPCH submitted to me in my open document request. Quoted amounts started at $498,191 went up to $627,572 and down to $563,208 and finally down to $546,142 stated on the invoice dated 5/20/2000.

I went to the Internet and easily found a competitive company in the same market as PREFAB, Inc. The representative explained they had been in business a comparable time and frequently bid against PREFAB, Inc. I'll refer to this company as COMPETITION, Inc.*

On November 4, 2004 I received an estimate on a modular building from COMPETITION, Inc. based upon the exact floor plan of the GPCH Doctor's building. Acting under an alias, I contacted the Sales Coordinator at PREFAB, Inc. and sent the floor plan redrawn by the

---

* *Company names have been changed.*

competitive company with a request for a quote. On Friday, November 12, 2004, I traveled to Mansfield, Texas and personally met with the Sales Coordinator at PREFAB, Inc.

Both companies quoted on the same floor plan. The Sales Coordinator at PREFAB, INC. quoted $310,000 to $320,000 compared to COMPETITON, Inc.'s quote of $277,668. I wanted to compare apples to apples to know that both companies would quote close to each other.

In late March, 2005, I went to the City of Borger and picked up a copy of the approved building specifications PREFAB, Inc. had submitted. I sent these specifications to COMPETITION, Inc. Both of these companies frequently bid against one another. COMPETITION, Inc.'s estimate was $369,091.

PREFAB, Inc.'s invoice in 2000 was for $546,142 compared to COMPETITION, Inc.'s current (2005) estimate of $369,091.

This was $177,051 less than PREFAB, Inc. invoice 5 years ago. Take into consideration that steel and material costs have risen over 5 years. What's wrong with this picture?

There were other things that did not add up. Remember in the Board Meeting notes from October 5, 1999, Norm Lambert stated, *"When a new hospital is built, the building can be moved. The estimated cost is $552,789. This includes furnishings and equipment."* Lambert's stated $552,789 is uncannily close to the invoice of $546,142. The estimate dated October 29, 1999 from PREFAB, Inc. presented a preliminary proposal by the Sales Coordinator with a floor plan that totals $498,191.

What happened to the furnishings and equipment? This was never a true statement. Even up to 2005, a board member defending the building told me the building included furniture and fixtures. Why was there only one estimate from one company when a competitive bid was so effortless to find?

Just for fun Sherlock, let's do some elementary math. Take PREFAB, Inc. invoice amount of $546,142 and subtract a nice round figure of $200,000. That equals $346,142. How interesting is it when the sum of all things come uncannily close to the $369,091 that PREFAB, Inc bid in 2005 on the exact approved plans from the City of Borger. Now, let's take $369,091 and subtract $346,142. This equals $22,949. Now, wouldn't $22,949 be a reasonable amount of increase in steel cost or whatever five years later?

The District's Enabling Legislation states in SECTION 5.07 CONTRACTS. (b) . . . board may enter into construction contracts that involve spending more than $10,000 only after competitive bidding as provided by Subchapter B. Chapter 271. Local Government Code, or other applicable law. (b) The advertisement must be published as required by law. If no legal requirement for publication exists, the advertisement must be published at least twice in one or more newspapers of general circulation in the county or counties in which the work is to be performed. The second publication must be on or before the 10th day before the first date bids may be submitted. A copy of a Legal Notice ad was sent to me but there was no information about where and how many times it was published.

This was the same company Larry Langley had contracted for a similar building in Dumas, Texas. Dr. Quiros in Borger said that according to the CEO at the Dumas Hospital, the similar building constructed by PREFAB, Inc. cost approximately $350,000.

I collated all the documents in an 88 page binder titled, "INVESTIGATION: GPCH Doctor's Building, 202 S. McGee, Borger,Texas, April 10, 2005". I took a copy to the FBI office in Amarillo where it was suggested I contact the Texas Rangers and set a meeting with District Attorney Clay Ballman. I was reluctant to meet with Ballman because of what I had learned when the other group of citizen's met with him in 2000. My expectations were that Ballman would look the other way and do nothing.

Author's Note: Following submission of this material to the District Attorney and some others, I attended a hospital board meeting where the CEO made a slide presentation to the board showing his version of the building cost. Why did he go to such an extreme when he could have easily handed out paper documents? His actions reminded me of his overwrought explanation over the MRI scandal. The administrator concluded his presentation by saying, "We are just good honest people."

Whenever, I raised my hand to present my information to the board, I was out of order and not allowed to speak. That's just the way democracy works in Hutchinson County.

MEETING WITH TEXAS RANGER AND DISTRICT ATTORNEY

On Monday May 2, 2005, I was surprised when I looked out the window to see about 3 inches of snow. Stopped by the post office and picked up documents I requested from GPCH . . . airport hanger and insurance policy. I drove to the courthouse in Stinnett to meet with Texas Ranger Todd Snyder and Clay Ballman for meeting at one PM.

I arrived early at the courthouse, walked inside, looked at the directory and took the elevator upstairs to the 3rd floor. The receptionist greeted me. She said Mr. Ballman had not returned from lunch, so I took a seat to wait.

Shortly thereafter, Todd Snyder arrived and walked over to shake my hand. I followed him into the Grand Jury room. Ranger Snyder is about 6'2" tall. He is clean cut in his early 30's and looked like his clothes had been dipped in a vat of starch. We exchange small talk about the late snow.

District Attorney Ballman enters the room and introduces himself. He is sharply dressed in a business suit, clean cut, square jawed and stocky built. This was my first time to see Ballman. Some pretty reputable sources had told me Ballman had a drinking problem and claimed drunken behavior at the Country Club and an incident in Fritch, Texas. These could have been rumors. I really didn't have facts to go on.

Ballman takes a seat opposite me. The Ranger has already given him the binder on the 202 S. McGee Doctors Building. Apparently he and the Ranger met before I arrived. Ballman says, "Okay, what's this about."

I proceeded telling about my return to Borger and my experiences with the Invest in Yourself committee, etc. He listened most of the time with his right hand covering his mouth. I wondered why?

For some reason, the only rise I got from him was when I mentioned the hospital board had voted to get a $400,000 line of credit from Wells Fargo Bank. *Was that an improper or illegal action?*

I brought up the Borger Police Detective, Charlie Keys who claimed Leon Mitchell, attorney, reported pornography to Keys and not "child" pornography which is a felony. Wouldn't any rational person think this was a lame story from an attorney? Wouldn't any attorney know the difference? I don't remember Ballman responding.

I asked Ballman if he knew where Langley was living. He said he knew Larry Langley was in Austin (Travis County). As I kept talking about two witnesses who would collaborate, Ballman continued to seem totally uninterested. My intuition was that Ballman was not at all comfortable with the conversation. He excused himself for another appointment and left before the meeting concluded.

I continued talking with the Ranger and the District Attorney's associate. Near the end of the meeting the Ranger said: "I was hoping we would have some criminal evidence coming out of this meeting. Something I could act on. This is no different from other hospitals in small towns." *This statement almost made me speechless!*

I explained that what is needed is a forensic audit. That's what the taxpayers who support the hospital need. What does Mr. Lambert and others have to hide?

The investigator said, *"There's no such thing as a forensic audit."* This statement switched lights on in my brain like a pinball machine.

I recalled that Jerry Strecker had told me, "Leon Mitchell, hospital attorney said in the past . . . there's no such thing as a forensic audit. I was told by Garret Spradling that in a meeting in July, 2004 between BBC (himself, Garry Hannon, Chuck Litteral) and (Invest in Yourself)Leon Mitchell and Conny Moore, Leon Mitchell replied, "Do you know what a forensic audit is?" And he continued to say, "There's no such thing as a forensic audit. That was a term coined by a past hospital board president."

The Ranger seemed to agree with the investigator that there is no such thing as a forensic audit. He didn't say anything but to ask about the hospital's auditing firm. I explained that Lambert had always used a firm from Houston. That's where Lambert came from. But the board had changed firms on the last audit. The firm is out of Lubbock, Texas. The Ranger said, "I'm going to Lubbock on other business tomorrow and will stop by the auditing firm to check it out." I replied, "I'll find the name of the firm and call you this afternoon."

The three of us stood up and I shook the Ranger's hand to thank him for his time. I left the court house feeling puzzled and at a loss. *The Ranger would not be able to find anything by looking into a regular audit. A forensic audit looks for fraudulent acts and missing documents.* The question still persisted, "What does the hospital have to hide?"

The district attorney didn't seem to be at all interested in investigating the doctor's building or any of the witnesses referred to him. My intuition was that he had made up his mind to do nothing before our meeting. I felt as though I had walked in the same footsteps of the same citizens who had met with the DA years earlier. It must have frustrated the hell out of them! Was it too much of a political risk for Ballman to get involved? What would it take to have someone investigate and gather evidence?

When I arrived home, I picked up the telephone and called the president of the hospital board. He told me the name of auditing firm in Lubbock. Later in the day I contacted the Texas Ranger and gave him the name of the firm. The Ranger going to the auditing firm would be futile because a regular audit only looks at the surface.

Were people in Hutchinson County so backwoods that they were ignorant about forensic audits or was this a diversion. Looking at my computer screen, I typed in the words "forensic audit" and entered a search on Google. In a flash, there was endless information on forensic audits.

"Forensic auditing is the investigation of a fraud or presumptive fraud with a view to gathering evidence that could be presented in a court of law. Auditors need to be alert for situations, control weaknesses, inadequacies in record keeping, errors and unusual transactions or results which could be indicative of fraud, improper or unlawful expenditure, unauthorized operations, waste, inefficiency or lack of probity."

MYSTERY OF THE AIRPLANE HANGER

When I arrived home, I looked at the open documents I received and the lease contract on the Airplane Hanger. While interviewing the past hospital board President, Pat Cleveland, she told me about the airplane hanger.

"It was a long time before I found out that records were being kept in an airplane hanger. I was there about 4 years before I found out about it. In my opinion, they seemed to want to keep that quiet.

Mr. Nives, a local citizen, was going to donate us a building as a tax right off on the appraised value. It was a nice building on Main Street with air conditioning where we could store records. Lambert and his members of the board didn't want anything to do with it.

I couldn't understand why they would want to continue storing records at the airport in an airplane hanger with no air conditioning and where rain could possibly leak on the records. During that time, one of the board members kept an airplane at the airport."—Pat Cleveland, past GPCH board president

When I looked at the documents sent through open records, I read on the contract that the hanger was leased month to month until such time it would be needed for an airplane. In fact, the hospital lost the lease when the space was needed for an airplane in July, 2003. Why didn't they accept a free building when taxpayer's money was being spent to lease space on a temporary basis? This was another thing at Golden Plains that went beyond common sense.

Were these records moved into local storage where more taxpayer dollars are frivolously being spent today?

Many locals are aware of the past history of drugs being flown in and out of the Panhandle of Texas. Theories and rumors about drug diversion run amuck. Like other irrational things, the Airplane Hanger brought suspicions leading to rumors and questions. Questions that are seldom answered in Hutchinson County.

WHAT IS DRUG DIVERSION?

I remembered a copy of a Memo addressed to All (GPCH)Personnel, from COO/Director of Nurses (initialed), on 3-15-05 with the subject of Medications stated:

Everyone needs to be aware that stock medication, found on the patient care units, are disappearing. In particular, we have noticed that Levaquin is disappearing by the box. Pharmacy is closely monitoring medications that are disappearing. This is the same as stealing medications and charges will be filed, when the person responsible is identified.

RN's please note: If you are pulling medications from the Pharmacy, a copy of the order should be left in the Pharmacy when you pull any medication. Do NOT take a medication out of the Pharmacy without the order in hand, and please write the number of doses you are taking to the department.

Thank you for your help in this matter.

Why wasn't the 24/7 pharmacist there to control and dispense medications by personally handing them out? This memo sounds like the nurses are on an honor system to pull what they want.

Theft of medications from any hospital or health care facility can be classified as drug diversion. It is very easy to find extensive information of the Internet.

Drug diversion can be best defined as the diversion of licit drugs for illicit purposes. Prescription drug abuse accounts for almost 30% of the overall drug problem in the United States, representing a close challenge to cocaine addiction. It is estimated that millions of Americans are addicted to prescription drugs. A large majority of these addicts are average citizens, with no prior history of drug abuse, who became addicted after first using prescription drugs for legitimate medical reasons. Often times however, these diverted prescription drugs end up on our streets where illegal drug abuse is an ever growing problem.

Pharmaceutical diversion reaps large profits for the traffickers, and devastation for the abusers. This eventually affects their friends, families, and their workplace.

The diversion of pharmaceutical drugs means that prescription drugs were illegally obtained by a variety of methods and a variety of offenders. This may have been accomplished by deception, or an outright theft of the drugs. Health care professionals face the prescription drug abuser on a daily basis. These drug seekers prey on physicians, pharmacists, dentists, and their staff, in a relentless attempt to obtain pharmaceuticals. A large majority of these pharmaceuticals are obtained illegally via fraudulent prescriptions.

Drug seekers often alter a legitimate prescription by use of a pen with the same color ink as the original prescription. Often times these drug seekers alter the number of refills on the prescription. Other drug seekers forge prescriptions from scratch. The forger begins with either a blank piece of paper or a legitimate prescription blank from a practicing physician. In the former case, the forger stencils a physician's name and address (as well as the telephone number of an accomplice) in black lettering onto a blank page and then uses a photocopier to reduce the sheet to the size of a prescription. To the drug seeker, a blank prescription is like a blank check. Prescription blanks are frequently stolen from emergency departments and in clinics, in part because of the *carelessness of the medical staff.*

LETTER TO THE DISTRICT ATTORNEY

After thinking things over for a couple of days, I wrote Mr. Ballman this letter.

May 4, 2005
Mr. Clay Ballman
Box—
Stinnett, Texas 79083

Dear Mr. Ballman:

Thank you for allowing me time to meet with you, your associate, and Texas Ranger Todd Snyder on May 2, 2005. I would like to review some things presented in our meeting that I believe remain relevant.

There appears a pattern at Golden Plains Community Hospital managed by Mr. Norm Lambert that may signal potential public corruption, gross mismanagement, waste, or theft of public money. I am not alone in my opinion. Many others in this county have the same opinion. There are those who would like to dismiss it as perception. But, if it is only perception, it began in 2000 when Mr. Lambert and a majority of his board members refused to allow a forensic audit of the hospital as requested by signatures of over 1000 taxpayers.

If there was nothing to hide, why didn't Mr. Lambert openly agree to the audit and why did Mr. Leon Mitchell, Attorney for the hospital dismiss it by saying there is "no such thing as a forensic audit." I found it noteworthy that following your departure, your associate stated to me that there is "no such thing as a forensic audit".

For your associates information and others concerned, I have enclosed information on forensic audits. A forensic audit looks for criminal fraud. It is not a normal audit that is performed annually for the hospital or any other business entity. These audits are being conducted in increasing numbers, i.e. Enron.

In my opinion, the documents I presented on the Doctor's Building speak of possible construction fraud. Either PREFAB, Inc. may have fraudulently overcharged Golden Plains over $100,000 *(Note: up to $200,000)* or possibly public money went under the table at the hospital.

(Omitted paragraph here because testimony of individuals named requested confidentiality)

At the end of the meeting, Ranger Snyder said he needed criminal evidence to proceed. As a public citizen, it's not my job to find and present criminal evidence. Your office is responsible for criminal investigation to provide evidence. I only brought forth information for investigation. There are many other areas of serious potential fraudulent activity at Golden Plains that need to be investigated.

A forensic audit of Golden Plains Community Hospital has been asked for and ignored twice. Please explain to me and others in the community how to go about ordering a forensic audit. A majority of taxpayers in Hutchinson County would like to find out why public money has been wasted, lost or possibly stolen. I look forward to hearing from you with your action plan.

Sincerely,
Glenn Baxter
cc: Texas Ranger Todd Snyder, Dumas, Texas

District Attorney Clay Ballman never responded with a phone call or a form letter.

CHAPTER TWENTY FOUR

WHERE THERE'S SMOKE THERE'S FIRE

After I completed the letter, I picked up the phone to call the FBI contact in Amarillo. We talked and he agreed to meet with me at 1:30 the next day. I walked into the FBI office on Thursday afternoon. In a brief meeting, I submitted a copy of the letter that was mailed to the district attorney and several other documents. I expressed my frustration to the agent. The agent said, "You might try asking the county auditor for a forensic audit and contacting the Texas Hospital Association." I thanked him for his time and started to leave. His departing comment was, "There appears to be a lot of smoke there."

Entering the elevator to leave, the old phrase, "where there's smoke there's fire" came to mind over and over.

BRANDED A LIAR!

On Thursday evening, May 5, 2005 I was blind sided by this FRONT PAGE HEADLINE "Hospital: Lee questions Baxter's veracity." By Nancy Young, editor.

Will there be a meeting between Dr. Jock Lee, DVM, and Glenn Baxter regarding the hospital issues?

The Borger News-Herald received a letter from Baxter stating that Lee has not responded to a request he made March 28 to meet. Lee said Wednesday that Baxter was lying.

Lee, who is a member of the Golden Plains Community Hospital board, answered a request made by Baxter in a letter to the editor published in the March 26 and 27 weekend edition to meet with the hospital board member. In the letter, Lee said he would meet with Baxter and he suggested that a representative of the County Commission also attend the session, along with the editor of the Borger News-Herald.

Baxter represents an organization, Citizens Who Care About Hutchinson County. He campaigned heavily against the election held in September 2004 to build a new hospital, and has said the hospital administration needs to be changed.

Lee, responded to Baxter's allegations on Wednesday by saying," that's a lie."

He said that when Baxter contacted him two days after the letter was published that Baxter said he would meet with him but said that he wanted Dr. Ed Quiros, as a local doctor, to attend the meeting. Lee said that Baxter said he would have to contact Dr. Quiros about attending the meeting and that he would get back in touch with Lee.

According to Lee, Baxter said he would have to get Dr.Quiros to attend the meaning.

"He (Baxter) has not been gotten back in touch with me," he said." That really upsets me," he said." Their needs to be a meeting to discuss the issues of misinformation.

After reading this article that evening I was really outraged at the editor and what in my opinion was biased support for Lambert and his cronies. She had allowed Jock Lee to call me a liar without contacting me to get my side of the story. How convenient was it that an article calling me a liar was on the front page two days before the school board election.

My night was spent restless waiting for the next day.

The next morning I walked into the Barber Shop and announced, "I'm here to tell lies and spread lies!" The Barber and others laughed. The Barber responded, "Don't feel bad. I have a customer who took his pet duck to a vet. The vet looked at the duck and exclaimed, "This duck in dead!" The customer replied, "Are you sure this duck is dead? Isn't there anything more you can do?. The vet whistled and a his black Labrador retriever walked over, took one sniff of the duck and walked away. The vet said, "See, the duck's dead." The customer asked, "Isn't there anything else you can do. I really like this duck."

The vet picked up a black cat and placed it next to the duck. The cat sniffed the duck and scampered away. "See there, that duck's dead. You owe me $150." The customer said, "What . . . $150 just to tell me my duck's dead?" That's right. Fifty dollars for the office call, fifty dollars for the lab work and fifty dollars for the catscan."

I replied to the Barber, "It sounds like that vet learned how to charge high prices like the ER at the hospital."

It was about 11 a.m. when I left the Barber and drove my pickup in front of the Times-Herald. The sound of the train whistle filled the air as I stepped through the front door of the newspaper. I saw Nancy Young at her desk and asked if I could speak with her.

I began to let off steam, "Why didn't you call me before printing this on the front page? You allowed Jock Lee to call me a liar! I'm not going to lower myself and call him a liar, but what he said is not true. I had already talked with Dr. Quiros and he agreed to be there in a meeting with Lee. Dr. Quiros will back my story.

This is slanted journalism!" I refrained from saying yellow journalism. The editor asked me more questions and said she would print my story in the newspaper. As I walked out, I mumbled to myself "better not hold my breath."

WHO WOULDN'T THINK THIS WAS A SET UP?

The editor did not print my story on Friday or in the Weekend edition. How coincidental was it that this front page article proclaiming me a liar came two days before the Borger School Board Election where I was a candidate? Was this an attempt to set me up to look bad before the election?

Back in March, I placed my name in nomination for the School Board. Running for the BISD board was my statement against what I considered to be hypocrisy of those school board members who also served on the hospital board and Invest in Yourself Committee. The Superintendent of Schools, and the President of the School Board, and a hospital employee who served on the school board also served on the Invest in Yourself Committee. The hypocrisy was that these people were supporting a Hospital Administration involved in an attempted child pornography cover up and at the same time representing the best interest of school children.

After I submitted the proper paper work to the school administration office to be on the ballot, I left on an out of town trip. Upon my return, I became suspicious because there was a request from the District Office to complete a criminal history report. I asked "why" when the proper forms were submitted with a signed sworn statement that I had never been convicted of a felony.

The threatening e-mail on Sunday, September 12, 2004 and the comment "I will attack your personal character, as you have done to so many. I will find out every ugly detail I can. I will publicly announce every questionable business decision you have ever made," quickly came to mind. The probability was that these people did a background check on me. Lexis/Nexus is a wonderful electronic source. Something smelled!

Therefore, I called the State of Texas and talked an attorney to find out the information I included in this letter.

Mr. Frank Henderson
Assistant Superintendent/Business
Borger Independent School District
Borger, Texas 79008

Dear Frank:

I am returning the attached form entitled "Criminal History Record Information Consent & Release Form" to your office.

This form was handed to me 2 weeks following my completing and submitting the original packet of forms for eligibility qualifications to run for the School Board. I meet all the listed qualifications on the official forms. Therefore, this additional form is not a requirement according to the Secretary of State under Chapter 141.

I am not applying as an employee. Serving on the school board is a voluntary position and is decided on by voters.

Best regards,
Glenn Baxter

When I said to the State attorney, "If I was a 500 pound sweaty, green giant with body odor, they couldn't discriminate against me from running for the School Board." She laughed and responded, "You're right."

BORGER POLICE DEPARTMENT PARTNER WITH CURNUTT, BAXTER

I called John Curnutt and told him I was going public with my DWI before others could smear me in the campaign. My arrest occurred in March of 2002. I discussed this with John and how it opened my eyes. Although a DWI is embarrassing, I had nothing to hide.

John had been the victim of a head on collision with a drunk driver in 1974 that led to his confinement in a wheel chair for the past 31 years. He had a great idea and I agreed to go with it. We decided to join together and speak to groups about the dangers of driving while intoxicated. We put together a press release for the newspaper and met with Chief Jimmy Adams of the Borger Police Department.

On April 12, 2005, the article on the front page of the News-Herald read, BPD partner with Curnutt, Baxter. The article covered what happened to John, and he was quoted, "If sharing our stories makes a difference and saves one life, it will be worth our time."

The story quoted me as saying, "When you come into contact with the law, you'll find out a secret nightmare. Anyone drinking and driving is subject to arrest, whether or not it is afflicting their driving ability. Three beers can register over the limit. One beer with prescribed medications, fatigue, or sleep deprivation can result in impaired driving. Driving impaired is against the law. I learned one big lesson . . . never drink one drop and drive. A DWI is very costly in dollars and time."

Admitting mistakes, being forthright and honest is always the best policy in serving others in a community. I didn't campaign to win for the school board election and lost, but my victory was in rocking their hypocritical boat. Robert Bradley and Gary Sneck were re-elected.

BAD EXPERIENCE IN EMERGENCY ROOM

The Letters to the Editor had a story submitted by Mrs. Alicia Boston about taking her 21 month old daughter to the Emergency Room at Golden Plains. She explained that her daughter has a history of urinary reflux and gets UTI's that need antibiotic treatment. The male nurse asked, "Did you just bring her to the ER to for a dose of Tylenol." And, she said they wanted to see a doctor. All the doctor did was look at my daughter and told me it was a viral infection and there was nothing he could do. They didn't even bother to check her blood or urine for infection. But they did give us some eye drops for drainage.

My daughter was miserable all day Sunday and most of Monday until she was diagnosed and received proper treatment from her doctor. I understand why people go to Amarillo. I don't think a new hospital will solve this problem. The doctor at the hospital could have examined her more closely instead of getting in a hurry to send us home. Similar complaints about the Emergency Room at Golden Plains had become common place throughout the community. The comment heard in the medical community is that "Rent-A-Docs" for the ER create inconsistent service to patients.

BLAGG DEFEATS BARKER

On Saturday, May 6, the great news was that the candidate we were supporting, Donna Blagg soundly defeated Julia Barker for her seat on the hospital board. Donna won by a landslide of 298-136 votes. Now, there was one other vote on the board that would support the citizens in selling the hospital or terminating the hospital administrator.

Garrett Spradling won a seat on the Borger City Council. This was an upset for others who challenged him in a re-count to no avail. Now, Borger had a young independent thinker who would be looking at making changes for the better. Heaven Forbid!

COMMISSIONERS MEETING MONDAY MAY 9, 2005 10:00 AM

Following the election on Saturday, an insider called me at 8 AM on Monday to tell me about a Commissioner's meeting at the court house in Stinnett. He said Lambert was going to be there to recommend appointing Dr. Boyd in place of Jason Vance. I quickly showered, dressed and drove the ten miles to the courthouse.

When I entered the courthouse, I saw County Commissioner Eddie Whittington standing next to R.D. Corneilson. Eddie asked, "What are you doing here dressed in a suit?" I replied, "I've got some business to attend to in the Commissioner's Court meeting this morning." I could see discern on the face of Commissioner Corneilson.

When I entered the court room, there sat Norm Lambert next to Dr. Boyd. Was that shock and awe on their faces? I certainly hoped so!

The Judge started the meeting and these are the exact comments taken from a tape recording.

Judge Jack Worsham: I think we'll go to 19 first considering appointment to the hospital board. As far as I know there are only two applicants Jason Vance served on the board this last round and he desires to be re-appointed. Then we have Dr. William Boyd. I don't know how long Dr. Boyd has lived in the county, I feel that I know him rather well because *we go to church together*. He and his wife have been *active in the church*. And I also know that it's not unusual for doctors to desire to serve on the hospital board. Do we have anybody who wants to speak in behalf of any one of the applicants? *Note: Doesn't it seem that the Good Judge is doing a selling job in behalf of Dr. Boyd?*

Baxter: My name is Glenn Baxter. I would like to speak in behalf of Jason Vance for reappointment to the hospital board. Mr. Vance has worked for Conoco Phillips over the last 2 years in Borger. A lot of times the Doctors will leave after a short time of coming here. Jason Vance has worked on the board representing both side of the issues. He has made comments about potential new management for the hospital.

A majority of citizens voted 68% verses' 32% against the hospital bond issue. They no longer have confidence in the hospital. They have no confidence in some of the board members. The voting record was a landslide in Stinnett and a landslide in Fritch. The citizens in this county deserve good health care. They haven't been receiving it. The hospital is in very poor financial condition . . . no matter how sugar coated it is. There have been many things that have happened in the past that citizens are upset about. I'd like to address one in particular, the MRI machine and the other is the Doctor's Building on 202 South McGee. The building has been researched to show that there is a discrepancy of $150,000 that may or may not be construction fraud. I do have that information in hand and I have given it to other people.

Dr. Boyd has been hired by Mr. Lambert and have voiced his opinions in the newspaper in support of Mr. Lambert. I see Dr. Boyd as being a rubber stamp.

The last point I would like to make is this. Commissioner Whittington is a car dealer and I've got a used pickup truck in the parking lot. Here's my keys. Would you or anyone else in this room give me $20,000 for that pickup truck without starting it up.

LAUGHS heard in the room.

Norm Lambert: I'm Norm Lambert, the hospital administrator that Mr. Baxter spoke about. I'm not here to necessarily promote one candidate verses the other. I think that for one thing in the past is that we have had Phillips employees or ex employees represented on the board. I think Phillips is well represented on the board. Mr. Baxter has noted that we have had physicians come and leave on the board. I think that is unfortunate. There's lots of reasons why they have been driven away by powers that be here and choices of spouses or whatever it might be. Dr. Boyd and his wife are *active in their church* and active in the community. I think it's time for us to consider representation from a physician who will represent the needs of the physicians in the community. I don't think there's a conflict of interest there as Mr. Baxter might indicate. But Mr. Baxter has indicated a lot of things over the last few months that have been . . . . I would just like to say that I would certainly support Dr. Boyd, but I have a good working relationship with Jason Vance also.

There's a new board member coming to the board after the election that already indicated that she wishes to sell the hospital. I believe that Dr. Boyd does not believe that way. Jason also has indicated that he would also like to sell the hospital. I think if this community wants to keep control of a local hospital they need to keep an appointment so they want lose control. That's all I got to say.

Jack Worsham: Dr. Boyd, do you want to speak for yourself.

Dr. Boyd:	I would just like to begin to say that I am here to stay. We really enjoy it here. ***God led me up here*** about ten years ago when I drove through here the first time and I just had a feeling. I don't know what it was I just want to say that I want to do what's best for this community. Especially being a health care professional And that's really what's behind my motivation for keeping health care in Hutchinson County non-profit
Jack Worsham:	Any member of the Court have any questions from any of these speakers? (No Response) Do I hear nominations from the floor?
Red Isbell:	I nominate Jason Vance for the hospital board
Eddie Whittington:	I second.
Jack Worsham:	Jason Vance is nominated to the hospital board. All those in favor. THREE VOTES SOUNDED OUT (MAJORITY IN FAVOR)!!!

Lambert and Dr. Boyd were visibly shaken as they stood up to walk out of the Commissioner's Court. I stood up to leave and told the commissioners, "Thank You," as I walked toward the door. When I entered the hallway, the two conspirators were standing there talking. I walked toward them, smiled and nodded as I passed them on my way out of the building.

I had been right seven months ago about Jason Vance becoming a target of Norm Lambert. There was an ecstatic feeling that I held inside until getting into my truck in the parking lot. I let out a victory whoop! Nothing had felt this good since the defeat of the bond election on September 11th.

THANK GOD! The church cards did not win the hand on this day.

GPCH WELCOMES NEW BONE DOCTOR

This was the headline in Monday night's paper. Lambert had recruited another Orthopedic surgeon at Golden Plains. In a past board meeting Lambert alluded to this plan because of all the money another orthopedic surgeon, had brought into the hospital. Did Lambert believe that repeating the past would be his salvation? Was this more management insanity?

CHAPTER TWENTY FIVE

CRITICALLY WRONG FOR HUTCHINSON COUNTY

The board's decision to convert to a Critical Access Hospital was nagging at me. I was suspicious that it was a tactic to avoid selling the hospital and keep the hospital CEO and his good ol' boys.

On Thursday evening, May 12, I began investigating Critical Access Hospitals on the Internet. I found that there were approximately 60 in the state of Texas. These hospitals were all in very small communities. While surfing the net, I came across the Texas Center for Rural Initiatives. I jotted down the telephone number to call the next morning.

On Friday the 13th when I called the Center for Rural Health Initiatives and I was directed to Mr. Quang Ngo. I introduced myself and our conversation centered around Information Sheet titled "GPCH to Convert to Critical Access" distributed by Norm Lambert to hospital employees and to the community on Monday night 5-9-05 in celebration of National Hospital Week.

I read the following statement (paragraph number 6) from the CAH information sheet to Mr. Ngo:

"Golden Plains Community Hospital is still looking into viable mechanisms for funding the building of a new hospital. Critical Access Hospital designation allows for a greater portion of new construction capital cost to be paid by Medicare. One accounting study that was performed under this CAH showed that another $700,000 per year of new hospital funding could be paid for under this CAH program in addition to the $600,000 mentioned above. This would pay for a significant portion of a new hospital . . . but not all."

Baxter: When I look at that (paragraph), I really can't believe it's as clear as stated.

Quang Ngo: It isn't that clear.

Baxter: Is it like blue sky?

Quang Ngo: Yeah, for the reason that when Golden Plains submitted an application to us to get a grant to do the feasibility study.

Baxter: Yes.

Quang Ngo: I was thinking that's part of the things you were reading off to me. I don't know for sure if but I'm pretty sure they completed their study and I have a copy of it here. It surprised me that a hospital of your size, that size . . . 99 beds I think it is would want to go all the way down to a 25 bed limit. (Laughs) It would essentially would require to de-license ¾ of your beds and again you're right if you're serving a base of over 24,000 (Approx. County Population) I'm assuming your staffing more that 25 beds if you got 99 operating beds. It didn't seem . . . this was probably the biggest hospital that ever wanted to plug up to Critical Hospital Status the whole time that I've been here. It was surprising to me but we don't disallow anybody who wants to take a look at it. It didn't seem to make sense to be honest with you and like I mentioned, right now everybody is funded with some pretty serious deadlines that if he were proposing to go through a construction mechanism route and then the critical care process, he would not make either one deadline. He wouldn't be able to construct the facility and be designated before the end. And if he decides to apply for the critical access. *In the current facility, everyone in the community should have the question: How are you going to maintain the same level of service if you're going to reduce your beds from 99 to 25?* That seems there has to be a reasonable explanation and I'm not sure there will be. It didn't seem to make sense . . . yeah, I'm not sure . . . their explanation is very clear. There are certain time restrains that will prevent them from things that will prevent them from going the route they want to go. He won't make it.

Baxter: In my opinion, he's just trying to use this as a way to convince people to keep his job.

Quang Ngo: Yeah . . . right.

Baxter: on the Board and other people who don't investigate things.

Quang Ngo: And yeah and all those people have to be aware of is the time constraints and the facts you know . . . I seriously doubt that if the study shows that critical access model would be favored and that the community would benefit from it. I seriously doubt it. I don't have the study but I don't think it would.

Baxter: I explained the background of GPCH hospital. The bond election, management, etc.

Quang Ngo: It's quite a story from somebody (hospital) your size. We've heard of similar stories. *It seems clear as daylight that whoever is administrating now is not doing a good job and is primarily the cause of the downfall of the facility, yet the local politics are such that it's nearly impossible to get those people out and get folks in with new ideas that can help. Yeah, that's a tough one there.* But certainly if he's hanging his hat in part, based on that information (CAH Information Sheet handout) that is provided that can be defensified.

Glenn Baxter: Is there any other thing you could add that would bring light on this?

Quang Ngo: In short of reading the study myself and be able to pick areas I can refute or whatever. Basically the short of his proposal is that it is impossible for him to meet that deadline. To me it's a dead proposal from the start. It's a proposal that doesn't bring any alternative to the hospital. Critical Access doesn't appear the way to go I mentioned that the program does allow you for capital expenditures and for a lot of the hospital that have converted they do see an increase of revenue. But, These are very small hospitals that naturally fit the model. You've got people who are probably 30 to 40 (licensed) beds. Even if they are only 40 licensed beds, they only staff 20, 18 to 30 beds. For you to go from 99 down to 25 I can't imagine why the community would support that. And your best bet for the community would be to educate what the Critical Access model is for. And It's certainly not intended to support a community of 24,000. (Laughs)

Baxter: *Your name again . . . I'm going to take this information to the newspaper.*

Quang Ngo: *My name is Quang Ngo and I am the licensed coordinator for the State.*

   I purposely asked Mr. Ngo to repeat his name and position because I was releasing his statements to the press. I couldn't have said it any clearer.
   These are other comments made during the conversation:

Baxter: My concern is it seems strange to me that there will be $700,000 per year through Medicare because Medicare reports it doesn't have a lot of money these days.

Quang Ngo.   Yeah. It's probably not as clear as it could have been. The CAH program allows for the reimbursement of capital expenditures but if your converting . . . In many circumstances if you're the right configuration you can see an increase in reimbursement through the cost basis of one percent above cost of critical access reimbursement. It will vary any where between from $100,000 all the way up to 6 to $800,000. But that's very specific to the facility. Here in Texas when we did the survey about 3 years ago of critical access hospitals, the average reimbursement benefits appears to be averaging about $400,000

Baxter: Is that per year?

Quang Ngo.   For the year that we were studying it. That's not a guarantee. I have anecdotes about administrators ... some of them will say that after conversion you can see a million dollar increase the first year and then in settlement cost in the second year they could be $400,000 in the hole they have to pay back. It's not one of those things that are constant, it really has to do with the specific hospital's operation and how they manage it. I would take that with a grain of salt. It wouldn't be applicable to every hospital. The bottom line is that an allowable reimbursement cost is capital expenditure and capital investment. By no means is there a study that shows that that is a constant.

Baxter: And even if there was a study done that shows there was an amount for hospital funding ... that wouldn't assure or guarantee that would be the constant amount received year to year.

Quang Ngo: Exactly.

Glenn Baxter: So, If a hospital wanted to build a 25 million dollar facility then there's no guarantee of what amount would come from Medicare. Is that correct?

Quang Ngo: Yes. And the other complication for anyone right now considering construction of a facility By the end of this year if you haven't been designated critical access, more than likely you will never be designated critical access because you have to be 35 miles away from the nearest hospital. There's a sunset provision that eliminates state authority to be at least 35 miles away from the nearest hospital.

Baxter: I'm in Borger with a population of 14,000 and Pampa has an acute care hospital. Pampa's 30 miles away.

Quang Ngo: If you don't get designated by the end of the year ... Borger would not qualify.

Baxter: How many Critical Access Hospitals are in Texas?

Quang Ngo: There are 67 CAH hospitals in Texas. 64 certified and 3 in the pipeline.

Baxter: I see that most communities where CAH hospitals are located are very small communities.

Quang Ngo: Most CAH's that qualify have 1 to 4 patients per day. We have a couple that go up to 8 and a couple at 10 to 12.

Quang Ngo: Historically most of the hospitals that come around to convert, they do so at the last resort. Either convert or close the door. The model we are going after is for people that convert before they *run into the red too deeply and not to take advantage of the program.*

TAKING THE NEWS TO AMARILLO

I was excited about what I just heard. After hanging up the phone, I called John Curnutt. When John answered the phone, the first thing he told me was that on the police scanner the previous evening, there was talk about the District Attorney Clay Ballman being involved in an DWI accident. I said, "That's shocking news! John replied, "I'll make some calls and we'll see what's in this evening's paper."

I said, "I've got more news for you. I just hung up from talking to a Mr. Quang Gno with Texas Rural Initiatives and he is the official who was familiar with the CAH application for Golden Plains Hospital."

Our conversation continued as I conveyed what was said and ended by my saying, "I've got to hurry and take this story to the Amarillo Globe News. I don't believe the Borger New-Herald will publish the story. They've been keeping things out of the news about the hospital.

That afternoon, my mother and I went to meet with the reporter at the Amarillo Globe News. We walked into the lobby at 2 p.m. and asked for the reporter. We waited for about 45 minutes until the reporter came over to meet with us. I was familiar with this person from a meeting months earlier. She appeared to be detached from what I was attempting to convey to her. She was rushing me when she said, "I've got another meeting and a story to get out. Usually another reporter handles the hospital." I knew who she was talking about and for some reason, he ignored other stories I submitted to him. That's why I didn't call him with the story.

I started talking faster and finally felt that just maybe she was getting interested in my story. She seemed to become more relaxed and asked my mother a question related to senior health care.

As we left she said, "I'll confer with the other reporter." My heart sank upon hearing her comment. In the following weeks the story never surfaced.

We drove back to Borger and when we arrived home, the first thing I did was go out the front door to pick up the newspaper. ***The headline on the front page read, "District Attorney Arrested for DWI."***

This was a Friday the 13th that I will never forget.

DA ARRESTED FOR DWI

On Saturday morning I began reading about the mishap of a District Attorney who I had first met eleven days earlier. The article read:

84th District Attorney Clay Ballman was arrested for driving while intoxicated shortly before midnight Thursday. By Nancy Young, editor.

He was taken to Hutchinson County Jail in Stinnett where he was released on the order of a district judge after approximately 35 minutes at the jail.

Borger Police Department received a cell phone call from a female motorist that said her car had been hit and she was following the 1998 Chrysler that struck her.

The DA was arrested for driving while intoxicated, first offense, a Class B misdemeanor.

Hutchinson County Sheriff, Guy Rowh, said this morning that Ballman was taken to the county jail at 12:28 a.m. and was released from the jail to a family member at 1:06 a.m. Ballman placed a call to 84th District Judge William D. Smith upon his arrival at the jail and that Judge Smith ordered Ballman released.

The article went on to say that when Judge Smith was asked why he released the District Attorney, Judge Smith said, "I just ordered them to release him. No one indicated there was any type of problem."

When asked if there was a law that someone must be kept in jail a certain amount of time after an arrest for DWI. He responded, "I don't know about that."

The irony was that in May, 2001, the child pornography cover up surfaced in the newspapers following the meeting between the group of citizens and the District Attorney. These people felt like Clay Ballman looked the other way and did nothing to investigate their concerns at Golden Plains. Was Karma paying a visit on the District Attorney? The old adage, "what goes around comes around", came to mind.

THE TAPE RECORDER LIED!

In the same newspaper, the hospital CEO attacked me in the Letters to the Editor. He wrote

"Dear Editor: I want to respond to your paper's headline and article that appeared in Tuesday, May 10th edition of the News-Herald. Since *your newspaper was not physically represented at the Commissioner's meeting on Monday, though your tape recorder was there, I believe that some misleading information was contained in your article.*" Lambert continued to explain that he was *innocently* invited to the meeting by Judge Jack Worsham and not to support either candidate.

UNBELIEVABLE!!! HOW CAN SOMEONE BLAME A TAPE RECORDER FOR NOT REPORTING THE TRUTH! BY THIS TIME, EXPERIENCE TOLD ME THAT THE

ONLY WAY TO GET AT THE TRUTH WAS WITH A TAPE RECORDER OR A LIE DETECTOR!!!

Here is an excellent example of how Lambert twists words and misleads. He writes, "Baxter claims that there was "construction fraud" surrounding the building of the medical office next to the hospital. Such slanderous statements are very malicious and are intended to injure the reputation of hospital management. He has made many statements before, making accusations and offering no proof of any of his accusations."

*My exact recorded statement to the County Commissioners was, "The building has been researched to show that there is a discrepancy of $150,000 that **may or may not be** construction fraud." I never said **it is** construction fraud and the CEO's claim that "slanderous statements are very malicious and are intended to injure the reputation of hospital management" is untrue, or as some others would say "outright exaggeration."*

Every citizen has first amendment rights to question those in government office or in paid positions in government entities who benefit from taxpayer dollars.

RESPONSE TO NORM LAMBERT'S LETTER

I replied to Lambert's letter and it was printed in Letters to the Editor:

IMMEDIATE RELEASE, May 14, 2005
Norm Lambert proclaims misleading information. Is this statement meant to say that Mr. Lambert has never and would never consider misleading the general public in Hutchinson County?

He blames the newspaper for not physically being there. He blames the tape recorder for misleading everyone. When has this hospital administrator ever blamed himself for his management blunders?

He protests too much! He shouts words like inflammatory and unproved statements, accusations, etc. My exact statement on Nancy Young's tape recorder was, "There have been many things that have happened in the past that citizens are upset about. I'd like to address one in particular . . . the MRI machine and the other is the Doctor's Building on 202 South McGee. The building has been researched to show that there is a discrepancy of $150,000 that may or may not be construction fraud. I do have that information on hand and I have given it to other people."

Mr. Lambert, I felt Nancy Young was generous to you when she excluded the following from her tape recorder. In reference to the MRI—"The last point I would like to make is this. Commissioner Whittington is a car dealer and I've got a used pickup truck in the parking lot. Here's my car keys. Would you or anyone else in this room give me $20,000 for that pickup truck without starting it up." The tape picked up laughs from the court room.

How can you say I was not informed about the MRI because I was not here in 2000. It doesn't take a rocket scientist to research past newspaper articles and interview others who were here in 2000. I will admit that I haven't been able to talk with everyone of the 1,041 who signed the petition.

How outrageous is it for you to point your finger at me and say I am critical of all 225 employees at GPCH? The quality of management determines the quality of health care. Ask the employees who have recently been laid off from bookkeeping and other areas in the hospital about how they feel about your management style. The hours of other employees have been decreased. When it comes to doctors how can you justify to the board . . . the number of Doctors run out of here before I returned to Borger.

After Mr. Lee referred to me as a liar on the front page article, I called him and told him it was useless to meet with him over decided issues. I was kind enough not to call him a liar. I realize he is a very close friend of yours. I requested that he cut to the chase, get to the truth and go to the board and convince the board members to agree to a forensic audit. He said he wouldn't spend the taxpayers dollars in that manner. It makes one wonder "what's to hide?"

The board will approve hundreds of thousands of dollars to pay Quorum for consulting fees and will not approve paying for a forensic audit to get at the truth.

Does your last statement, "It is time for everyone to begin to work together for a more constructive outcome," mean we should all fall in line, praise and follow your leadership into a 25 bed Critical Access Hospital? Mr. Lambert are you telling everyone in the county that there is no falsehood in your statements and plans for a CAH hospital? If all 225 employees still have their jobs because of the CAH, what other reasons will you let them go or decrease their hours?

Some of these people are friends. They have bills to pay and families to support.

TAKING IT TO THE BORGER SUPPRESS!

On Saturday morning, I walked into the newspaper and gave a copy of the taped conversation between Quang Gno and myself to the News-Herald Editor. She asked me questions and took notes. She lived up to all my expectations and never a story was published in the following weeks. I wondered who's big ears were burning when I left her office?

CHAPTER TWENTY SIX

DISTRICT ATTORNEY GETS HEAT

In the Letters to the Editor, Mr. Jack Harvin in Borger proclaimed, "I fail to understand why someone like Mr. Ballman should get preferential treatment of the magnitude reported!!! This is ludicrous and unacceptable!!! This man knew the consequences of his actions and preferential treatment was NOT THE ANSWER!!!

Now that the public knows his lapse of judgment, if you want to call it that? I believe Judge Smith should be held accountable as well as Mr. Ballman to their actions. Favors of this type we as a county and city DO NOT NEED!!!"

Ms. Helen Klapper responded, that she and others were witnesses to the culmination when Ballman was removed from his car. She questioned, "Why was he not placed in jail?" And would any other Borger citizen be let off without any punishment after leaving the scene in a drunken state and be set free?

The BIG question is, 'Can people in high positions be set free with no punishment when regular citizens pay a penalty—jail, fine or both?'

Judge Smith also stated that he was not informed of the problem. Is driving and drinking while intoxicated and causing an accident not a problem?"

NO ADDITIONAL CHARGES AGAINST BALLMAN

The May 16th front page story in the News-Herald stated, "Borger Police Department Detective Sgt. Jeremy Hundley told the Borger News-Herald Monday morning that it is unlikely charges for hit and run will be filed against 84th District Attorney Clay Ballman.

Hundley said that since the DWI is a Class B Misdemeanor and is a higher charge than the hit-and-run which is a Class C Misdemeanor as there were no injuries reported in the wreck. He said that this is a routine procedure.

He also confirmed that officers broke out the right rear passenger window of the 1998 Chrysler to gain entry to the vehicle. He said the doors to the vehicle were locked and that Ballman was unresponsive towards the officers.

JUDGE SMITH GETS HEATED CRITICISM

On May 19th, Mr. A.B. Hunt wrote a very passionate Letter to the Editor.

"This letter regards our "esteemed" DA, Clay Ballman. However, it is directed to District Judge Smith. If you were correctly quoted in the Borger News-Herald, "no one indicated there was a problem"—my question would be just this. Just how much of a dunderhead does one have to be to not realize that there is a problem when some joker calls at midnight for a "get out of jail free" card? All the more so, if that joker is the DA.

Rumor his it that he was in your company while doing his imbibing. If so, were you not aware of his condition when you parted company? Perhaps the question of shared responsibility should be raised here! Your action, while less potentially deadly, is not one whit less contemptible.

Regarding the "no one indicated there was a problem" statement. I learned something interesting. I spoke with someone in the Sheriff's Office whom I am confident was a high ranking deputy but I did not get his name and would not state it if I had. I was told that "we don't usually question the judge." When I put forth the idea that to do so would be tantamount to questioning the king, he readily agreed. As we all know, no one questions the king because the king can do no wrong.

Letter writer Kenneth Gibbs professes to know Smith as a good Christian. I submit that, with his ordering of Ballman's release, he becomes an enabler. I would agree with Gibbs that he did not have all the facts, since the booking officer would not dare to question the judge, as informing him of Ballman's obviously drunken condition. To do so would have been potentially dangerous to the health of this individual.

Since Ballman had not resigned, it is clear that he places his personal well being above that of the 84th Judicial Court system.

Finally, since Smith failed to recognize that there was a problem, may I suggest that he resign. (Big Joke!) Then, perhaps, we could get a judge, who, rather than showing judicial arrogance, would have the common courtesy to ask, "What do I need to know about this situation?" Then, the booking officer could answer the judge's question rather that be in the position of "questioning the judge." A.B. Hunt, Borger

Judge Smith is a reputed good Christian and Deacon at the First Baptist Church. Judge Smith never responded nor denied he was with Clay Ballman before his DWI accident. Were his intentions good when he gave Ballman a "free get-out-of jail" card? Did he do a good, kind thing for Clay Ballman? Would he have done the same good kind thing for an ordinary citizen in Hutchinson County who would call him at 12:30 AM?

THREATS SILENCE FREEDOM OF SPEECH

I contacted Ray Shoemaker (Healthcare Engineers), in Mississippi a couple of weeks before their group was to make a presentation to the hospital board on Thursday,

May 19th. He agreed their group would attend the following day and speak before business managers representing companies in the community. We arranged to set up a sandwich luncheon in the large meeting room in the Phillips Building. I contacted Dr. Paul Anderson and he accepted my invitation to introduce the people from Healthcare Engineers.

At about 10:00, I got a call telling me the Mississippi group would not be able to attend the meeting. We had spent days contacting people to invite them and there was no way to call it off. I became outraged when I made a phone call and found out the real reason they canceled the meeting.

I did my best to remain calm and greet people at the door as they arrived. About 50 people filled the meeting room. I stood at the podium and apologetically told the audience that Healthcare Engineers had an emergency and had to return earlier to Mississippi. I called on Brother Paul Anderson to come up and lead us in prayer.

Following Paul Anderson's prayer, he said, "What I liked about the meeting with Tri-Lakes was they were so positive. Their outlook was such that they could do about anything. I like that outlook in people and they proved it. This one doctor gave up his practice to become the administrator of the hospital. Being a doctor, he has the personality that's special to doctors in order to be respected. They begin to fill the hospital up and doctors came together to change things considerably. There are some very positive things they had to offer. It showed you can get some things done if people will just come together and cooperate. We asked a lot of question and they always had a good answer. It was good close management. They actually have less population than we have in Hutchinson County and yet they were able to successfully turn a hospital around on a situation similar to ours.

I thanked Brother Paul and added, "Their original proposal was a blending with the county hospital with a partnership and a 20 year written agreement not to sell the new facility they would build. They offered up to $40 million to invest in a new hospital and assisted living facility. I felt that was very generous because if the 25 million dollar bond issue had passed the extra money taken away from Phillips and other large companies in taxes could be saved and possibly used for other charitable things in our community.

Another thing that impressed me with Tri-Lakes being that I have a marketing background, is they saw the opportunity of having a facility in Borger that could reach a 60,000 population. A new facility located in Borger, Texas with proper management, management without past baggage that treats people with excellent health care."

Then, I opened the floor to questions and concluded the meeting by saying, "In my heart I want the truth. I want the truth for people in Borger, Texas and Hutchinson County. There are some of the best people here . . . people I've known all my life. They're good, honest people. They need good health care. It's about taking care of people in our community. It's not about a few people's salaries at the hospital. It's about a community that's like a family. That's what I've contributed my time to.

People have called me a radical and a trouble maker. That's fine, I'm big enough not to let words bother me, because in my heart I know who I am. It's just a matter of exercising the power in speaking out to get at the truth. Again, I apologize for the people from Mississippi not being able to be here today."

It was reported that political pressure was applied to the group from Mississippi. They felt if they attended the luncheon, they might as well forget being one of the companies under consideration to buy the hospital. Once again, freedom of speech was suppressed in Hutchinson County.

I'LL BUY AN AD TO GET THE STORY OUT

I was absolutely fed up with excuses from the News-Herald editor. It was May 26, and twenty-one days had passed and she had not published my rebuttal story to Jock Lee's front page story branding me a liar. I decided to buy a quarter page ad and if the newspaper refused to run the ad, we would picket the paper and call all the television stations in Amarillo. I could visualize a dozen or more people marching in front of the paper with signs reading "BORGER NEWS-HERALD SUPPRESSES FREE SPEECH".

I pulled up in front of the News-Herald and walked inside. Looking at the receptionist, I asked, "Is L.W. here?" One of the women standing in front directed me to his office.

"Hi. How are you?", he responded when I entered. "Just wanted to stop by and visit with you," I said when taking a seat across from his desk.

We exchanged pleasantries. He commented on my casual dress. I was in a suit following the meeting at Phillips Building when he saw me last. We exchanged small talk about his working in Houston, Texas and having to suit up everyday.

"I want to discuss this article," (showing him the front page of the Thursday, May 5, 2005 edition).

"This bothers me because I was never contacted to get my side of the story." I talked to Nancy the next day and told her this is wrong when someone can call me a liar on the front page of any newspaper without giving me the opportunity to defend myself. This is not fair impartial journalism."

I've waited 21 days and if my only alternative is to pay for an ad to get the other side of the story out I'll do it."

I handed the print ad across the desk to L.W. and waited while he read the ad.

McCall said, "I'll run this in the paper."

I thanked him and left. I was surprised because it was not the response I expected. I remembered how the previous publisher had refused to run the ad with the child pornography documents. Maybe L.W. McCall is a stand up man.

The ad ran in the May 28-29 Weekend.

What's There to Lie or Hide About?

On May 5, 2005, a front page article in the Borger News Herald quoted Jock Lee, GPCH board member referring to me as a liar. He claimed that "I contacted him and said I would contact Dr. Ed Quiros to attend the meeting to discuss issues of misinformation and that I would call Lee back to set a meeting." **The truth is that Dr. Quiros agreed to a meeting before I called Lee. Lee's statement is untrue. Dr. Quiros has been a local doctor for 27 years and will back my story.**

This article upset me very much because the newspaper editor did not contact me to get the whole story before going to press. Following the story, I went to her office and she interviewed me. I have asked her numerous times when my side of the story will be published only to hear that she doesn't have time. I explained that I called Lee and said I was so frustrated with his story and to forget about meeting on things that are already decided. **If Lee wants to get to the truth, go the hospital board and convince them to vote for a forensic audit. What's there to hide?"**

This is not the first time the editor has omitted the other side of the story:

Most recently, the paper has not published comments made by **Mr. Quang Ngo, licensed coordinator for State of Texas Center for Rural Health Initiatives regarding GPCH proposal for Critical Access Hospital**. He is quoted saying, "It surprised me that a hospital of your size, 99 licensed beds, would want to go all the way down to a 25 bed facility. **This is probably the biggest hospital that ever wanted to plug up to Critical Access Hospital Status the whole time that I've been here. It was surprising to me but we don't disallow anybody who wants to take a look at it.** It didn't make sense to be honest with you. **In the current facility, everyone in the community should have the question, "How are you going to maintain the same level of service if you're going to reduce your beds to 25?"**

The majority of the citizens in Hutchinson County know about the horrid management at the Hospital. **It doesn't make sense when an intelligent man like Dr. Jock Lee doesn't get it?** A forensic audit has been asked for twice to no avail. Maybe Lee would agree to a mutual lie detector test. We'll bring our questions and he can bring his questions.

THE TRUTH COULD HURT!

Paid for by Glenn Baxter, Chairman-Citizens Who Care About Hutchinson County

LAMBERT RESPONDS TO BAXTER'S AD

The following weekend of June 4-5, I opened the newspaper to page 4. At the top of the page there was a Guest Column with a picture of Norm Lambert. The headline read: ADMINISTRATOR LAMBERT RESPONDS TO BAXTER'S AD.

How outrageous! After paying for freedom of speech to get out the other side of the story, Lambert was getting free space to respond to my ad.

Lambert attacked and attempted to spin the truth to manipulate public opinion. In his article he says, "He (Baxter) quotes a State official after misleading him with hypothethetical questions that did not identify Borger as the subject."

This was an untrue because Golden Plains Community Hospital was clearly identified on the recorded tape

What surprised me was that he quoted Mr. Ngo as stating, "due to Baxter's underhanded recording of their conversation, he was advised by the State's legal counsel not to get involved further in what appeared to be a political matter in Borger. Mr. Ngo did assure me that he was aware of our situation and fully supported our decision to Convert to Critical Access."

I wondered what kind of political pressure changed Mr. Ngo's tune. There was nothing underhanded about recording his statements. Reporters record interviews all the time. I purposely and pointedly asked him to repeat his name and position because I was releasing his statements to the press in Borger and Amarillo.

FOUL PLAY AT THE NEWS-HERALD

On Monday, I went to the News Herald to see the publisher. I walked into his office and said, "What's going on?" He responded, "I hate to rush you but . . ." I quickly said, "What's this about Norm Lambert responding to my ad"

He replied, "I didn't know we had that in there. I haven't read Sunday's paper yet." I didn't stop talking, "I paid for an ad to get an opinion out and then he (Lambert) gets a Guest Column to respond to my ad. That didn't cost him anything!"

"I'll have to ask Nancy about this," replied McCall. "I'm going to have to have a long talk with her."

I went on to question the doctor's survey and asked, Why was Dr. Rogers mentioned in the newspaper and why is the survey being split up over two days. It seems this will confuse readers."

"Dr. Rogers said that he wanted to have his name used with his questionnaire. And we saw no reason not to print his name. Any of the doctor's could have had their name printed with their survey. All the others wanted anonominity. We're doing this in two parts because I had serious doubts about the 5 that came in all at once being legitimate. Four of the 5 were typed and one was hand written. They were all in the same envelope and same stationery. I'm just very uncomfortable about it but we are going to report them.

I told McCall that I was in Dr. Quiros office when he was filling out his survey. I knew for a fact that all 5 of the doctor's were sending their surveys to the newspaper in one package and they were legitimate.

I called the publisher on Wednesday, June 8th to see what he had decided about a Guest Column.

"Hello, this is McCall, how can I help you?" I replied, "L.W. this is Glenn Baxter and I'm getting back with you about the Guest Column."

McCall responded, "Glenn, you get to have the Guest Column one time. Then, we're going to end pretty much all of this. The calls back and forth are not productive anymore. But, you do have one Guest Column."

My response was, "Okay, I'll get it together for this weekend edition. Thank you L.W., bye.

DOCTORS GIVE VIEWS ON GOLDEN PLAINS

The News-Herald conducted the survey of the doctors at Golden Plains Community Hospital where they could voice their opinions. The doctors were not required to place their names on the survey forms. They did not want to become bigger targets by expressing their views. They feared retaliation from the hospital administration.

Six out of the nine doctors who submitted survey forms said the number one change that would benefit the hospital would be to terminate the CEO and the COO. The majority spoke and again were ignored.

A GUEST OF THE NEWS-HERALD

The following weekend on June 12 my guest column ran with headline: BAXTER RESPONDS TO LAMBERT CONCERNING HOSPITAL.

I wish to respond to Norm Lambert's Guest Column on June 4-5, 2005. Our goal is to work together where each citizen prospers from an inspired community life based on a shared vision for all citizens and not only a few who decide for others at Golden Plains Community Hospital.

On September 27, 1999 Lambert signed a contract for a refurbished $615,000 MRI that was financed over 60 months for a total of $703,131. The Board was never given the contract to review. This equipment was purchased unseen. In the agreement, its states: There are no warranties, written or oral, provided otherwise: All service and parts covered under this agreement are provided as is. This equipment never functioned properly. Additional legal cost was incurred by the hospital and an FBI investigation of the vendor.

One thousand forty one citizens signed a petition requesting a forensic audit. A forensic audit is about a "fraud" investigation. Apparently, many citizens suspected fraud at GPCH at that time. The hospital's attorney stated there was no such thing as a forensic audit. Incredibly, Mr. Lambert in his article acknowledges that forensic audits are for real. I HAVE COPIES OF ALL THESE DOCUMENTS RELATING TO THE MRI AS PROOF!

The same Chief Financial Officer that Mr. Lambert blamed for the purchase of the MRI was the same CFO who Lambert presented a one month's severance pay check in the amount of $11,000 and allowed him to submit a letter of resignation following the discovery of 5 photos of child pornography that was sealed from others until its disclosure 15 months later. I HAVE COPIES OF THE CHECK, RESIGNATION LETTER AND ALL OTHER DOCUMENTS AS PROOF!

Mr. Lambert writes about my "quoting a state official after misleading him with a hypothetical question that did not identify Borger as the subject. This is not true. I did identify Borger and I did ask him to "restate his name because I'm going to take this information to the Newspaper." It's true that I recorded the conversation rather than taking notes. After I told him the background of GPCH, Mr. Ngo stated: "We've heard of similar stories. It seems clear as daylight that whoever is administrating now is not doing a good job and is primarily the cause of the downfall of the facility, yet the local politics are such that it's nearly impossible to get those people out and get folks in with new ideas that can help."

I HAVE THIS ON AUDIO TAPE AS PROOF!

I have findings on the Doctor's Building at 202 South McGee with present day estimates provided by the company who built the project and another competitive company. The estimate is based on the approved specifications from the City of Borger. Five years later, when costs have risen, the building can be constructed today for $150,000 less. On May 2, 2005, I gave a copy of this information to District Attorney Clay Ballman and requested an investigation.

Mr. Lambert, it is not up to me or any other citizen to bring you proof. It is up to you and others to prove they did not commit fraud. Those are the guidelines of a forensic audit that follows the paper trail.

My rhetoric is about focusing attention on the lack of leadership that has ignored the majority of tax paying citizens. Taxpayer dollars have been mismanaged. The Texas Tech Survey stated that the administration is the number one reason the bond issue was voted down. The recent doctor surveys obtained by the Borger News Herald clearly state that your leadership is the number one problem at GPCH. Two thirds of the Doctors who responded, strongly suggest a new CEO and COO would benefit the hospital. The majority of people in Hutchinson County know that new management will make the hospital better. What is hurting the hospital is your management and select board members who keep you in power.

Glenn Baxter
CCHC Chairman

After writing the Guest Column, I recalled how good it sounded when McCall saying "we're going to end pretty much all of this". I took that to mean that the hospital CEO wouldn't get to make a response to my Guest Column. I had received some telephone numbers of some people who were very upset over patient care at Golden Plains and wanted to talk with me. I decided to call them and get their stories.

CHAPTER TWENTY SEVEN

FAMILY MEMBERS LOSE LOVED ONES AT GPCH.

These are stories of people who lost loved ones at Golden Plains Community Hospital and a story of a doctor losing a patient. Interviews like these are never reported in the Borger News-Herald. What's reported in the paper are usually stories about complaints in the ER at GPCH. Then, there is paid advertising promoting 90% plus patient satisfaction at Golden Plains.

BILL SPELCE LOSES HIS WIFE.

"At about 4 o'clock in the morning on December 5th, She was having difficulty breathing and woke me up and said I think you need to take me to the hospital because I can't catch my breath. I jumped up and started to put my clothes on. She said why don't you just go ahead and call 911. So I called 911 and the fire department got here first. They came in and put an oxygen bottle on her. She said, "Oh that feels so good"

In a minute or so an ambulance came. They were talking to her. She said, I just can't get my breath as she walked to get in the ambulance. As she lay down she said, "Oh, I can't breathe laying down. Sit me up a little bit." They were going to take her on the ambulance and I wanted to go with them, but they said I would have to follow.

We went to the emergency room. I wasn't too far behind them and I noticed when they were on Cedar Street, they turned the siren on. When we got to the emergency room they wouldn't let me in. I sat there waiting for quite a while before the Doctor came out.

He said that before they got to the emergency room they gave her Albuteral. She immediately slumped on them when they gave her that. There was only one man in the back and one man driving. So, I guess the one in the back couldn't use the paddles on her and give her oxygen at the same time. So, they just rushed her into the emergency room.

When I finally got to go see her they had a ventilator tube and all kind of wires hooked up to her. She was completely out. She was taken on Lifestar to Amarillo. We finally got there in about 45 minutes and checked in. When I finally get to see her, she's still out

When the Doctors begin to check her in Amarillo, the heart Doctor says I'm not concerned about her heart, what has happened to your wife is that she's brain dead from lack of oxygen.

What it amounted to was that Verna left here walking and talking and she left the (GPCH) emergency room brain dead. She was 61 years old and in good health. She didn't have asthma and in all the reports I got, I can be heard clearly saying, "**NO, she does not**

have asthma," on the police recording. I've contacted several Attorneys and they won't take the case unless I have a pot of money."

*NOTE: Albuterol is prescribed for asthma patients. The stated side effects of Albuterol are: stop taking Albuterol and seek emergency medical attention if you experience an allergic reaction (**difficulty breathing: closing of your throat,** swelling of your lips, tongue, or face; or hives); or chest pain or irregular heartbeats.*

MARILYN REEVES LOSES HER FATHER

"My Dad apparently had gotten sick at his stomach and was starting to throw up, coffee grounds like old blood. He had a history of peptic ulcer disease but, it had been over 25 years since it had given him any problems. I took my Dad's blood-pressure, pulse and everything. I did what I could and when I saw what he was throwing up, I told him you're going to have to go and get checked at the emergency room.

Golden Plains Hospital has let me down so many times but I still thought I'd give them a chance to help my dad. I asked my dad if he thought he could go in to the Borger hospital if my Mom drove him there. My mother drove him to the emergency room and a doctor there examined him. They did do cardiac enzymes test but they didn't do an EKG. I figured that the hospital would admit him for overnight observation and give him some fluids.

They treated him and gave him some Pepcid for stomach and some IV fluids and some Phenogren. He did say that he was feeling better after that, and they sent them home and gave him his discharge instructions. They gave him prescriptions to be filled the next day at the pharmacy. This happened on a Sunday.

Halfway back home near Buena Vista, my dad starts throwing up blood again. My Mom turns the car around to take him back to the hospital. When they arrived at the hospital, he doesn't want to get out. He probably felt like that although he was sick, he gave them the chance the first time around and he didn't want to give them another opportunity. My Mom goes in the emergency rooms and calls me. I tell her to talk to one of the nurses in the emergency room and ask the nurse to go out and encourage him to come inside to be reevaluated.

On discharge instructions, it says, if your condition worsens then notify the emergency room and come back in. Well, the nurse goes out there and looks at what he's thrown up and says "that's just old blood, it's no big deal".

IT'S NO BIG DEAL! It's not normal for anyone to throw up stuff that looks like that. She didn't go out to encourage him to come in. She should have said, Mr. Nelson, your condition is getting worse. We need to get you back in the emergency room and do another assessment. We may have overlooked something. Let's go back and make sure things are going to be right because this is definitely abnormal. This is something she should have said to him. I was told she said, "It's no Big Deal". What kind of nurse or anybody in the medical field would say that?

Any way they go back home and arrive there about 6:30 PM. My Mom was exhausted and she fell asleep there in the chair in the living room. My Dad was up-and-down . . . very uncomfortable, fidgety and restless. You know that's a sign of internal bleeding. Then at midnight, she called and said he's still real sick. I told my mother to call an ambulance and get him to the hospital in Amarillo.

He arrived in Amarillo at about 2:30 in the morning and he passed away at 6:35 that morning. He didn't have the typical symptoms of a heart attack although his EKG in Amarillo indicated he had a heart attack.

All that Golden Plains did was cover up the symptoms on the surface. They did not know how to stop his bleeding and failed to admit him for 24 hour observation. I feel like they looked at my Dad and thought since he is 83 years old, let's do the minimum and sweep it under the rug. I believe that human life is so taken for granted by some health care professionals. They don't give a crap after you reach a certain age. That's wrong! I don't care if you're over 90 years old, no one has the right to discount life."

ONE DOCTOR'S STORY

Doctor: "It was a lady that had asthma and really what I thought was just a routine admission. She'd had it for a long time and she tolerated low oxygen levels pretty well. Then one night she went into respiratory failure and I think that because the Nurses were used to seeing her do that . . . she would pull off her oxygen and go into a really bad spell of hypoxemia but her body was used to it, so it didn't make her look all that bad.

So this particular night I think she pulled her oxygen off repetitively (they couldn't keep it on) and finally went into respiratory failure *and they never called me . . . all night.* And she died seven or seven thirty the next morning. *And it would have been pretty easy to treat.* But the nurses just never called me about it. The COO/Director of Nurses at the time convinced me that the nurses had done everything right. I just forget their exact ploy. The real thing was that the patient was in respiratory failure. She couldn't think because her oxygen level was so low. And she wasn't functioning as an adult. Even if she refused therapy, she was goofy because of the hypoxemia and wasn't behaving rationally because of that reason. It's not like you had a patient who understood everything and decided to refuse treatment.

They knew I was unhappy about it. And the COO/Director of Nurses probably tricked me into not applying heat. The other problem though was that *if I wanted to be aggressive about this case, they could turn it around on me. Because really in another sense I'm responsible even if they didn't call me I'm the attending physician. And they could make it hard on me so I just dropped it."* As far as I can tell they're not going to do anything official from the inside to investigate it or anything. *They have already done that to their satisfaction. It's very disappointing to say the least.*

Response: Did the patients relatives ever make a comment about it or anything.

Doctor: No. Not that I'm aware of.

Response: They just accepted it and went on?

Doctor: They haven't been in contact with us. This is a lady who has family out of town. And, I think another thing is that this ladies death was inevitable. This was a person that really did not take care of themselves and did not make much of an active effort to improve herself. She just abused her body, she was probably a drug abuser and smoked and if you got asthma and still smoking you've got a death wish. And so even with good medical treatment, the lady was killing herself by the way she lived her life and it was inevitable that something like this was going to happen.

Now it happened sooner than it should have in my view. And the lady still had the opportunity to clean things up and start living right. It probably was not going to happen. She did not strike me as someone who would be responsible about her own health care. So in that sense, she died prematurely but the same thing would have happened a few years later.

GOOD KIND THINGS FOR OTHERS?

Makes one wonder how many more patient stories and doctor stories go unreported. Doctors are afraid to say anything because of possible retaliation against them. The patients feel helpless because law firms refuse to take their cases and the newspapers seldom print their stories.

In Texas, the passing of Proposition 12 tort reforms in 2003 placed a cap of $250,000 per defendant. This has severely hurt Plaintiffs of malpractice suits and has led attorneys in Texas to turn down cases they would have taken on contingency in the past. Passing the tort reforms made it extremely better for business (hospitals/doctors) and extremely unfair for ordinary folks.

Medicine is about being compassionate over the suffering of others. It's placing the highest sanctity on life. When it becomes about greed and power, it becomes depersonalized. Patients are thought of as a heart in bed one, a broken leg in room two, renal failure in room four, or the drug addict in room eight.

SPECIAL PROSECUTOR APPOINTED

It was announced on the front page of the June 2, News-Herald that the Oldham County District Attorney was appointed to prosecute the driving while intoxicated cases against Clay Ballman.

Kent Birdsong was appointed by Judge Jack Worsham. Hutchinson County Attorney Mike Milner recused himself from the case.

The reason for the special prosecutors and judges is so the defendant gets a fair and impartial trial.

FIRM MAY HELP SELL HOSPITAL

In the June 7th edition of the News-Herald, the GPCH Board of Directors announced plans to contract Stroudwater, Associates to sell or lease the hospital.

Lambert was quoted, "There are three factors that the board is looking at in a company.

- provide the capital to build a new hospital
- provide needed health care to patients while working with the community and physicians
- and have experience in owning hospitals

Stroudwater is not promising a buyer, Lambert said. He said that if the local hospital was located in a high population growth area that it would be sold easily. However, since the area is in population decline, that it will be more difficult.

It was also announced at the Board meeting that patient revenues were down. Chief Financial Officer Bill Remming told Board Members that gross patient revenue is down 14.8 percent from the same period last year.

Was the decrease in patient revenues due to increasing distrust of the hospital administration and doctors sending patients to other hospitals outside of Hutchinson County?

It had been over 9 months since the bond election had failed. What happened to the fear factor of urgency to build or close? Why did the board continue to support the CEO? The majority of voters and the majority of doctors saw the administration as the number one problem. Why hadn't the board terminated the CEO?

WHO IS SELINA McCLELLAN?

On Monday June 13, 2005 in the News-Herald, it was intriguing to read the Letters to the Editor because of one of the two letters attacking me. One was from an individual who had written in the past. She was connected as a past employee (nurse) with the hospital who had been hired, fired, rehired or whatever. The other letter was written from someone new. I was curious about this woman and why she was writing. Did she did have any connections with the hospital?

Dear Editor:

I am so sick and tired of opening my newspaper and seeing another article or letter from Mr. Baxter to Mr. Lambert and vice versa. I feel that Mr. Baxter has a personal vendetta against not only Mr. Lambert, but our community as a whole.

I do not personally know Mr. Baxter, but my impression of him is that he thrives on making other people miserable. It seems he is out to ruin people's lives, take advantage of people and make everyone around him miserable.

This is just the impression I get from all the letters and articles he has submitted to the Borger News-Herald.

I am wondering if Mr. Baxter has a self esteem problem or something. I would love to see some of that negative energy be turned into something positive.

I sincerely hope that I am not the only person in Hutchinson County who is tired of his endless rhetoric.

Selena McClellan, Borger

Actually, I was getting sick and tired of writing letters to the editor! If it wasn't for my personal integrity, love of freedom, and belief in speaking up against injustice, I would have placed all the energy in my business and other matters. Unlike some others, I am not one to look the other way, stick my head in the sand and live a life of resignation.

I had become a target of unkind things. I was suspicious of Selena McClellan and her motives!

CHAPTER TWENTY EIGHT

WHAT HAPPENED TO LARRY LANGLEY?

Thursday, June 23, 2005. Today I felt exhausted over battling Lambert through opinion articles. Mentally, I was saying, "I'm through. There's nothing more I can write or say about that man or his administration."

I had asked around about "what happened to Larry Langley?" No one seemed to know.

I was able to search and find his address with an unlisted phone number in Austin. But, no one could tell me anything about Larry Langley's trial.

Predictably, the Borger News-Herald never followed up on the story to its conclusion at the Courthouse in Stinnett. Everything said and heard had been vague, so it was time to drive to the Hutchinson County Courthouse and research the case.

I arrived at the courthouse and walked upstairs to records. One of the clerks showed me how to use the computer to find felony cases. I typed in Larry Langley and pressed enter. A screen came up showing Langley, Larry Nelson with the Austin address.

The screen recorded two cases filed against Mr. Langley:

24071   9101   F-MISAPP FIDUCIARY/FINANCIAL 01/25/00 DISPOSED CSDC
21820   8702   F-POSS POSS PROMOTION OF CHIL 01/25/00 DISPOSED
316 DISTRICT
10/07/03 DISMISSED   INDICTED 06/26/2001
ATTORNEY: DAVID ISERN
PROS. ATTORNEY: CLAY BALLMAN
-DISMISSED—CONVICTED IN A 10/07/2003
PLED GUILTY TO IN # 9101
ON OCTOBER 3RD 2003, 84TH JUDICIAL ATTORNEY CLAY BALLMAN REQUIRES COURT TO DISMISS THE ABOVE ENTITLED AND NUMBERED CASE FOR FOLLOWING REASON-
DEFENDENT PLED GUILTY TO AN INFORMATION IN CAUSE NO. 9101 AND PLACED ON DEFERRED COMMUNITY SUPERVISION FOR THREE YEARS-
WHEREFORE, THE STATE PRAYS THIS ABOVE AND NUMBERED CASE BE DISMISSED-
SIGNED BY CLAY BALLMAN, DISTRICT ATTORNEY AND JUDGE JOHN LAGRONE

I left the courthouse with the copies of all the documents and drove back home. How and why did Langley get off so easily on child pornography felony charges? Something about the documents really bothered me.

Sitting at my desk, I read over another file of documents. I looked at the copy of the check for gross amount of $11,703.72. When I saw the date on the check I almost fell over. The check was dated on 01/31/00. Langley was paid 5 days after the date of offense on cause 9102 and 8702.

I had never really interviewed Cynthia Lagrone about Larry Langley so I called her on the telephone to discuss what I had found at the Courthouse. I was puzzled why she was not called or listed as a witness to the case.

Cynthia: "It was in the morning of January 27, 2000, when Norm (Lambert) brought me the sealed package. NO ONE IS TO OPEN THIS EXCEPT NORM LAMBERT, CEO OR HOSPITAL ATTORNEY LEON MITCHELL was marked on the outside of the envelope. It was sealed with tape and he told me to lock it up and I did."

Question: "Cynthia, are you sure it was January 28," I replied.

Cynthia: "Yes, and what was strange was the that Shirley Langley called me that afternoon. She remarked that Norm is trying to get rid of Larry and she mentioned "girlie pictures". The next day on the 28th, Leon Mitchell comes to Norm's office. Norm came to me and asked for the envelope. He carried the envelope into his office to meet with Larry Langley and Leon Mitchell. Leon left about an hour later at about 10:15 a.m."

Question: "Then what happened?"

Cynthia: "Ten minutes later, Norm brings envelope back to me and says, "Here, lock it back up." "When I looked at the envelop it was still intact. The tape had not been removed."

Question: "You're telling me it appeared that the envelope wasn't opened," I said.

Cynthia: "Yes. Then Denette called me saying that Norm needed to meet with Patty Wilhite and me. When we met in his office, he said, "Larry Langley was leaving. It was his last day." I looked at Norm and said, "I'm not surprised because Shirley Langley said you were trying to get rid of him over girlie pictures." Norm quickly said, "No that's not it!" At 10:30 A.M. Norm called a meeting of all of Langley's department managers to break the news. Later that afternoon of the 28th a Memo was sent out announcing that Larry Langley had resigned."

Question: "Tell me again how Lambert supposedly got the pictures," I asked.

Cynthia: "Denette, Patty Wilhite, secretary's offices were together next to Larry's office. He was gone that day and they went into his office to find papers for a report they were putting together. They said they found the pictures on top of Larry's desk in a folder."

Response: "That was stupid of Langley," I responded.

Cynthia: "Then Denette called Jolene and they took the pictures to Norm Lambert.

Question: "How long were the pictures locked up after Lambert handed the sealed package back to you?"

Cynthia: "I was in possession of the sealed package from January 28, 2000 until March 12, 2001.

　　　　　　That was about one year and two months. On March 12th, Mr. Brice, the investigator for the District Attorney came to pick up the sealed package. Previously he called me and said he wanted Larry Langley's Social Security number, driver's license number, and the sealed package. I told him I couldn't give him the information without someone's approval. He told me he could get a supeno and suggested I call attorney Leon Mitchell. I called Leon and he told me to let him have what he wanted."

Question: "Why was Langley's check dated January 31, 2000," I asked.

Cynthia: "He walked out on the 28th, so accounting must have processed the check and mailed it to him."

Cynthia Lagrone was really shocked when I told her the possession of child pornography charges were dropped against Larry Langley through a plea bargain where he pled guilty to the offense of MISAPROPRIATION OF FIDUCIARY PROPERTY and his punishment was a fine of $1,000, $287.25 in court costs and placed on community supervision (deferred adjudication) for three years.

She didn't know that Langley had suffered a heart attack. The records state that on March 12, 2003 a Motion for Continuance was filed because defendant (Langley) was continuing to recover from a heart attack he suffered.

In the case files was an APPLICATION TO WAIVE, AND WAIVER OF TRIAL BY JURY signed off on October 1, 2003. This effectively kept the case out of the public eye and the media.

Although Langley pleaded not guilty to the five (counts) photos of child pornography taken from Larry Langley's computer at Golden Plains Community Hospital, why didn't District Attorney Ballman prosecute to the fullest extent of the law? The disgusting evidence was there for everyone to see.

A warning that some of what you read is explicit. It is imperative that the horrific graphic descriptions of the 5 Counts be presented. As a father and grandfather, it sickens and angers me when I read the depiction of the photos. The reality and full impact of this crime need to be understood by readers and every citizen in Hutchinson County.

LARRY NELSON LANGLEY (hereinafter referred to as "Defendant"),

(Count One) did then and there knowingly and intentionally possess visual material that depicted a female child younger than 18 years of age at the time the image of the said child was made, who was engaging in sexual conduct, to wit: by lewd exhibition of the said child's genitals and breast below the top of the areola, in that said visual material depicts frontal nudity of the said child, and the Defendant then and there knew the said visual possess visual material depicted the said lewd exhibition,

(Count Two) did then and there knowingly and intentionally possess visual material that depicted a female child younger than 18 years of age at the time the image of the said child was made, who was engaging in sexual conduct, to wit: by lewd exhibition of the said child's genitals and one breast below the top of the areola, in that said visual material depicts frontal nudity of the said child while the said child has her fingers in her mouth, and the Defendant then and there knew the said visual material depicted the lewd exhibition,

(Count Three) did then and there knowingly and intentionally possess visual material that depicted two female children both younger than 18 years of age at the time the image of the said children was made, who were engaging in sexual conduct, to wit: by lewd exhibition of the said children's genitals and breasts below the top of the areola, in that said visual material depicts frontal nudity of the said children while the said children have an arm around each other, and the Defendant then and there knew the said visual material depicted the said lewd exhibition,

(Count Four) did then and there knowingly and intentionally possess visual material that depicted two female children younger than 18 years of age at the time the image of the said child was made, who was engaging in sexual conduct, to wit: by lewd exhibition of the said child's genitals, in that said visual material depicts frontal nudity of the said child while the said child's genitals were near the exposed penis of a male person, and the Defendant then and there knew the said visual material depicted the said lewd exhibition, and

(Count Five) did then and there knowingly and intentionally possess visual material that depicted a female child younger than 18 years of age at the time the image of the said child was made, who was engaging in sexual conduct, to wit: by lewd exhibition of the said child's genitals, in that said visual material depicts frontal nudity of the said child while the said child's genitals were in contact with the exposed penis of a male person, and the Defendant then and there knew the said visual material depicted the said lewd exhibition, and the Grand Jurors aforesaid, upon their oaths aforesaid, do further present in and to said court that all of the counts contained in this indictment are offenses which arose out of the same criminal episode by the Defendant prior to the presentment of this indictment,

AGAINST THE PEACE AND DIGNITY OF THE STATE

Signed: Robert Bradley, Foreperson of the Grand Jury

Found on testimony of C. H. Price—Criminal Investigator—DA's office Denette Ehrlich, Jolee Hoff, and Norman Lambert

I couldn't believe my eyes when I saw the name and signature of the Foreperson of the Grand Jury. Robert Bradley was the same individual I ran against in the May 2005 School Board Election. Mr. Bradley is an African American. Since Mr. Bradley serves on a School Board in the best interest of children, I wonder how the 5 photos impact his thoughts each day?

The waiver of a jury trial kept everything "hush-hush" and out of the news. District Attorney Clay Ballman through a plea bargain elected not to prosecute Larry Langley to the fullest extent of the law. WHY!!!

CHILD PORNO PREDATOR RELEASED ON AUSTIN, TEXAS

Mr. Langley was able to walk away quietly from Hutchinson County without a single headline appearing in the Borger News-Herald or the Amarillo Globe.

Questions still haunted me. Why wasn't Langley immediately terminated? According to his contract there was definitely cause to fire him without any severance. Why was he awarded severance pay 5 days after the date of his offense? Why wasn't a simple management decision made to terminate an employee over child pornography and contact the authorities? Why wasn't an emergency meeting of the board of directors called to disclose the problem? Why weren't these sound management decisions made? Wasn't there a flagrant abuse and waste of taxpayers' dollars on an accused child pornography pervert? Were the photos checked for fingerprints and if so, whose fingerprints were on the five photos?

Was there a deal cut in the DA's office? Finally, the most puzzling question; why is Norm Lambert still employed today in a community hospital owned by the citizens in Hutchinson County?

In 1996, the Child Pornography Prevention Act expanded federal powers over the distribution and possession of child porn. It requires a five-year sentence and up to 30 years for the production of computer generated child pornography or any visual simulation of a minor engaged in sexual activity.

LOOK IN THE EYES OF THE INNOCENT

This was the first time myself and others had learned Langley was simply convicted with Misappropriation of Fiduciary /Finance Property (computer). It was never reported in the News-Herald. Had the District Attorney and the Hutchinson County Judge done a good, kind thing for Larry Langley and the good ol' boys in Hutchinson County? Was justice served? What happened to "do the crime, serve the time."

Can others honestly look into the eyes of their children, grandchildren and school children in the community and believe that justice was served? How would they feel if their own children were in those pictures? How would the District Attorney have reacted if the pictures were of his children? Is it easier not to care and look the other way when the photos where not close to home? How can some people truly call themselves "Christians"? How can they say they had "good intentions"?

If Jerry Strecker and the other Doctor's had not spoken up, the public would have never known about Langley being accused of child pornography. Why were Dr. Strecker and others persecuted for standing for human decency and presenting the truth to the public? Good kind things were not done to them.

JUDGING CRIMES AGAINST CHILDREN LIGHTLY

Throughout July, I stopped sending in opinion articles into the News-Herald. I purchased a copy of Sonny Donaldson's book "Singing Too Loud in Church". I read about how he was railroaded by the good ol' boys, a District Attorney and the County Court system in Hutchinson County

I found irony in one of his accounts in the book:

"Sitting around with a legal pad and a ball-point pen, just waiting on one of the jailers to make a mistake, keeping up with what inmates could come back to court, which was one of the things I did every day. Friday is always a busy day in court; only this Friday I blew a fuse.

Three men out of my tank went to court. One was in jail on a D.W.I., one for child support and one for molesting a 4 year old stepdaughter. All three was being tried in Judge Hazlett's court. The one with the D.W.I. came back with a five year sentence, I didn't have a problem with that, and after all it was his 17th D.W.I.

The second one came back with an 8 year sentence. He explained that his ex-wife had been hired by Judge Hazlett as a secretary in his office and some time the year before and still worked for Judge Hazlett. I said did you appeal your sentence. He said no he didn't know he could. I told him he had every right based on conflict of interest. Judge Hazlett should have never even considered hearing your case. We will sit down tonight and get that case set aside. Bert said I don't know how to write. I said Bert I've heard that over and over in jail. Before you get out of here, you are going to. That is if you are in here for any length of time.

The 3rd one with the child molesting case came back to court with a 4 year sentence. I blew my top. He said the Judge gave me one year for every year of my daughter's life. I said if that's so, I wish she were 99 years old."

This wasn't the first time in Hutchinson County that crimes against children were taken lightly. I wondered about other times and considered researching records. Was there a pattern to all this insanity!

CHAPTER TWENTY NINE

LEAVING HUTCHINSON COUNTY

Mother's divorce was finalized in July and we were preparing our move to North Central Texas into another home. Mother was tormented by a negative "stigma" over getting a divorce after 60 years of marriage. Her attorney had told her she could get a partition of assets rather than a divorce. She offered that to the other side, which included my Sister, brother-in-law, and Father. They turned down her offer.

The family was split apart and fingers were pointed at me. I became the convenient scapegoat. My sister had placed an "Elect Robert Bradley" election sign in her yard when I ran in the School Board Election. My Dad hired the hospital attorney to plead keeping his driver's license before the Justice of Peace.

On August 1, 2005 we left Borger and Hutchinson County.

WILL THE FAT LADY EVER SING?

Throughout August, we spent our time settling in the lake home. The serenity of the surroundings is healing for both of us. Mom likes to watch the ducks, geese, squirrels and other wildlife. She takes pictures of sunrises and sunsets reflected in the water. She's beginning to smile more these days. Grandchildren and great grandchildren are within a short driving distance. I really believe it's true that their aliveness, laughs and hugs makes older people feel younger. Mom is beginning to heal and enjoy her freedom.

There are days when I think about my Dad. I envision him collapsed in his plush recliner. His body fatigued and breathing heavy before falling off to sleep in solitude. I remember earlier times when life belonged to my Dad preceding the disease that robbed him of reasoning. I admired him sitting in the same recliner when he gave me advice or told stories of friends who helped him in the oil field. I would marvel at how strong he was and how the lines in his face showed both laughter and years of physical struggle. I miss that side of him and always will.

We still subscribe to the Borger News-Herald to keep up with what's happening and talk with friends every week. It's been over a year since September 11, 2004 and nothing has changed at Golden Plains Community Hospital.

Each day I wonder if it ever will.

OUR SERENITY INVADED

During the first week in September, I walked to the mailbox to get the mail. I returned to the house and handed mother the Borger News-Herald. Her facial expressions dropped when she read the Letters to the Editor. I asked her what was wrong and she handed me the paper to read. I read the following article and remembered the writer's name from a previous attack article that I ignored with no response.

GLEN BAXTER HAS MOVED AWAY
Dear Editor:
I am writing this letter on behalf of a very sweet friend of mine. She let me know of some good news and I thought I would share it with the community.

Finally, after all the negativism and ugly continuous rhetoric, Glen Baxter has moved on. I am sure the citizens of not only Borger, but all of Hutchinson County are breathing a collective sigh of relief!! He truly did wreck havoc in our town and also with his own family. I pray for them and hope they will be able to get back to some semblance of normal living.

I truly hope he does not continue his ranting from a distance. It really has been nice opening my paper and NOT seeing his name there.

With that being said, I would like to urge the citizens of Hutchinson County to pray for the victims of Hurricane Katrina and always for our troops in harms way.

THE TRUE COLORS OF SELENA MCCLELLAN

My mother's feelings had been wrongly stirred and hurt all over again. She had spent sixty years making lifetime friends and contributions in Borger, Texas. Her record had been one of doing good kind things for her family and others. Now she felt violated by some stranger.

Who was this woman? Who was her very sweet friend? What does she know about wrecking havoc on my family? How can this "goody two shoes" have the audacity to say she will "pray for them and hope they will be able to get back to some semblance of normal living." Living with dementia is seldom normal.

I looked up her telephone number in the Borger directory. A woman answered the phone and I asked if she was Selena McClellan? When she said, "Yes" I responded by telling her who was calling and asked her if she worked for the hospital or had any connection with the hospital? She evaded my question.

I asked her who her good sweet friend was and she said, "the friend is your sister".

I wasn't really surprised and I said, "My mother's feelings were hurt and will be hurt worse now. You were wrong in what you wrote because you know nothing about what happened in my family."

I ended the conversation and went downstairs to tell my mother about the phone call.

FUTILE RESPONSE TO THE NEWS-HERALD

My mother had never written an opinion article in her life. She decided to respond and wrote, "Ms. McClellan's article about my family upset me. My son is truthful and honest. I am proud that he speaks up in support his family and community."—Norma Baxter

I wrote it was in poor taste when an outsider involves my family in her opinion article. Will Rogers once quoted, "We are all ignorant, just on different subjects."

Ms. McClellan did not and does not have all the facts on the subject of my family affairs to state her opinion. Her article angered and hurt my mother who has resided in Borger since 1946. My mother knows all these facts because she has lived with them for the past 60 years. Friends in Borger who have known my mother over the years know more facts on the subject than does Ms. McClellan. The real truth comes from facts known at the Hutchinson County Family Crisis Center and Shelter for Women.

I pray that in the future, Ms. McClellan will be compassionate and get all the facts before placing an opinion article in the paper. I also pray that her very dear friend will have the compassion to look at all the facts before spreading rumors.—Glenn Baxter

Our two opinions were e-mailed to the News-Herald editor and predictably never published.

SECRET SURROGATE?

I made some inquiries about Ms. McClellan. It didn't surprise me when I found she used to work for one of the Doctors in the prefabricated building on South McGee Street.

Golden Plains Community Hospital pays the salaries of those employees and were paying Ms. McClellan when she was working there. Did this link her as a participant in a pattern of disinformation and character assassination? Where my suspicions confirmed about her probable true motives to smear my mother and me?

In my opinion, Ms. McClellan unconsciously soothed her guilt when she writes about "victims of Katrina and caring about the troops".

American soldiers give their lives to protect our free democracy, freedom of speech and freedom of the press. These freedoms have been pervasively ignored, abused, manipulated and suppressed by a few in Hutchinson County doing unkind things to others.

There are those in Hutchinson County who think I folded the cards the day I moved away.

Thanks to Ms. McClellan, she stirred emotions that inspired me to write this book. So, I unfolded a chair on the patio and began to write. The good people in Hutchinson County need the entire story.

Taking the advice of the hospital pharmacist following my resignation from Invest in Yourself, I began spending days getting all the facts and organizing documents. By the middle of October, I began writing about Hutchinson County. The first draft was called *"Boomtown Documents . . . Corruption that happens in Hutchinson County stays in Hutchinson County.*

PETITION TO REMOVE DISTRICT ATTORNEY

Later in September, the News-Herald was reporting that Betty Holland was filing a petition to have the District Attorney removed from office under Chapter 87 of the Local Government code. The code states that a government official may be removed for an intoxicated offense. I kept up with all the news stories covering the DA going back to his arrest in May and decided to call to interview Ms. Holland to get her side of the story.

Holland: "My daughter, Gina, left her house that night and was sitting at the corner of Ocla and Fairlanes intersection.

She saw a car coming down the road weaving everywhere. He drove past her, over shot his turn and ran into her. He backed up and she thought he was backing up so they could talk about the wreck. He backed up into the oncoming traffic and went around her down Ocla Street. She turned around to follow him flashing her lights, honking her horn and hollering at him trying to get him to pull over. He doesn't stop until he reaches the middle of the intersection at Cactus and Dolomino. All the time my daughter is calling 911 on her cell phone.

When the police get there, the dash cam video is not there yet. Just a couple of officers. Ballman won't get out of the car, so the police break out the back window to get the car unlocked. Clay Ballman is inside of the vehicle passed out. They get the doors open where they can talk to him and that's when the dash cam video arrived. They repetitively ask him, "Clay, step out of the vehicle. Clay we need you to step out of the vehicle. And he doesn't obey them and says, "I'm looking for my wife".

He refuses to step out of his vehicle. The police officers told him over 30 times to step out of his vehicle. They never told him to step out like they would have an ordinary citizen.

"Clay step out. Clay are you going to take a field sobriety test?" They weren't getting any answers, so one of the officers walked over to another officer and says, "I'm going to ask him one more time on the field sobriety test and he doesn't answer or respond to it, I'm going to take it as a no."

The officer goes back over and asks him four to five more times. So they try to pull him out of the driver's side of the car and one of the officers says, "We can't get him out because his leg is locked in there." So another officer gets in the passenger side to unlock his leg and they finally pull him out. They got him on the ground and handcuffed him. Two of them tried to walk him to a police car. You could see how intoxicated this man was. It was unreal.

We thought resisting arrest should have been filed because they had to forcibly remove him from his vehicle. One of the officers told my daughter that night that Ballman would be charged with hit and run, leaving the scene of an accident, DWI, and resisting arrest. He asked her at the site if she wanted to press charges and told her this is the

District Attorney, Clay Ballman. The "District Attorney" didn't mean anything to an 18 year old girl.

She called me and I told her that the District Attorney isn't any better than you or me. If you want to press charges on him you should be able to do it without fear of what he's going to do to you. So, she went to the police station the next morning and filled out paper work and a statement to continue with the charges.

We thought they would get a hold of her before court. Then I heard through the grapevine that Ballman was going to court in Vega. So, I called Birdsong the prosecuting attorney in Vega, and I asked him "Why haven't you got a hold of Gina when she is the witness to all this?"

He said, "Well, we tried to call her one time and it said the phone had been disconnected. So, we didn't try again."

My exact words to him were, "If you were looking for her you would try more than one time and you had her address." I just think he just didn't want Gina there as a witness.

I asked him before the trial if Gina needed to be there and he said, "No not if you just want to come and watch."

After the trial, it came out in the paper that Ballman was charged only with the DWI. He did a public apology in the newspaper. To this day he has never tried to get a hold of my daughter to apologize.

I sent Birdsong a letter and said we felt it was his responsibility to remove Clay Ballman from office. Myself and others got together and decided we could remove him with Chapter 87 in Texas Statutes. That's when we started the petition.

I went to see Birdsong after the letter and finally went to see him when my letter was not answered. I asked him why it wasn't his duty to have Clay Ballman removed. He said, "I just don't feel like he's done anything worse than anybody else out there."

I said, "That's not the case here. He is the District Attorney. He prosecutes people for DWI's when he was out getting drunker than some of people he's sent to the penitentiary. His charges should have been hit and run, leaving the scene of an accident, a DWI, and resisting arrest.

Birdsong told me, "Mrs. Holland, we only did Hutchinson County a favor by taking this case because we didn't want them to get someone from Dallas coming up here and telling Hutchinson County how to do this." I said, "I don't think you're doing the people of Hutchinson County any favors."

I told him, "I didn't come over here to lie to you. I didn't come over here to hide nothing from you. But, if you don't remove him then me and some other people are going to file chapter 87 on him. He said, "There's nothing wrong with you filing chapter 87 on him. But, just remember that has not been practiced in over 25 years.

He didn't even know that Ballman been pulled over the year prior in Fritch that hit the paper. I talked to the Fritch police officer that pulled him over that night. There's a dash cam video out there, but nobody is giving it up. I talked to the policeman who stopped him and asked him where I can find the dash cam video. He said, "I was told to let him go and let his wife drive him home and Ballman was very belligerent and mouthing." This same man signed the petition.

Question: What about the tape?

Holland: Fritch police department told me they erase all their tapes after 60 days.

Question: What's next?

Holland: "We got an estimate to repair the truck and were told it was dangerous to drive. We got an insurance claim and sent it into the insurance company. The insurance company was State Farm in Borger. I contacted their Lubbock office. They sent an adjuster on Thursday and by Friday morning we had an insurance check for the full amount of $732. I thought that was strange that the check was sent over night. I think they were hoping that getting the truck fixed would shut me up and I would drop everything.

Question: Has Ballman ever called your daughter with an apology?

Holland: "Ballman has never tried to get a hold of my daughter or any one in my family."

The more I talked with Betty Holland, the clearer it became she was not going to give up. It would take stubborn conviction to remove some individuals living off the taxpayers in Hutchinson County. Citizen petitions mean nothing to these people. Where is the sense of integrity and honor in these public officials.

SUBJECT: PREACHER FIGHTS FOR LIFE AT GOLDEN PLAINS

I was thunderstruck when I opening up my e-mail on Tuesday morning, December 6, 2006. I couldn't believe my eyes as I quickly called the person who sent the message. What happened?

She answered the phone and I asked her if her e-mail was a joke? She responded, "A friend of mine works with Susan Youngquist and her husband died at Golden Plains early Sunday morning. His name is Pat Youngquist. He's a pastor of a small church in Borger and works at a radiator shop.

According to my friend, he had severe nausea, vomiting and stomach pain. His wife drove him to the Emergency Room on Friday and admitted him. Then, he was put into ICU.

He had a seizure late Saturday night. Six Borger Policemen went up there to hold him down and tie him to the bed. A few hours later, on Sunday morning he passed away.

She said the family heard the police inside struggling with him. They said the nurses sedated him and told the family he was fine, so they went home. An hour later, they were called and told he was dead.

When the family returned to see the body, they claimed his Adam's apple was pushed to one side and that he had bruises on him. *(I have not been able to confirm this as true.)*

The son said the doctor was rude in talking with the family and whenever they asked about an autopsy, he discouraged the family in telling how much it would cost. They are a poor family and felt pressured, so they agreed to send the body to Brown's funeral home.

My god, this was a small man weighing only 146 pounds!"

I asked her if that's all she knew and she said, "Yes." I told her thanks for the information and that I would make some calls to find out more.

Hung up the phone in disbelief. How much of this story was true and how much was wild rumors or exaggeration filtered through a third party? I wondered if the formaldehyde used to embalm a body would make it difficult to get toxicology tests? If so, that would be a perfect way to cover up a medical wrong doing.

When I called around, the rumors were rampant. One person said that one of the nurses in ICU (Special Care Unit) was married to one of the police officers who responded to the call.

The next day, December 7, the News-Herald the headline read "Autopsy results awaited". The story stated that the autopsy results conducted Monday in Liberal, Kansas on a local Borger man should be available at the end of the week. Pat Youngquist, 43, was the pastor of Missouri Street Family Worship Center

Borger Police Chief Jimmy Adams told the Borger News-Herald that police officers were requested by the hospital staff to restrain Youngquist. He said two officers were sent to the facility and additional officers were sent to restrain him until he could be sedated.

Judge Blanks said that completed autopsy reports should be available at the end of the week. Youngquist's funeral was today.

On Friday, I reached the Judge on the phone. One of the first questions I asked was, "Is there a toxicology report?"

She responded, "There was not really a full blown tox report because he was already embalmed. So there were some tissue samples being tested and some citrus fluid. I believe that's what I don't have back yet. I just have the rest of the autopsy back.

"I've heard all kinds of stories flying around," I said.

"So have I and so far that's what they are, just stories. The family called me because he was an inpatient and they didn't know what to do. I'd never been called up there on an inpatient before. I told them to all decide what you're going to do. If the doctor isn't going to sign the death certificate, then call me back. I'll come up there. Chances are there won't be an autopsy because he was an inpatient. At the time when I knew nothing of this persons history whatsoever. All I knew was that he was admitted on Friday night and this was at around 4 on Sunday morning.

They never did call me back. So, when the funeral director called me to ask about helping get this family an autopsy, I just went down to the funeral home and addressed the family. Because the doctor hadn't been contacted back at that point in time, I decided it might be the wise thing to do because I had a little bit of his medical history from the family at that point. And I felt that an autopsy needed to be addressed for the reason of the pain killers he was on.

"What about blood test (from the hospital)", I said.

"At this point, I haven't had time to read the complete medical records that I've ordered. But, I've been pretty well satisfied with my autopsy, so I haven't felt the need to take the time to do that at this point.

"It's another mystery?"

"Well it really is to some people. I don't know where it's all coming from. After meeting with the family and listening to all of them have their say, it's like they think there's some type of conspiracy and all this business. And I have released a copy of the autopsy to the family.

You know myself, I don't see a problem with the evidence I have. But like I said, I haven't read through all the medical details. I basically rely on that. Myself, I'm satisfied without getting a tissue sample back so far. The doctor sent me a paper to read on the condition that caused younger people an early demise because they do not know they have this condition."

I thanked the Judge for talking with me and hung up the phone.

Through other calls, I actually confirmed that one of the nurses in ICU was married to one of the Police Officers who was called to the hospital. This brought up many questions in my mind. Had an injection of a medication caused an adverse reaction that agitated the patient? When the patient became violent, who panicked and called the police? Did nepotism play any part in that decision? Why weren't other hospital staff called from other floors to help restrain the patient? In my personal experience with my ex-wife who was an ICU nurse at Baylor Medical Center for years, I don't recall a time that Police Officers came into the ICU unit.

I was still not satisfied and wanted more facts so I completed a public information request and sent it to the Borger Police Department.

When the police report arrived, I looked through the reports of the six responding officers. I found the report of an Officer Strope that matched the name of the Mellisa Strope listed as one of the three attending hospital staff. Strope's report was the first one I read.

"On 12/03/05 at approximately 0100 hours R/O (Reporting Officer-Strope) heard officer Bryant get dispatched to Golden Plains Community Hospital S.C.U. regarding a combative patient. Strope was finishing a call and went to back up Officer Bryant. Officer Strope is familiar with this area of the hospital and arrived on the second floor. He went to the S.C.U. and observed nurses David King, Melissa Strope and a female hospital staff known as Michelle.

The staff appeared to be having difficulty with a patient later identified as Patrick Youngquist. King told Officer Strope that Youngquist had been verbally and physically combative. Upon seeing Officer Strope, Youngquist appeared to calm down was told that he needed to cooperate with the staff. This cooperation did not last long as Youngquist again began giving the staff a difficult time. The patient was not staying in his bed and was pulling off cords that were on machines and attached to his person.

After approximately five minutes, Officer Bryant arrived on the scene. Officer Strope placed latex gloves on his hands and began to assist the staff in restraining Youngquist by placing his hands on top of Youngquist's knees to attempt to keep him in bed. Youngquist did not appear lucid as he was talking to someone named "Joe" and stating he needed to go pick up his car.

Staff was contacting the Doctor on call and requested that officers stand by for the safety of the nursing staff until the doctor arrived and could sedate the patient. Youngquist was still struggling with officers and repeatedly pulled off his wires and attempted to hit, kick and bite officers and staff. Officer continued to assist for a short time until Youngquist was secured with restraints. Youngquist was still able to kick and punch at the staff as the restraints were being pulled by Youngquist. A catheter was put into Youngquist, which he began to attempt to pull out.

Officer Strope assisted in keeping him from doing so by controlling his arm, as this would have caused serious pain and possible medical problems. Sergeant Gipson asked what the status was and was told that Youngquist was still combative and that Officers were still assisting the staff.

A short time later Sergeant Gipson arrived with Officer Soler to assist if necessary and to relieve Officers. Officer Strope was at this time holding the right leg of Youngquist. Youngquist managed to get his leg off the bed, then kicked Officer Strope in the strike plate on his vest causing pain to the Officer's right ribs and mid-section.

Officer Strope stepped out of the room and took a short break. He was fatigued from holding down the legs of Youngquist as he was struggling quite aggressively. The On Call Doctor arrived and the staff began to attempt to sedate the patient.

After a time the sedation began to appear to take effect as Youngquist started to fight less. Once Youngquist appeared to be sedated to the point that he was no longer a threat to the hospital staff, the officer left the scene.

Officer Strope ended by reporting visible bruise and slight laceration to his midsection from where he had been kicked by Youngquist."

Author's Note: The following Supplemental Reports filed by the individual Officers duplicated Officer Strope's Report. I have omitted that redundant information and only written about the additional information that was not in Strope's Report.

SUPPLEMENT REPORT 2—Officer Jason Gipson

Officer Jason Gipson's report reveals it was approximately 45 minutes from the time he heard the dispatch sending Strope and Bryant, that he called to check status and Officer Strope advise Gipson that they were still struggling with Youngquist.

Youngquist had been tied down to the bed, but the restraints were largely ineffective, and he had pulled out enough slack to actively kick and punch at Officers.

Youngquist kicked Gipson on three separate occasions during the struggle. Gipson did strike Youngquist on the leg of his left calf in an attempt to make him comply and stop his resistance. Youngquist did not comply, and Gipson repeated the strike to his left calf two additional times.

After about 15 minutes of struggling with Youngquist, Gipson witnessed the nurse administrator a shot to Gipson's buttocks, apparently to sedate him.

After about 20 more minutes, Gipson told Melissa Strope that officers could not remain at the hospital for much longer. Melissa Strope advised that the Doctor on call was the one making the decisions, and he was seated outside the room.

SUPPLEMENT REPORT 3—Officer M. Bryant

Upon arrival, Officer Bryant made contact with an ER nurse that showed where the SCU was located. Bryant walked into a room, which (2) nurses were attempting to hold down Patrick Youngquist. Bryant knew one of the nurses to be Melissa Strope. The other nurse was a white female, with blonde hair and glasses (nothing further known). Bryant observed Officer Strope putting on latex gloves to help hold the patient down.

Author's Note: Strope stated in his report that Strope heard Officer Bryant getting dispatched to Golden Plains and Strope went to back Bryant up. Bryant report reads as if Strope was already in room putting on latex gloves. Officer Gipson states in his report he heard dispatch send Officers Bryant and Strope to GPCH. Are these inconsistencies?

There were (2) occasions where Youngquist asked Bryant for a kiss and Officer Bryant replied by saying, "I don't kiss other guys." *NOTE: Doesn't this indicate the patient was out of his mind?*

During the time that Officer Bryant was in the room, he observed nurses King and Melissa (Strope) inject 2 doses of an unknown medication into Youngquist IV. Bryant observed Melissa give 2 shots of an unknown medication into the buttock of Youngquist. After the second injection into the buttocks, Youngquist fell asleep a short time later.

SUPPLEMENT REPORTS 4-5 Officers Webster and Soler

Officer Soler stated in his report, "The patient later identified as Patrick Youngquist, whom had been under some type of drug that was making him react in this manner. Soler also noticed the subject to be in 4-point soft restraints as well as officers and hospital staff attempting to hold the patient down.

Author's Note: A family member claimed bed sheets were used as 4 point restraints.

Looking through the reports, I could only come up with 5 Officers and 3 hospital staff excluding the Doctor on call.

According to the police reports, this man struggled for approximately one hour and twenty minutes. What caused this man to become so agitated that it required eight people to struggle to restrain him? Why couldn't the hospital staff restrain the patient? Couldn't they have called staff from other floors?

Why wasn't the Doctor on call there sooner where sedatives could have been administrated? You can drive anywhere in Borger, Texas in 10 minutes. Why was the doctor outside the room and not in the room?

Another person I talked with said Youngquist died of a heart attack because of an unknown preexisting medical condition (condition that caused younger people an early demise) of the heart. If this is true, isn't it conceivable that the medications and the physical struggle may have agitated a heart attack classified as a natural cause of death in an autopsy?

No one knows what was going through the mind of Pat Youngquist. The reports read like he was hallucinating and suffering from delirium. How did he perceive the Officers in uniform?

I called the Texas Hospital Association and talked with their legal department. When asked if they had ever heard of police officers entering into an ICU unit in Texas, they said NO. Emergency Rooms are another story.

Searching the National Library of Medicine, I could not find a similar incident with police officers. I did find to quote that, "*minimal* restraint practices can be safely implemented in intensive care using a comprehensive program . . . that supports the patient's dignity of risk." Does GPCH have continuing education to improve nurses' knowledge and attitude toward restraint in ICU patients?

I called the Society of Critical Care Medicine, American Nurses Association and searched the Internet for news stories of police in ICU's to restrain patients and found nothing.

It is the responsibility of the administration's hospital staff to evaluate patients and be professionally trained to use restraint that enhances the quality of care in ICU patients. Is it the responsibility of a hospital to maintain a non-threatening, caring, peaceful and healing environment.

I don't believe the police intentions were bad. They may have been naïve in getting pulled into the Special Care Unit (ICU) of the hospital. The whole thing is so bizarre, who knows what to believe !

The family has retained a law firm. I called and talked with the attorney. He told me it was odd because there were no nurses' notes from 11 AM to 7 PM on Saturday in all the medical records received from Golden Plains.

Looking over the police report a second time, I found that Nurse Melissa Strope did make the dispatch call into Officer Gipson at 10:41 to 10:42 PM. Strangely, that's approximately 2 hours and 20 minutes before her spouse, Officer Strope reported being first to arrive at the hospital room.

What happened in the lapse of the two time periods? Why weren't the nurses' notes turned over to the attorney? Where are the nursing notes?

Hopefully, the answers to these and other questions will come out in the courtroom.

It's been over two months and the Youngquist story only ran once in the Borger News-Herald. Friends and fellow workers remember Pat Youngquist as a kind, gentle, caring man and are upset to see him gone, to see his family broken up emotionally and financially, and to see foreclosure on their home.

The story has stayed under the radar and away from the eyes of the world for over two months. Too many times what goes on in an island in the Texas Panhandle stays there

ATTORNEY NEEEDED!

By mid January, Betty Holland was running up against roadblocks in hiring an attorney to represent her. Holland said, "I've called over 15 law firms. When I call attorneys in the Panhandle, they say they don't want the case or they say the lawyer's schedule is full and they can't take the case. One attorney expressed fear of reprisals the next time he represented a case in Hutchinson County. Some said it would take too much of their time to learn Chapter 87 of the Local Government Code."

The four-page section allows jurors to decide whether a county official should be removed for incompetence, official misconduct or "intoxication on or off duty caused by drinking an alcoholic beverage."

She said, "If I can't find any lawyers to help, my complaint could get tossed out next month." Following a story in the Houston Chronicle, Holland was contacted by a law firm in Houston, Texas who consented to take the case

I've heard it said by an attorney, "We are all somewhat brothers and sisters when it comes to our profession."

97% PATIENT SATISFACTION AT GOLDEN PLAINS

It's now been one year and five months since 9/11 in Hutchinson County. It looks like the CEO's regime at Golden Plains Hospital is resuming its old habits. Dr. Sal Kramer, originally a supportive surgeon, had fallen from grace at Golden Plains and left the community without a whisper in the newspaper.

It appears the Borger News-Herald revenues are up from GPCH advertising. Ads and articles are appearing in the News-Herald almost weekly proclaiming 90% plus patient satisfaction. Articles are more frequent spreading Lambert's photo and good will throughout Hutchinson County. It appears the administration's plan to build a facility through Critical Access along with disinformation tactics is slowing down the process of selling the hospital or changing the management. What happened to Tri-Lakes, Blackhawk and others interested in the Request for Proposals.

The administration knows there only needs to be three or more board members applying time and rhetoric to assure a victory in keeping Mr. Lambert. Are they betting apathy will lead the citizens astray?

The trust in Golden Plains Community Hospital is bankrupt. The future for health care in Hutchinson County remains up in the air?

CHAPTER THIRTY

CHILD PORNOGRAPHER RETURNS HOME

Before ending this book, there was one more thing to research. I received a call from a woman in tears telling me the story about some children molested in Hutchinson County. I phoned an associate in Borger and asked if she or someone else could check records at the Courthouse. There was a hint of a rumor that Langley had violated his probation, so I asked to see if there was anything new on his case.

The day was February 17th,2006 on a Friday evening when the phone rang. On the other end my associate said, "Are you sitting down?" I said, "What did you find?"

"You were right about Larry Langley. The case number is 9101 and it states: Larry Nelson Langley violated community supervision by committing a felony in Travis County, Texas on or about June 27, 2005 of possession of child pornography. There were 71 separate images of intercourse, unknown female and unknown male and male children. There were 16 separate visual exhibition of breasts and vagina areas of male and female children.

The case was set for Langley to appear at the Hutchinson County Courthouse on January 11, 2006 and has been reset for February 27, 2006 at 10 AM."

"You won't believe what I found on the other case you asked about! The sex offender was indicted in February 1996 and in July 1996 received 10 years deferred adjudication for child molestation. District Attorney Clay Ballman was quoted as saying, "If he lives by the rules and lives out his probation and no new offenses, then he won't end up with a conviction."

Then the record read that three years later in 1999, the guilty party admitted in a polygraph test in the Sheriff's office that he molested another child. His defense is that "he is not competent to stand trial. The psychiatrist who examined the sexual offender stated, "he fakes mental illness and is volatile."

In court on April 10, 2003, District Attorney Clay Ballman stated, "No sense in trying the case, he'll just be back out." With the 3 years left on his probation from 1996 left, another 10 years was added in deferred adjudication. At this very moment he walks the streets today as a free man although he is listed on the Texas DPS Sex Offender Records."

I said, "All this is unbelievably disgusting!

Is the criminal justice system in Hutchinson County more concerned with the rights of the criminal than the rights of protecting innocent children. This demonstrates another case where a DA and a Judge have taken an lenient approach and allowed a child molester to re-offend without incarceration. Studies show that child molesters cannot be rehabilitated. This man is walking the streets as a high risk of destroying another innocent life.

Before hanging up the phone, I asked my associate to help with some other records. I had been researching another idea of looking through the DPS Sex Offender data base for other child pornography cases previous to Larry Langley's case. I was curious what type of sentences Mr. Ballman enacted on these individuals? I could only find one other conviction of child pornography with a DPS photo. I gave my associate the name of the convicted offender to return to the Courthouse and retrieve a copy of the files.

HEAR THIS!!! CHILD PORNO IS A VERY SERIOUS CRIME

All of this was mentally overwhelming. It was totally unthinkable and outrageous that every thing written in this one book had occurred and is continuing to occur in a small town in America.

More questions came to mind. Why did the District Attorney lightly slap Larry Langley's hand in 2000? Did the District Attorney look the other way because the hospital attorney is a good old boy, a fellow attorney, a Deacon at the First Baptist Church and a mutual member of the Country Club?

The hospital attorney was aware it was *child* pornography found in Larry Langley's office. Why did he omit the word "child" when he claimed he reported it to Police Detective Charlie Keys. Did the attorney tell the whole truth to the DA and explain why the alleged child pornographer was rewarded over $11,000 (TAXPAYER DOLLARS) and sent freely on his way? Was the Judge privy to all this information when Langley stood in front of him?

A District Attorney is elected to protect citizens, individuals, families and children from criminals. The hospital's "good intent", as stated by District Attorney Ballman in the News-Herald, allowed a potential sexual predator to walk away with the freedom to prey on other children in Travis County.

It was becoming clearer why Hutchinson County is nationally rated above average in crimes of Rape, Robbery, Assault, Burglary, Larceny, Vehicle Theft and Arson.

BAD NEWS BECOMES A MYSTERY

It was after five o'clock, Wednesday evening, February 22nd, when I heard the phone ringing and ran up stairs to pick the receiver up.

"I've got bad news for you," said my associate from Borger.

"What is it," I replied.

"I drove to the Courthouse this afternoon and couldn't find what you wanted. Every time the sex offender's name was typed in on the computer, the name would come up but nothing else would. The District Clerk tried to help me. She was perplexed that the name would show and there is nothing else. I could tell she was shocked."

I responded, "Well I can pull up his photo and record on the DPS Sex Offender Web Site.

That's really strange. I'll check into it and call you back."

The thought of what happened kept creeping into my mind. This was the only case I found on a child pornography conviction in Hutchinson County while searching the DPS Data Base. Had the records been tampered with?

COURT RECORDS HAVE DISAPPEARED

All day Thursday, I was busy e-mailing media in Amarillo and Borger the news of the Child Pornographer returning to Hutchinson County on Monday.

Friday morning, February 24th, I called the court house and asked to speak to the District Clerk and waited for her to get the phone.

"Joan I need your help. I read her the sex offender's name. His registration record in on 10-08-1999 in Hutchinson County. She repeated the name to me on the phone. I said, "That's right"

"We normally don't look things up on the phone Mr. Baxter, but I'll see what I can do. "Well, there are no cases found in criminal and it was in 1999?

Yes, and I'm looking at this guy's picture on the DPS Sex Offender data base. This was child pornography, one photo of a 15 year old girl and ten (10) year probation in 1999," I responded.

"If it was in 99 and it's not coming up on our index. It is either an un-indicted case where they did a pre-diversion agreement and it was never filed as an indictment in which case it may be in record in the District Attorney's office that were never filed or it is a sealed record," she said.

I said, "The date of disposition was 02/09/1999."

"Well it should be in our system. If it was actually filed in which case you might get that information from the District Attorney's Office, but I'm not saying that you can. I just know that it's not in this office."

"Okay, thank you very much."

I hung up the phone and immediately called the District Attorney's office.

I asked, "Can you help me find a file please?"

"Okay, what on?" she responded.

"I checked downstairs with the District Clerk and she couldn't find this file," I said and gave her the name.

"I'm not showing anything. Is it something we've handled?" she replied.

"Yes, if you look on the DPS data base you'll find it there," and I gave her the information

"She said, "We don't have it in this office, so it must be out of State."

I said, "That doesn't make sense because it states 10/08/1999 TX1170000 Borger So Hutchinson County.

Note: What I read to her was where out of state was listed on all the other records. For example, when looked at all the other photos in Hutchinson County some would say Kansas, etc.

I'm looking at the data base and it says disposition 2/09/99.

"Hmm, let me let you talk our investigator. He might be able to answer the questions a little easier,"

"This is C.H."

"Yes, I'm trying to find this file," and continued to repeat the information.

"I don't know why we would have anything where a guy was on probation in our records and wouldn't be in the clerks office," replied the investigator.

Next, I called the Texas Department of Public Safety.

When the woman answered the phone, I repeated the information.

"What do you want on him?

"He shows up as having a record in Hutchinson County, but he shows up as a ghost."

"Where do I get this information?"

"Hutchinson County should be able to give it to you," she said.

"They don't have it! I've talked to the District Clerk and the DA's Office."

"I can't tell you where else to go because that's where we would go," she replied.

"You're looking at the same screen that I am, right," I asked.

"Yes." (her voice was showing she was rattled as she was looking at DPS NUMBER 04788186)

"Now doesn't the information on the screen tell you that this guy was prosecuted in Hutchinson County."

"YES, and you would go to Hutchinson County Courthouse. Maybe you should take a copy of this screen there and show it to the clerk," she said in an uncertain voice.

"I appreciate your help.

Next, I called the Borger Police Department and nothing was found there.

Finally, I ran a national criminal check and a background check on this individual. The only address that came back on his background was the exact one listed on the DPS data base. There was no record of any other locations where this individual had lived. It was bizarre that there was not more information. When I looked at the criminal history check "Offense ID" with a blank next to it. I had come to a dead end.

The Big Mystery is what happened to this sexual predator's court files?

DOES ANYONE CARE ABOUT CHILD PRONOGRAPHY IN THE TEXAS PANHANDLE?

It looked like Karma was speeding faster than a freight train toward Hutchinson County in a collision course toward the District Attorney and others who have ignored the severity of child pornography, other sex crimes against children and groups of citizens who have asked for investigations.

District Attorney Ballman was to appear on January 9, 2006 in court to face his Chapter 87 removal from office supported by a petition signed by over 800 citizens. Two days later on January 11, 2006, Ballman was scheduled to be in court at 10 AM for the Larry Langley homecoming.

The attorney representing Ballman filled to dismiss Ballman's Chapter 87 removal from office case on Friday, January 6.

This action stalled Betty Holland Chapter 87 case and gave her 30 days to respond to the motion or the case will be dismissed. Langley's case was reset for February 27, 2006. On Monday, February 27, 2006 at 10:00 AM, the case was reset for a third time and moved thirty days.

After e-mailing releases on Larry Langley's return to face 71counts of child pornography, not a single newspaper or television station reported the story in the Texas Panhandle. How and why was the news purposely kept below the radar?

I called the editor of the News-Herald to make sure she received the release. She had, and when asked if she was going to cover the story she replied, "I don't know what I'm gonna do. L.W. is out today and I'm going to show it to him Monday when he comes back. She spoke as though she didn't want to be bothered with reporting the story.

When no story appeared, I called the Publisher at the end of the week.

"L.W., I e-mailed information last week." He responded as though the editor did not inform him. I'll check and see where we are. We're short two reporters and doing the best we can."

I continued explaining how the public deserves to know and how serious child pornography is in the community.

"I agree with you that it's bad stuff, but we're going to do the best we can." I'll look into it on Monday."

This would prove a good test for the publisher. Will the story tell the whole truth or be written in half truths? Will he choose not to report the story, make like it never happened and never have to deal with the consequences.

God forbid if the newspaper advertising dollars are placed at risk. After all, what's wrong with placing profit as a priority over the lives of innocent children? Why would the readers care to know anyway?

If anyone would like to know if the story is printed, only time will tell. Citizens in Hutchinson County who care, mark this date: March 3, 2006.

WHO'S YOUR NEIGHBOR

A few months ago, DATELINE NBC broadcast an episode where hidden cameras investigate computer predators who troll the Web looking for young teenagers. Working in conjunction through decoys at Perverted Justice, grown men were coaxed into showing up for sex with 12 to 13 year old teens home alone.

I was surprised to see the hidden cameras catch an ER Doctor, a New York City Firefighter, and a rabbi among others. These prominent men lead double lives as secretive Jeykl and Hyde personalities.

The addictive behavior of these sexual predators cause them to repetitively violate children. One never really knows the numbers of children these men have abused. Since they are better educated, and are employed in prominent positions, they should not be exempt from being prosecuted to the full measure of the law.

This is becoming a growing national epidemic. If not stopped, these evil men that prey on innocent souls through child pornography rings on the Internet will destroy the future of our nation.

INVESTIGATION AUSTIN

On Thursday morning, March 9, 2006, Mother and I drove to Austin, Texas. We arrived outside the Travis County District Clerks Office at about 2 o'clock in the afternoon.

The weather was unseasonably warm. The temperature was nearing the mid 80 degrees mark. I parked and pulled Mom's walker out of the trunk of the car. We entered the Courthouse and passed through security.

We walked up to the clerk's window and I asked for the files on Larry Nelson Langley. We took a seat and waited a few minutes for the clerk to return. She handed me the files and I returned to sit next to Mom and read over the files.

The Affidavit for Warrant of Arrest stated that a Detective of the Austin Police Department assigned to the Child Abuse Investigations Unit had good reason to believe that Larry Nelson Langley on or about the 15th day of July 2005, did commit the offense of Possession of Child Pornography, 3rd Degree Felony.

The warrant is based on the following information:

On July 27, 2005 a call was received from an individual who repairs heating and air conditioning systems at the Austin State Hospital.

Sometime during the month of May, this repairman had an order to work on a vent in the office of Larry Langley, building 781 on the 3rd floor. This individual arrived around 7:20 AM and found the office door locked. When he started to unlock the door, Langley opened the door and let him in. The repairman saw Langley's computer screen had a picture of a young girl that was nude. Langley tried to keep his body between the repairman and the screen. The repairman left the room and returned and the image was still on the screen.

The repairman described the image as a female "easily recognizable" to be 9 to 10 years of age with brown hair. The female was sitting up right with her legs crossed at the feet. The female had no clothing and her underdeveloped private parts were clearly visible.

On July 18, 2005, the Director of Internal Affairs for the Office of Inspector General, contacted the Detective with instructions to seize the computer in Langley's office.

On July 27, 2005, the computer was taken to the Austin Police Department Computer Forensics Unit. On July 28, 2005 the Detective viewed several images. Sixteen images of young females, aged 9 or 10 years old to no more than 14 years old were pictured nude in a variety of poses causing the focus of the picture to be on the private parts. These images were "thumbnail" or smaller preview images of jpeg image files that had been placed, and then deleted, on the computer's hard drive.

There were 71 similar image files and close-up's of underdeveloped sex organs engaged in copulation residing in the hard drive's unallocated clusters and "lost files".

On August 8, 2005 Larry Langley arrived at the Child Abuse Unit and was read his Miranda rights. Langley signed a confession stating that he did view "Child Pornography" at his office and as he described as "nude pictures of underage children". Langley stated that he frequents another web site with a password to access information including child porn. Langley said, "I have pursued that information, viewing the child porn and other porn, with a curiosity and fascination."

This outright treachery of filth was occurring daily under the nose of the administration at The Austin State Hospital. This hospital promotes a Child and Adolescent Psychiatric Services Department on its web site.

The patients are composed of troubled children up to age 12, including an adolescent girls' unit and an adolescent boys' unit. Certainly, there must be adolescent children there because they were abused by sexual predators.

How did Langley get employed there? How did he get employed at the previous hospital in Yoakum, Texas? Who provided him letters of recommendation? Why didn't these two hospitals thoroughly research Langley's background?

ENOUGH IS ENOUGH!

Child pornography is addictive behavior. Pediphiles cannot keep from repeating their perverted behavior over and over again. The following information from www.crimelibrary.com explains the three categories of pedophile collectors. There's also good information on the FBI web site.

The pedophile collector falls into three general categories: closet, isolated and the sharer. The closet collector maintains and views his erotica in secret and does not molest children. This type of collector builds his collection in a clandestine manner and keeps its existence a secret. Sometimes, he will maintain this collection for years without the knowledge of a live-in spouse.

The isolated collector is actually engaged in molestation and will display the material to a victim. The sharer-collector trades and displays the material with others and may do so for profit. He also will molest children and keeps company with other pedophiles. Since other criminals, like burglars, muggers, car thieves, rarely collect artifacts relating to their criminality, why do pedophiles collect? The answer to that question lies in the psychological characteristics of his condition.

He has a twisted sexual compulsion for children whose origins are separate and apart from criminality. His deviance is defined as criminal only because society has deemed it so. Some pedophiles believe that they have done nothing wrong and are simply more enlightened than the general public. They feel they are part of a special progressive movement and one day society will come to accept, what they see as, their sacred ritual of adult/child sex.

What category does Langley fall into? What rational person wouldn't suspect that he was likely escorted out of the Dumas Hospital for the same reason before being hired at Golden Plains? Why did Lambert hire Langley in the face of protest from some board members? He defended Langley (11/02/97) as having the highest degree of integrity? He placed Langely as a major link in a chain of events that lost approximately a million dollars in a taxpayer supported community owned hospital.

Who would disagree that a moral and unethical offense was committed and paid for with taxpayer dollars in Hutchinson County? Langley worked in hospitals with children in pediatrics units. The citizens in Travis county should be outraged that the legal system in Hutchinson County allowed a sexual predator of children freewill in their community. Citizens in Hutchinson County should be equally outraged. No one knows the full extent of Langley's crimes. Seventy one photos may be just the tip of this iceberg.

Laws needs to be passed where individuals who mislead, do not accurately report and attempt to cover up any alleged felony crimes against children can be held accountable for obstruction of justice in felonies (federal and state), and (financially) aiding and abetting the escape of these pedophiles into other communities.

WHERE'S EQUALITY IN THE EYES OF THE LAW?

District Attorney Clay Ballman made a choice to ignore a petition of 800 citizens for his removal. He's chosen to hire an attorney to fight to keep his high paying job and government retirement.

The board of directors and others at Golden Plains Community Hospital chose to ignore two petitions, one of 1,041 signatures and another of 200 signatures with a request to the Hospital Board of how many signatures will it take for you to act. The response was we don't have act on anything!

How well does this speak of those who serve the public in Hutchinson County? Obviously, they believe they can ignore citizens, look the other way and people will forget. Are those in power and privilege accountable to a lower measure of justice while the average citizen is held accountable to a higher measure of justice?

In Ballman's case, what if the shoes had been on the other foot? Consider what would have happened to 18 year old Gina Holland if she had been driving drunk and hit the District Attorney! Would Judge Smith allowed her to go home or would she have spent the night in jail. How many charges (DWI, hit and run, leaving the scene of an accident and resisting arrest) would she have faced? And what if she was a school teacher or a nurse in Hutchinson County. Would she still have a job today? She would definitely have difficulty finding a job with a DWI permanently on her record.

I viewed the entire police video cam showing Clay Ballman's arrest. I felt sorrow watching it. His mother taught me in grade school. My memory of her is one of a caring lady of quality and class. I can't imagine how much it must have broke her heart.

Nonetheless, Mr. Ballman is an adult who can make choices. Reputable sources have reported his problem with alcohol way before the fateful night on May 12, 2005. Why didn't he, a friend or family member intervene to help long ago before this tragedy?

I have walked in his shoes and made the mistake of drinking and driving. I am not an alcoholic, but made a stupid choice out of peer pressure to drink in a business meeting, chose to drive and got stopped. The Officer did not have to pull me out of my vehicle because I got out and walked on my own free will. I was scared and had been told "never take a breath test" and I said, "No". My hands were placed in one set of hand cuffs. They were tight and hurt my wrists. I spent the night in Jail, was humiliated, hired an attorney, spent thousands of dollars, and sat through all the hours of classes and reporting. I sat next to people who had multiple DWI's and couldn't understand why they repeat the same behavior. I got it right the first time and will not drink one drop and drive ever again. It never leaves my mind as I worry and remind my daughter in College never to drink and drive. I went through all of this without special treatment and I live with the hell of it on a permanent record.

Mr. Ballman did get special treatment. The police officers didn't immediately pull him out of his car. They repetitively asked him 30 times to get out of his car. Finally, three Officers forcibly pulled the DA out of his car and onto the ground. Then one of the them says, "I'm going to put two pairs of handcuffs on him." Two pair linked together are more comfortable and don't hurt as much.

Then, he didn't have to spend the night in jail when the judge let him go home.

The law should be equal in all eyes, and it simply is not in the case of Clay Ballman. The District Attorney should be an example of integrity. He should be held to the highest degree of the law. He is in office to protect the citizens and set high moral standards.

He has a law degree and can find employment elsewhere. A person with integrity would resign.

CITIZENS ACT IN BEHALF OF YOUR FREEDOM

Whenever those elected to government office are receiving lush salaries for themselves and their friends, maintaining power and position becomes and end to itself. When rules no longer apply and they believe they are above the law, corruption erodes everything around them. Using position to control others and subvert rivals to undermine the system to keep their positions, increases cynicism and kills off trust in basic democracy. The balance of power is undermined when a simple majority vote cannot cause the dismissal of a government employee or a government official.

The Hospital District bylaws requiring 5 out of 7 director's votes to terminate a hired employee (CEO/Administrator) changes the balance of power in Hutchinson County. It breeds self righteous arrogance in a few who believe they can never fall from power short of legal prosecution.

Through my experiences and during the time spent writing this book, I have often pondered the insanity of what has occurred at Golden Plains Community Hospital. So many things go beyond common sense. Too many questions have gone unanswered. Little has been investigated.

In attempts to present the truth through seeking rational examination of the events, I became a target of disinformation. I could see through the ongoing, old pattern of lies, deceit, half truths, suppression of truth, press manipulation, censorship, smear and ridicule to lead the public astray from the truth.

This book presents many questions, but it also presents a pattern and links in a chain of events. It allows the reader to place these links in a rationale order to find some answers.

John Curnutt, a paraplegic, confined to a wheel chair and other good honest people have sacrificed so many hours speaking up against the administration at Golden Plains. He and others are not getting paid a damn dime for their efforts to change toxic hospital management, while those in control at Golden Plains rake in hundreds of thousands of dollars in salaries and benefits. All John and so many others really desire is good health care they can trust in their hometown.

I think back when I was kid sitting in the Morley Theater on Main Street in Borger. I remember my little brother sitting next to me on the edge of his seat. His eyes wide open watching Cowboy and Indian movies.

Back then, the Calvary were the good guys and the Indians were the bad guys. Later in life we learned we were blind. Hollywood had conned and deceived us to make a profit.

In truth, the Calvary were the bad guys. The soldiers, righteously "looking good" in their uniforms, shamelessly robbed the Indians of their land and food by protecting greedy hunters who annihilated all the buffalo.

Tribes of these native Indians roamed the Texas Panhandle. The spirit of freedom in these proud people was killed off and they no longer live on the Great Plains. It was a shameful death of a Nation.

Although my brother and I were blind to the truth, near the end of every movie, we would feel a sense of victory whenever a conspiracy or wrongdoing was exposed and the bad guys were stopped or punished when the story ended. This is the story ending I envision for Hutchinson County.

It can only happen if people open their eyes, look in a mirror and decide if they like what they see. If they don't, then do everything in their power to make changes. Never give up and let others break your spirit. Change the community by changing leaders who strongly protect truth, individual freedom and the innocence of children.

It's up to the 68 percent silent majority who turned out to vote "against". It's time for these people to become the vocal majority . . . organize, speak out and show up in force in support of *"good kind things for others".* *

tsaatʉ mahi ʉrʉ hanikatn *

Translation courtesy of Comanche Nation Language Department
Lawton, Oklahoma

Death of Innocence

Child playing in a sandbox
A sunny, cool spring day
Pure aliveness
A miracle of God

A black ominous shadow
Abruptly rips up the child
Thoughtlessly ravaging
Tearing life from innocence

Inflicting bewilderment
Pain guilt and confusion
A child's soul dies
Four year old remains

Tears in the sandbox
Inner death of the child
A childhood stolen
Aliveness nevermore

-Glenn Baxter

"**The world is a dangerous place to live, not because of the people who are evil, but because of the people who don't do anything about it.**"—Albert Einstein

One of the most successful applications of the RICO laws has been the ability to indict or sanction individuals for their behavior and actions committed against witnesses and victims in alleged retaliation or retribution for cooperating with law enforcement or intelligence agencies.

The RICO laws can be alleged in cases where civil lawsuits or criminal charges are brought against individuals or corporations in retaliation for said individuals or corporations working with law enforcement, or against individuals or corporations who have sued or filed criminal charges against a defendant.

Anti-SLAPP (strategic lawsuit against public participation) laws can be applied in an attempt to curb alleged abuses of the legal system by individuals or corporations who utilize the courts as a weapon to retaliate against whistle blowers, victims, or to silence another individual's speech. RICO could be alleged if it can be shown in retribution and retaliation for themselves having been brought before the courts.

USEFUL RESOURCES

Child Protection Resources

www.childseek.com
Network for Missing Children

www.crimelibrary.com
Excellent educational source on crimes
against children.

www.enough.com
Lighting the way to protect children
and families from the dangers of illegal
Internet Phonography and Sexual Predators.

www.familywatchdog.com
Free National Data Base of Sex Offenders

www.fbi.org
Federal Bureau of Investigation
Report Internet Child Pornography

www.jessicamarielundsfordfoundation.com
Helping children in crisis

www.opra.com
Oprah's Child Predator Watch List

www.passjessicaslaw.com
National initiative to pass laws that would
sentence convicted child rapists to a
minimum of 25 years in prison and lifetime
monitoring. Click on and vote "YES"
to this National Poll.

https://records.txdps.state.tx.us
Texas Department of Public Safety
Sex Offender Registration Data Base

Health Care Resouces

www.alz.org
Alzheimer's Disease and Related Disorders
1-800-272-3900

www.hospitalconnect.com
American Hospital Association

www.hospitalvictims.com
Helps uninsured deal with excessive hospital bills.

www.ndvh.org
National Domestic Violence Hotline
1-800-799-SAFE

http://cms.hhs.gov/medicaid
Medicaid 1-410-786-3000

http://www.thaonline.org/
Texas Hospital Association Box 15587
Austin, Texas 78761-5587 1-512-465-1000

Legal and Law Enforcement Resouces

www.cpiu.us
Counter Pedophile Investigation

www.corporatecrimecontrol.com
Investigative and Protective Services

www.policeworld.net
Online forum on Law Enforcement

http://www.oag.state.tx.us/
Texas Attorney General

http://www.sll.state.tx.us/
Texas State Law Library

http://www.usdoj.gov/
United States Department of Justice

http://usdoj.gov/usao/offices/index.html
United States Attorneys' Offices

www.dea.gov/
Drug Enforcement Association

Freedom of Speech Resources

www.aclu.org/
American Civil Liberties Union

www.ncac.org
National Coalition Against Censorship

www.usccr.gov/
U.S. Commission on Civil Rights

SAMPLE OPEN DOCUMENT REQUEST

Every citizen has the right to request open documents from government and tax supported entities.

(date here)

ABC Community Hospital
ATTN: Public Information Officer
(address here)

RE: Information Request

Sir or Madam:

Under section of 552.221 of the Texas Government Code, this letter comprises an official application for public information. The information requested is as follows:

(Write in the information you are requesting)

As required under section 522.221 of the Texas Government Code, we expect a prompt response. Payment will be made upon itemized estimation of charged or completion of inquiry. As specified in the Texas Government Code, we will be expecting to be informed of the production of the documents or the date of production within 10 days.

You may contact me at (telephone number). The completed copies may be mailed or you may call and I will pick them up.

Sincerely,

(Your name and address here)

DOCUMENTS

This story is ongoing and readers wanting more information will find updates on news events relating to and occurring in Hutchinson County.

Log on to **www.goodkindthings.com**.

January 28, 2000

To: Norm Lambert, CEO

From: Larry Langley

Please accept my resignation from employment as Hutchinson County Hospital District effective February 25, 2000. This resignation is made freely and voluntarily.

Larry M. Langley

Larry N. Langley

Received & accepted 1-28-2000

Norman J. Lambert

Hutchinson County Hospital District dba
Golden Plains Community Hospital
200 S McGee • Borger, TX 79007

LARRY LANGLEY

761

REGULAR HOURS	OVERTIME HOURS	HOLIDAY HOURS	SICK LEAVE HOURS	VACATION HOURS	OTHER
200 00		8 00		130 16	

GROSS PAY			VACATION & SICK LEAVE			DESCRIPTION	DEDUCTION CURRENT
	CURRENT	YEAR TO DATE					
REGULAR	6922 00		VACATION REMAIN				
DEFERRED			SICK LEAVE REMAIN			TML LIFE	41
OVERTIME			TAXES			HEALTH INS B-4	138
HOLIDAY	276 88		DESCRIPTION	CURRENT	YR. TO DATE	DENTAL B-4 TAX	22
SICK			FEDERAL	3450 37		GIFT SHOP	17
VACATION	4504 84		FICA	883 03			
OTHER			STATE				
GROSS	11703 72						
	160 86						

TAXABLE PAY				TAXES		DETACH & RETAIN THIS STUB FOR YOUR RECORDS	DEDUCTION
11542 86				4333 40			58

EARNINGS STATEMENT

Hutchinson County Hospital District dba
Golden Plains Community Hospital
200 S McGee • Borger, TX 79007

01/31/00

$7

* * * * * SEVEN THOUSAND ONE HUNDRED FIFTY DOLLARS AND 52/100 * * * *

LARRY LANGLEY

⑈047158⑈ ⑆111900659⑆ ⑆120607754⑈

GOLDEN PLAINS
COMMUNITY
HOSPITAL

....
... ., ...
...., .
... .

ADMINISTRATION

MEMO

To: All Departments, Board Members & Physicians
From: Norm Lambert
Subject: **Larry Langley Resignation**
Date: January 28, 2000

Please be advised that Larry Langley, Chief Financial Officer, turned in his resignation today.

I will be meeting with those departments that organizationally reported to Larry over the next days and weeks to determine a new organizational structure for Golden Plains Community Hospital. In the mean time, should you have any financial related questions, please feel free to contact me or .   .
.   .   .   Controller.

CEO Self-Evaluation

Norm Lambert, CEO   November 2, 1999

note: these are paragraphs from page 2

Management Team Development. I have spent a considerable amount of time during the early part of my tenure here hiring and developing a management team that can effectively lead this hospital. The current team is a group of strong individuals who each have experience and expertise in their corresponding areas to effectively lead this institution to new heights. I have empowered each of these administrative leaders to aggressively make changes to improve our operations. Their leadership styles vary with each individual, and while their individual styles may produce discomfort for some individuals, they have achieved positive results. My role has been to bring leadership, direction and motivation to them while trying to produce a balanced approach as an Administrative Team. Additionally, my leadership style has tried to empower middle managers to take action and accept responsibility for those actions. This apparently was not the style of the past. The previous culture here appears to have been not to empower anyone to take action even to the point that there was a fear about taking action.

When I arrived in late 1995, it was obvious to me early on that the then CFO did not know how to manage the financial administration of this hospital. I replaced him with the current CFO. While Larry Langley does have an abrupt leadership style and at times lets his demeanor get away from him, he has aggressively tackled many critical financial issues and has been of great value to me in achieving this financial turnaround. Larry's integrity has been challenged, in most part from rumors preceding his arrival here. In working with Larry from day-to-day, he has exhibited only the highest degree of integrity contrary to the rumors. In fact responding to the negativity of these rumors has cost us additional dollars for unnecessary audits. I have counseled Larry on his demeanor and the need for him to pay more attention to details. However, his more direct style of management has produced positive financial results.

Pat Cleveland, President, HCHD Board
_____

    Please distribute a copy of the enclosed memo to each Board member at the start of the Executive Session. This is a memo from Leon Mitchell marked "Attorney-Client Communication" and, therefore, should be distributed in the closed session.

    I am unable to attend the meeting due to a prior engagement with several physicians at my house.

        thank you,

        Norm Lambert

        6-26-2000

Amarillo
Heart Group

Joaquin Martinez-Arraras, M.D.
Marc Moreau, M.D.
Prakash K. Desai, M.D.
Jon Luigi Haddad, M.D.
Robert E. Jackson, III, M.D.

D. Gary Soya, M.D.
Agustin Cabrera-Santamaria, M.D.
Ismaile S.H. Abdalla, M.D.
Ernesto Rivera, M.D.

November 3, 2004

Hutchinson County Hospital District
Attn: Norm Lambert, CEO
200 S. McGee
Borger, TX 79007

Dear Mr. Lambert,

We recently received the payment for the balance due on the indigent patient account in
response to the letter of demand. I appreciate every effort you made to resolve this issue.
I do hope that all future billing will be handled expeditiously as to avoid a re-occurrence
of this negative situation.

All of the physicians in Amarillo Heart Group wish to continue a good working
relationship and expect reimbursement within forty-five (45) days of the statement date.

Sincerely,

Ron Welty

Ron Welty, C.M.P.E
Executive Director

cc: Mr. Jack Worsham, Hutchinson County Judge
Mr. David Brandon, President of Board
Mr. Edgar Davis, Hospital Board Member
Mr. Ken Benton, Commissioner
Mr. R. D. Cornelius, Commissioner
Mr. Glen Baxter, Chairman of Citizens Who Care about Hutchinson County

Advanced Diagnostic Solutions
MRI, CT and Ultrasound Services
755 Ole Hwy 15 #66 West Monroe LA 71291 - Phone # (318)397-8255 - Fax # (318)396-2895

Golden Plains Community Hospital	Page 1
Borger, TX 79007	Date: September 27, 1999
Att: Steve Price	Quotation Number : SE1.065Y9

ADVANCED DIAGNOSTIC SOLUTIONS LLC is pleased to submit this quotation for the products described herein, subject to the enclosed Standard Conditions of Quotation and the following:

- Warranty Term: 60 Months
- Terms of Delivery: Completely set-up and delivered
- Terms of Payment: Leasing Company

ADVANCED DIAGNOSTIC SOLUTIONS:

Submitted by:

_____
James Gandy (President ADS)

BUYER:
Hospital

Agreed to by:

_____   11/4/99
Authorized Customer: Date:
Representative

_____CEO_____
Title

QUOTATION

Golden Plains Community Hospital   Page   2

Borger, TX 79007   Date: September 27, 1999

Att: Steve Price   Quotation Number : SE1.065Y9

QTY	CATALOG	DESCRIPTION	PRICE

USED 1.0 TESLA SIEMENS IMPACT MRI SYSTEM

GE531   Used Siemens Impact 1.0 Tesla Mobile MRI System.
               Includes:
               - Preinstallation in the 8' x 48' Portable Trailer
                 with wheels, Delivery, Final Calibration and 60 Month
                 Warranty.

               - Does include Cryogens and Magnet Maintenance.

               - **Laser Camera**

               - System will include: Sun Spark2 Computer, Optical Disk
                 Body Coil, Head Coil, Knee Coil, C-Spine Coil, Shoulder
                 Coil.

               - Warranty includes all parts, labor and Cryogens for 60
                 Months.

QUOTATION

Golden Plains Community Hospital

Borger, TX 79007

Att: Steve Price

Page   3

Date: September 27, 1999

Quotation Number   SE1.065Y9

QTY   CATALOG   DESCRIPTION   PRICE

Site preparation will be included (except power)
Including all pad work, wall way, fencing, awning and
all guard railing.

Tech Training on site for 2 Weeks if needed,
and daily phone support.

TOTAL MONTHLY PRICE, WITH APPROVAL OF LEASING COMPANY..............$12,822,83

615,000.00

Cash Price: :................$625,000.00

*per phone conversation
11/4/99 @ 3:56 p.m for
James Dardy / Denita Ehlich*

ADDENDUM

ADDENDUM

Golden Plains Community Hospital

Borger, TX 79007

Att: Steve Price

Page   4

Date: September 27, 1999

Quotation Number :   SEI.065Y9

This Addendum is to serve as a buy back policy. If after 180 days of full-time service and the hospital is not able to realize a profit with the MRI, then ADS will Buy the unit back at that time. The hospital will make ever effort to make this unit profitable.

ADS will pay what ever is owed on the lease at that time. This deal will start After 180 days of service and stand for 120 days after which this buy back policy will expire.

James Gandy (President of ADS)

9/27/99
Date:

Date:

DEFAULT:

Default shall be deemed to have occurred should client:
- Fail to perform any of its other obligations under this Agreement.
- Fail to perform any of its obligations under any other Agreement with ADS or its affiliates.
- Commit an act of bankruptcy or become the subject to any proceeding under the bankruptcy act, or become insolvent, or if any substantial part of the Client's property should become subject of any levy, seizure, assignment, application, or sale for or by any creditor, or governmental agency

Should a default occur, ADS may declare all outstanding amounts due from Client immediately due and payable, may immediately terminate this Agreement and may exercise any other right or remedy available at law or in equity.

WARRANTY DISCLAIMER:

ADS's full contractual obligations are provided in the Agreement. There are no warranties, written or oral, provided otherwise.

All service and parts covered under this Agreement are provided as is. No warranty of merchantability or fitness for a particular purpose applies to anything provided by ADS or it service contractor.

LIMITATIONS OF REMEDIES AND DAMAGES:

The total liability of ADS and its representatives to Client and Client's exclusive remedy relating to this Agreement and the service to be provided under it is limited to the fees for the service which is the basis for the claim. Client agrees that ADS and its representative have no liability to Client for: 1) any penal, incidental or consequential damages such as lost profit or revenue 2) any assistance not required under this Agreement, or 3) anything occurring after the end of this Agreement. This is a commercial service transaction. Any claim related to this Agreement will be covered solely by commercial legal principles. ADS and its representatives will not have any negligence or other tort liability arising from this Agreement.

SURVIVAL, WAIVER, SEVERABILITY, CHOICE OF LAW:

All of ADS's rights, privileges and remedies with respect to this Agreement will continue in full force and effect after the end of this Agreement. ADS's failure to enforce any provision of this Agreement is not a waiver of that provision or of our right to later enforce each and every provision. If any part of this Agreement is found to be invalid, the remaining parts will be effective. The laws of the State of Texas shall govern any dispute arising out of this Agreement.

April 6, 2005

Estimate from   . Building Systems, Inc.

Note: This estimate is based upon
Released Specifications for Golden Plains Community Hospital
Medical Office Clinic 82'-6" X 70'-0" that were obtained from the
City of Borger, Texas Building Code Enforcement.

Estimate Total is $369,091
original company . . . Invoice $546,142

Difference of $177,051

Note: (original company) completed the Doctor's Building in 2000.
The cost of steel and construction has gone up over the past 5 years.

Note: Company names have been omitted.

BUILDING SYSTEMS, Inc.

~~~~~ ~~~~~ • PO BOX ~~~ • ~~~~ ~ TX ~.

Telephone :·   ` FAX

April 6, 2005

Mr. Glenn Baxter
Horizon Southwest Medical Center
P.O. Box 542,
Borger, TX 79008.

Dear Mr. Baxter:

Thank you for your interest in .... Building Systems, Inc. The price reflected below, for a 70' x 76' (nominal dimensions) modular Medical Clinic, located in Borger, TX, is based on the attached specifications and floor plan.

1. The purchase price as specified is **$369,091**. This includes delivery, poured concrete footers, set up, skirting and poured concrete handicap ramps and steps. The price does not include canopies, self-contained fire alarm, low voltage equipment, utility hookups, site work, taxes or permits. It is assumed that the site can support the building, is relatively level and easily accessible.

2. Engineering takes two weeks from the time the order is finalized. Third party plan approvals will take an additional week. An approved engineering package will then be provided for your review. Once you have approved the package the materials will be ordered and the building will go into production. This normally takes four to six weeks depending on the materials involved with an additional week for installation. Sales that are finalized prior to receipt of your order will have precedence and may affect the delivery schedule

3. The building will be built in compliance with the International Building Code, Americans with Disabilities Act, and the National Electric Code. The building will be engineered to meet local floor and roof load requirements and will have electrical, heating and cooling loads sized in accordance with NEC and IBC codes. Cost to comply with local codes beyond the attached floorplan and specifications is the responsibility of the owner.

4. Prices are valid for 14 days. Because of extraordinary daily raw material price fluctuations, this quote is subject to price adjustment after this 14 day period up to the time the order is placed. You will be notified of any required price adjustment before and order, contract or purchase order is accepted on the building.

Please call with any questions.

Sincerely,

Project Manager

Memo

To: All Personnel
From: . ... ------- . , RN *(MP)*
Date: 3-15-05
Subject: Medications

Everyone needs to be aware that stock medications, found on the patient care units, are disappearing. In particular, we have noticed that Levaquin is disappearing by the box. Pharmacy is closely monitoring medications that are disappearing. This is the same as stealing medication and charges will be filed, when the person responsible is identified.

RN's please note: If you are pulling medications from the Pharmacy, a copy of the order should be left in the Pharmacy when you pull any medication. Do NOT take a medication out of the Pharmacy without the order in hand, and please write the number of doses you are taking to the department.

Thank you for your help in this matter.

Note: Name of COO/Director of Nurses has been omitted

ADVERTISING

Would You Invest $600,000 to build this Portable Building?

This is no joke. Drive by and examine this Doctor's Building at 202 S. McGee in Borger. Your property tax dollars helped pay for it.
Do you really want your tax dollars increased 150% to support a $25 Million Bond to build a new Hospital under the current management?

IT'S YOUR HOMETOWN
VOTE NO
SEPTEMBER 11

Get all the Facts. Click on www.VoteNo911.com

Paid for by Citizens Who Care about Hutchinson, County Box 542 Borger, Texas 79008

Vote YES and Have Your Head Examined.

August 12, 04 Financials show $500,000 is over 90 days past due with over $600,000 up to 90 days. Financial loss of $1,457,395 Million over the past four years. *Wouldn't any good businessman or banker need their head examined if they handed over $25 million to a losing operation?*

$600,000 spent for Prefabricated Doctor's Building at 202 S. McGee. *Drive by and check it out. Wouldn't you need your head examined, if you paid for what you see.*

$800,000 wasted for a MRI machine that never worked. *Created a petition signed by 1,040 citizens calling for the Hospital Board to perform an forensic audit to no avail. Board refused audit and thought citizens heads needed examined.*

Three Chief Financial Officers have resigned over the past 4 years while the present Chief Executive Officer has remained in office. *What was wrong with their heads? Can anyone answer where they are or what happened.*

Numerous complaints from Hutchinson County citizens over improper and negligent medical care. *The hospital wants everyone to think these patients need their heads examined.*

Don't lose your head when you vote. A new or updated medical facility makes sense. But, does it really make sense under the track record of present management?

IT'S YOUR HOMETOWN
VOTE AGAINST
SEPTEMBER 11

See your tax dollars in use. Click on www.VoteNo911.com

Paid for by Citizens Who Care about Hutchinson, County Box 542 Borger, Tex

Don't Let Spin Doctors Mislead You.

The Blame Game

Brought to You by the GPCH Administration of Spin.

Blame the Doctors

Blame the Patients

Blame the Vendors

Blame the Numbers

Blame the Building

Blame the Citizens

RULES: We're NON-PROFIT stupid. As of August 12th we're only $501,638 past due over 90 days. You can't blame us. Believe us when we say that we have a 93% approval rating. Don't believe all the negative patient stories you read in the newspaper. Don't believe the stories about our own Doctor's checking into Amarillo Hospitals. Our reputation is built upon facts and excellent patient services. Trust us. It's only $25 Million in tax dollars. We only pay our CEO $140,000 plus bonuses annually.* Vote for us. Don't worry, you're in good hands with GPCH. Buy us a new building and we'll get even better.

Are you fed up with the them playing games with your tax dollars. Maybe it's time you really show your appreciation by voting <u>Against</u> on Sept. 11.

See your tax dollars in use online at www.VoteNo.com

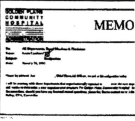
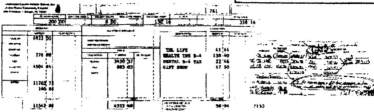

ORDER FORM

INTERNET: www.goodkindthingthing.com
e-mail: goodkindthings@yahoo.com

MAIL: Send this form with check, or credit card info to:
Glenn Baxter
Box 6761
Granbury, Texas 76049

Please send_____copies of *Good Kind Things for Others* book:

Company_____

Name_____

Address_____

City_____State_____Zip_____

Phone(_____)_____

E-mail_____

Texas Sales Tax: Add for books shipped *within Texas*
Example: One book: $18.00 + 8 ¼ % (.0825) Sales Tax = $19.50 plus shipping

Shipping U.S.: Add $4 for the first book and $2 for each additional

Total $_____Check enclosed (No COD)

ORDER BY CREDIT CARD (Please check one)
_____Visa   _____American Express   _____MasterCard

Full Name on Card_____

Account Number_____

Expiration Date_____

Signature_____

BVG